Contents

189 PRI

MEDIE 2006

An In   on

B. 1   rice

BLACKWELL
Oxford UK & Cambridge USA

First published 1992
Reprinted 1992

Blackwell Publishers
238 Main Street, Suite 501
Cambridge, Massachusetts 02142, USA

108 Cowley Road, Oxford OX4 1JF, UK

Library of Congress Cataloging in Publication Data
Price, B. B. (Betsey Barker), 1951–
  Medieval thought: an introduction/B. B. Price.
      p.   cm.
  Includes bibliographical references and index.
  ISBN 0–631–17508–3 — ISBN 0–631–17509–1 (pbk.)
    1. Christianity—Middle Ages, 600–1500.   2. Philosophy,
  Medieval.
  I. Title.
  BR252.P67   1992
  189—dc20   91–10668
                                                                        CIP

British Library Cataloguing in Publication Data
A CIP catalogue record for this book is available from
the British Library.

Typeset in 12 on 14 pt Bembo
by Best-set Typsetter Ltd, Hong Kong
Printed in Great Britain by T. J. Press Ltd, Padstow, Cornwall

This book is printed on acid-free paper.

Preface

The European Middle Ages is a period very deserving of study, for it had a lasting impact on western thought and culture. Spanning at least ten centuries, it might seem unavoidable for study due to its length alone. It is, however, the importance of the events between about 400 and 1500, still reflected in many components of western society, which commands attention. Certainly for those interested in the history of the Christian Church or its religious ideas, the contributions of the Middle Ages are central. Perhaps less well known is that in the medieval period almost all areas of life found intellectual expression, and that the study of medieval thought can therefore embrace subjects as diverse as agriculture and metaphysics.

A common thread, none the less, underlay all the activity of medieval society: the importance of Christian beliefs and Church doctrine. The entire period can be characterized as one with a unifying and forceful set of Christian ideas about moral and intellectual conduct which were considered to be the foundation of all human activity. The first serious step facing the historian of the Middle Ages is thus the need to recognize that corpus of fundamental ideas. From today's perspective, it may seem inordinately difficult, for example, to take seriously the oft-repeated medieval papal threat of excommunication, or to see what was at stake in the constantly recurring struggles between the popes and kings of the period. It requires answering the question, according to what intellectual construct did medieval men and women act? With that question broached, one could ask yet others: why should the ideas of a single social institution have been so compelling at the time? how might one account for its ideas being so long-lived and geographically so widespread? and how did they come to permeate all areas of western medieval life?

Historical evidence is interpreted in the present book with the conviction that all aspects of the Middle Ages reflect its intellectual side. Recently the social history of the medieval period has become more and more interesting as scholarly devotion to it grows and paints a fuller picture. The new details and the generalizations they foster are fascinating. Some of the research findings reflect a common Christian ritual, without, however, depicting a society connected through a common body of ideas. For those particularly interested in social history to forgo the study of medieval thought is to fail to avail themselves of a possible richer understanding of the whole culture.

The objective of this volume is, however, not really to build a bridge between the recent contributions in social and intellectual history. Its aim is instead to offer a reassessment of medieval thought which can be used to complement the new contributions of social history. Within its focus on intellectual history, the purpose of the present book is to identify and trace the activities and ideas which had an impact on thinking in the Middle Ages. The book should serve to illustrate the importance of the study of thought in gaining an understanding of the period, by making its often complex ideas available for general comprehension. Both constancy and change in the ideas of the Middle Ages are given consideration. In the very variety of cultures – classical-pagan and religious, Christian and Jewish or Muslim, religious and secular, Latin and vernacular – lay the seeds of medieval intellectualization.

Medieval intellectualization was a process by which the activities and practices in all areas of human endeavor took on during the Middle Ages an intellectual quality in their description and pursuit. Human activity was over the course of the Middle Ages increasingly to be characterized by its counterpart, human thought. This evolution toward intellectualization is traced and described. The elevation of activity to an intellectual plane does not often occur instantaneously, but is most frequently the outcome of a process. Material and political crises whose effect may be an abrupt break with the past are indeed a historical reality; the intellectual responses they provoke usually reflect, however, some unsevered connection to past thought.

The emphasis here, then, is on the continuity of Christian thinking running throughout the Middle Ages, despite the more sensational political and material crises of the period. The viability of the medieval Christian Church demanded unity in its rituals and subsequently in its ideas. With that necessity for unity came the need to suppress, or at least channel, variety in thought and expression. As is well acknowledged in the history of religion, the suppression of specific beliefs and practices by the Roman Catholic Church at the end of the Middle Ages resulted in the schismatic division of that

Church into Reformation Protestants and Catholics. It is not the purpose of this study to describe any particular instance of disagreement, but rather to analyze how tension and antagonism between the religious and non-religious components of medieval culture, its Church and State, its Latin and vernacular languages, were a creation of the western Christian cultural environment of the Middle Ages and resulted in sophisticated intellectualization with in that culture.

Given the introductory nature of the present study and the subject of its analysis, it goes almost without noting that there are omissions. Some thinkers of the medieval period may have undeservedly gone without mention, and those identified could have been awarded much more space. Necessary compression of ideas has also meant forgoing thorough treatment of Jewish and Arabic religious and cultural influence on western European medieval culture, as well as neglecting the vital and interesting eastern Christian Greek culture of the Middle Ages. Each of these omissions is acknowledged and could well be the subject of a separate volume. It is hoped that the interested reader will pursue these areas of medieval history in other works, some of which have been noted in the bibliography.

My interest in writing this book stemmed from my experience teaching medieval intellectual history to undergraduate university students in North America. Their interests and needs have guided its organization and content and to them I am grateful. I am also extremely grateful to colleagues, especially historian of medieval philosophy J. M. Hackett, with whom I have talked and corresponded about many of the ideas this study embraces. To the closest among them, O. F. Hamouda, I owe the conception of the volume and invaluable critique of the manuscript. Susanne Rose also read the final draft of the book and provided useful editorial suggestions. The publisher's referees and the desk editor, Jenny Tyler, offered helpful guidelines and direction for the book in progress and further astute comments on the completed manuscript. I thank both them and my editors, Stephan Chambers and Alison Mudditt, for having made publishing with Blackwell Publishers such a pleasant experience.

Introduction

The world of the Middle Ages has long been manifest in its catchy, "eternally" valuable items, its cathedrals, castles, jewelry, tapestries, and perhaps even its written remains. To hope, however, for rewarding insights into the artifacts of any period involves taking the time to settle into the whole of its historical landscape. Social and political upheavals of the Middle Ages are perhaps its most obvious features, but the *ideas* of the period are in many respects what formed the foundational bedrock for those changes. The tangible social and political structures of the Middle Ages – in fact, all its dimensions – are inextricably linked with the intellectual activity of the period. To reach a full understanding of any aspect of the Middle Ages inevitably means acknowledging medieval thought; a direct approach to the intellectual aspect of the Middle Ages is provided in this study.

It is difficult to turn from the secular horizon of modern western culture to appreciate a landscape truly permeated with religious ideas. There is little alternative than to observe the religious topography of medieval ideas from historical distance, but this need not entail determining the scale of their importance in the Middle Ages with the sole aid of the ruler of today's values. Every segment of the past, and the Middle Ages is no exception, demands interpretation of its content in its historical context. The context under discussion in this book is abstract expression in the Middle Ages and the content is medieval thought. The attempt is to learn whether and how changes in abstract expression and in the content of that expression had ramifications for those alive at the time. For example, political events during the Middle Ages were affected, if not effected, by their being conceived abstractly and in the current mode of thought.[1]

Medieval Thought is an introduction to a very long period of time and touches many aspects in the development of ideas, thoughts, and culture. Intellectual changes discussed chronologically and methodologically are easy to follow without a great deal of knowledge of the period or its languages. In addition to the book's general bibliography, each chapter ends with a select bibliography for further reading, and seven appendices are included to help readers interested in extending the study. No knowledge of Latin is demanded to read the present book; all titles and quotations have been provided in English except in instances in which they are virtually untranslatable or have passed into English parlance and are readily recognized or understood. Appendix 4 may, none the less, inspire some readers to acquire some facility with Latin.

The objective of *Medieval Thought* is to introduce the Middle Ages, which, designated here as from the late fourth through the late fifteenth century, was an intellectually vital era. The book will function as a guide in which the main characteristics of the intellectual vista will be pointed out. Further, *Medieval Thought* will analyze the intellectual features of the Middle Ages. Little familiarity with Christian theology is required to approach the present study. While medieval religious ideas will receive predominant consideration, little about the emergence of Christianity will be assumed as common knowledge, and important aspects of many religious ideas of the Middle Ages will be explained. General questions of what effect religious ideas had on those who did (and did not) entertain them, and in just what way they formed part of the intellectual fabric of medieval thought, will be addressed. Finally, *Medieval Thought* will examine how medieval intellectual ideas are a product of their context which encompassed the reception of classical learning into Latin, the rise of European monasticism, the "discovery" of vernacular languages, and scholasticism.

The book is divided into eight parts. All of its contents will be discussed in the light of the first part, where the basic concept of the medieval Christian is introduced. Next follows a discussion of the importance of early medieval religious thought. Then two sections pertaining to classical learning are presented: the roots of education in the medieval period and the influence of the greatest classical philosophers, Plato and Aristotle, in medieval thought. The role of the vernacular as an alternative to the Latin of the Church and as a vehicle for expression of medieval lay culture is next discussed. Two chapters then present a general description of the evolution of medieval philosophical ideas, from early scholasticism to the late medieval tension between the Church and intellectuals. Finally a survey of all domains of intellectual activity in the Middle Ages will establish the extent to which all aspects of medieval life were intellectualized.

Somewhere in between the romantic and ruthless auras of the medieval period lies the image of its having been an intellectually unenlightened and arcane era, full of superstition. This impression is due in part to the lack of understanding of the formative impact of the institution most appropriately associated with the European Middle Ages, the Roman Christian Church. In chapter 1 this study of medieval thought will begin therefore to explain in what way Christianity molded a concept of the person, his world, and his God, as well as how it offered every man and woman a new community to which to belong after the demise of Rome's unity and the migration into Europe of the barbarian hordes. The success of Christianity depended pragmatically upon its being adopted by organized groups; or rather, by their leaders. A growing corpus of ideas and writings, however, was also to foster the intellectual attractiveness of Christianity and to interpret its social and political roles.

Some studies of the rise of Christianity fail to emphasize the early medieval period as a time of transition in which the seeds of Christianity as an intellectual endeavor were being sown. In chapter 2 the contributions of this period, necessary antecedents to high medieval thought, will be discussed in light of their intellectual affirmation of Christianity. Already evident from the fourth century AD was a formative aspect of medieval religious thought, the presence of "schools" of theology and the debates and controversial abstractions they imply. In addition to its efforts to define an orthodox school, early medieval Christianity developed by consciously debating its posture with regard to the pagan past. Both processes continued to be important intellectually throughout the Middle Ages.

The most important of several intellectual preoccupations of the medieval period which were to contribute strongly to its thought was the medieval Christian reaction to classical languages and learning. From the earliest medieval teachers, the attitude that the pupil should be led away from or beyond (*educare*) classical knowledge to Christian understanding was manifest. Chapter 3 will present in general as well as in greater detail a look at the two distinct views which the medievals held on how to reach their goals as educators: either to avoid the distracting and deleterious effects of classical scholarship as much as possible and keep to scripture as the sole 'textbook,' or to embrace and use the earlier learning as a cultural and educational springboard into Christianity. Both approaches are represented early within the Latin monastic movement, the first by Benedict of Nursia, the second by Boethius. By the ninth century the Carolingians with their palace schools exemplified the strong support of the medieval lay community for the integration of classical learning into the Christian life.

To appreciate the full importance of classical learning in relation to the ideas of the Middle Ages, as well as the ideas themselves, it is necessary to understand the way in which the writings of the classical philosophers, Plato and Aristotle, were received and absorbed. This will be the undertaking of chapter 4. For the first time since Boethius' translations of the early sixth century, Plato in the twelfth century and Aristotle in the thirteenth made their way into medieval culture, though rarely free of accompanying or incorporated interpretations. Considered authoritative by those who studied them, Plato's and Aristotle's writings very quickly became normative, and hence their pagan limitations troublesome. In arguing and striving to demonstrate that the message of the classical philosophers could be circumscribed by the word of God, both Christian Platonists and Aristotelians battled other believers who insisted on the authority of scripture alone.

After Christianity, the next major sign of an intellectual divorce of the Middle Ages from its classical heritage was the use of the European vernacular languages. As is explained in chapter 5, despite their being geographically limited and of frail history, Anglo-Saxon, Middle English, *langues d'oc* and *d'oïl*, Middle High German, etc. were extremely successfully employed to reflect a new medieval expression of culture, the arts, religion, and politics. Latin still remained the dominant language of education, religion, and politics throughout the Middle Ages, and the vernacular tongues traversed a difficult road to legitimacy. It is not surprising that their progress was considered a threat by the Church, especially as more than a new mode of expression was being tested. The vernaculars were a catalyst to stating new religious ideas, to trying new forms of political involvement, and to registering a new literary commentary on medieval life. Medieval lay culture had acquired an independent form of expression and was fast making the content its own as well.

Medieval thought continued to flourish in Latin, however, as exemplified by scholasticism, probably one of the most rigorously rarified intellectual movements in all of human history. Chapter 6 will discuss scholasticism, the medieval movement which, instigated by a desire to justify religious belief logically, flourished from 1200 to 1500. The practice and influence of Latin scholasticism were at their strongest in the medieval universities. Its impact extended, however, well beyond academe into contemporary attitudes toward, for example, law and architecture. To understand the complexities of the medieval scholastic movement itself, it is helpful to view it in light of some of its most important philosophical and theological distinctions (e.g. realism and nominalism, Averroism, Thomism, and Aristotelianism, metaphysics and natural theology), the questions it deemed important (e.g. In what way do things which seem to exist really exist? What is the relationshiop between God and his world?), and the roles of its principal adherents (e.g. Albertus Magnus, Thomas Aquinas, Duns Scotus, William of Ockham), as this chapter sets out to do.

By the fourteenth century it was very clear that the authority of the Church was becoming the subject of considerable criticism from factions both within and outside its ranks. With time, even the strong positions taken by its theologians or administrators could not disguise its vulnerability. Chapter 7 will look at its vulnerability through, most notably, the opinions of William of Ockham and Nicholas of Cusa. Needless to say, the Church attempted to hold its ground. None the less, in the late medieval period all learning, including philosophy, was defining, albeit somewhat defensively, a new role for itself beyond that of handmaiden to the Church and its theology.

In all but the last chapter, the fundamental theological views of the Church are presented as the dominant feature of medieval thought. When effectively controlled by the medieval Church, theological ideas were intentionally used to foster or to stifle intellectual activity. They fostered the groping of the scholastics to extend the scope of the Aristotelian corpus, but they also condemned heretical dissension and literary frivolity, not to mention political independence. In chapter 8 an analogy to the leitmotif of the role of the Church in society will be shown to have existed in the rapport between theology and all other intellectual spheres.

Gradually over the course of the Middle Ages, the intellectualization of all areas of medieval life strengthened. The process of intellectualization was definitely enhanced by the high medieval consolidation of all thought under the rubric of Aristotelian logic and the close integration of the intellectual roles of medieval theology and metaphysics. An abstract corpus of ideas for each area of thought came increasingly to be written, codified, and often even taught as an "art" or "science." This trend, which would continue well beyond the limits of the Middle Ages, came to yield the secularization of most of the intellectual activity we know today.

1

The Christian Impress

The ideas of Christianity so permeated thinking in the Middle Ages that it is fitting to preface a chronological discussion of medieval thought with a general introduction to the components of medieval Christian self-definition. The components to be considered here are the individual believer, the religious community, and the orthodox text. This chapter is primarily restricted to a discussion of the emergence of these three components. Their roles in the medieval Christian context were undeniably multifaceted and complex. Even as they rapidly evolved beyond their initially social and institutional forms, they became intricately interwoven, as will be seen in the following chapters. It should, none the less, be helpful in this opening chapter to examine independently the Christian individual, community, and written word, which together are at the core of medieval thought and which were each to acquire an increasingly influential intellectual dimension during the Middle Ages.

The Christian individual will be sketched both as a follower of Christ, in the sequential interpretations of that role (e.g. disciple, martyr, hermit), and also as a creation of the Christian God. Next, the Christian community will be discussed both in light of a more restrictive concept of the individual as somehow apart from Christ, the natural world, and God, conceived thus as a social being and defined particularly by and among other fellow believers, and in light of the institution which formed the focus of that community, the Catholic Church. As in the whole of this study, special emphasis will be placed on the medieval western Christian community and its Church of Rome. In a third section, the larger social and religious context of medieval Christianity will be summarized. The last component by which medieval Latin Christianity was defined, its major texts, will be briefly noted in a final section, devoted especially to the Old and the New Testaments of the Bible and the writings from the religion's first centuries.

The attempt is to provide a framework for what was throughout the Middle Ages almost universally encompassed by the notion "Christian." For the purposes of this chapter, few nuances of the notion need be emphasized. It might, however, be useful at the outset to clarify the term itself. The name "Christian" derives from the acknowledging of Jesus of Nazareth as the "Messiah" or *Messias*, an Aramaic title which translated into Greek as *ho Christos*, or "Christ," the "Anointed One" (John 1:41; 4:25). It seems to have emerged first in Antioch, Syria, among the non-Christian community as an appellation for the followers of Jesus shortly after his death. Appearances of the term in the New Testament as well as many early non-biblical references reveal that it was a title of reproach, used to identify those of morally reprehensible conduct or irrational beliefs, deserving of repression or denial of rights. For example, in his *Annals* Tacitus recounts that Nero punished with the most elaborate torture *"those whom the mob* hated for their abominable practices *and called Christians"* (italics added).[1] It carried a predominately derogatory connotation throughout the years of late Roman history. By the Middle Ages, however, the term "Christian" was used relatively innocuously by Christians and non-Christians alike to denote the institutions, practices, and individuals recognized as "of Christ" either during or after his lifetime.

With the tremendous growth in all aspects of Christianity in the Middle Ages, designations of the religion and its followers became increasingly modified. There was Gnostic, Celtic, Roman (or western), Byzantine (or eastern), Latin, Greek, orthodox, and unorthodox Christianity. Further distinctions were made as well by using completely different terminologies. It was popular to distinguish, for example, those who knew Christ during his lifetime, by the terms "disciple" (one of the Twelve), "apostle" (one sent out by Jesus to preach), or "witness," from later followers. In the Middle Ages, believers would be identified by titles denoting their Christian lifestyle (e.g. anchorite, cenobite, cleric, layperson), their place in Church hierarchy (e.g. presbyter, pastor, parson, dean, deacon, cardinal, bishop, archbishop, metropolitan, patriarch, pope, monk, nun, mendicant, abbot, canon), or even their state of grace (e.g. virgin, widow, priest, martyr, saint, gentile, sinner). While none of these differentiations can be overlooked for a detailed understanding of medieval Christianity, some will be easily clarified in the context of discussions in later chapters.

The Medieval Christian as Individual

It might seem today that the concept of the Christian as individual would not be particularly associated with any specific geographical place, but only with the pervasive persona of one charismatic individual – Jesus of Nazareth. From the start Christianity was an evangelical movement, concerned with extending Christian teaching far and wide. Jesus himself never envisaged that geographic location should impose any restrictions on the following of his words. His teaching and the continuation of that activity by his disciples had merely begun in one location, Palestine, and were to spread. His activities during his lifetime lent new or renewed interest to specific sites, and brought them, and by extension others like Rome, into play in the lives of Christian followers. Second-century pilgrimages to Jesus' birth site in Bethlehem, to the Mount of Olives (where Jesus delivered his most famous sermon), or to Jerusalem, especially for Palm Sunday (the day commemorating Jesus' triumphal entry into that city) and Easter (the day of Jesus' resurrection) are examples of the attachment of early Christian identity to geographic sites. The significance of the Holy Land sites became all the more important as Christian teachings spread to a non-Palestinian audience. The expression of that importance became extreme in the Crusades of the eleventh and twelfth centuries, when European Christians felt compelled violently to wrest the Holy Land from the Seljuk Turkish Muslims. Despite such examples, for the most part in the Middle Ages the significant events in the life of Jesus were to be associated with symbols or relics, rather than with specific sites.

Jesus, the Model Individual

Jesus of Nazareth himself was the focus of Christianity and the earliest model for Christian followers. Since Jesus was clearly revered as "someone apart," (as a great rabbi or prophet; see for example, Matt. 7:28–8:1), it was in his words that many of his first followers sought guidance for their behavior. Whenever he stressed his own humanness or similarity with mere mortals (as in the power of anyone to perform miracles, for example, see Matt. 12:27), followers, however, also saw clues for his defining a behavior of emulation. Thus, from the combination of directives and example derived a programme for the Christian as individual. From it also stemmed a programme of conduct for the Christian Church and Christian society. Although a religious programme, it would encompass social, political, and economic aspects, as well as developing a theology. Each aspect would receive different emphasis at different times throughout the history of Christianity.

Jesus had found himself regarded during his lifetime as the leader of a social and political reforming movement which seemed to some contemporary observers to be offering a new political and religious order for the Jews, a people at the time under the domination of imperial Rome. But, unlike the role projected on him by the politically active religious Zealots (there was one among his disciples; Luke 6:15, Mark 3:18) or the advisors of Rome's Procurator of Judea, Pontius Pilate (Luke 23:2, where Jesus was accused of preventing the payment of tribute to Caesar), Jesus was in fact remarkably self-composed in advancing his espoused reforms. Furthermore, he did not meet with the worldly success contemporary rulers feared. Jesus' movement during his lifetime was limited geographically to the Roman Palestinian provinces of Judea and Galilee and numerically to about 100 followers (though this number had grown to 3,000 by the first Christian *Shavuot* or Pentecost, less than two months after his death). Except among a small group of close followers, Jesus' understanding of the role of the individual, peaceful and loving, does not seem to have attracted a great deal of attention, particularly among those in that era of sentiments calling for armed Jewish revolt against the Roman presence who saw such a posture as ensuring that the stronger would retain its control of the weaker.

Under the immediate impact of Jesus' teachings on the formation of the Christian individual came the first missionaries, the most notable being the convert Paul. With Jesus' immediate followers, the concept of the Christian individual as "Christ-like" gains ascendancy. Two kinds of behavior were thought to render one like Christ. To a desire to emulate the leadership attributes of Jesus (in his role as caretaker of the marginalized, teacher, and especially preacher) were joined rituals symbolic of events in Jesus' life on earth. Jesus' flesh-and-blood experiences were indeed the most important inspiration for the adopting or establishing of certain rituals as Christian. For most believers Jesus' death and resurrection came to be the source of the most profound meaning they found in most Christian rituals.

The role-modelling after Jesus "on earth," enhanced with "after-death" symbolism, was an extremely important phenomenon. It was the first sign of an emerging intellectual dimension to the concept of the Christian individual which, along with its social dimension, would be enhanced during the Middle Ages. Worship, baptism, and the Eucharist were the three activities undertaken by the earliest believers in Christ as symbolic ways to be like Him. During his life, it had been the custom of Jesus to go to the synagogue for worship (Luke 4:16ff.). Synagogues throughout Galilee were sites of his teaching and healing (Mark 1:39), and he continued to worship in them despite his distaste for some of the practices he observed there (Matt. 23:6; 6:2, 5). For several decades Jewish Christians, following the example of Jesus, continued to worship in synagogues on the Sabbath. As an even more sustained effect of Jesus' example, the role of early Christian worship and its rituals were modelled also among Gentiles closely after the synagogue patterns that had signified worship to Jesus (and his Jewish followers): prayer, confession of faith, reading of scripture, exposition of the text, and closing blessing.

Baptism was another older ritual adopted into Christianity for its role in Jesus' life. Before beginning his own mission, Jesus was baptized by John the Baptist in the Jordan River (Mark 1:2; 2:27). Interestingly, however, Jesus did not go on to baptize others. Thus, when in their early preaching the disciples of Jesus baptized others with water (John 4:1–2), they did so by analogy to John, not Jesus; the believers who underwent baptism, however, were emulating Christ. This ritual, which was to acquire increasingly abstract theological meaning, was the second to be taken up and continued from the earliest days of the apostolic Church.

The Lord's Supper or Eucharist was a third ritual inspired at least initially by its importance during Jesus' presence on earth. "Do this in remembrance of me," Jesus had said, referring to his eating of bread and drinking of wine with his disciples at the Passover meal on the eve before his capture by the Romans. However slowly the "breaking of bread with Christ" was to distinguish itself completely from the traditional Passover meal or the weekly meal to begin the Sabbath, the words of Jesus were probably already included in such common meals during the apostolic era (I Cor. 11:23ff.). Thus like the other two religious practices, the Eucharist became reenacted within the early Christian Church both in remembrance and in recreation of part of Jesus' life.

In Imitation of Christ

In addition to specific rituals, three whole lifestyles, that of the suffering martyr, the religious recluse or hermit, and the believer within a society of believers, presented themselves to the early Christians as ways in which parts of Jesus' life could be emulated.

The martyr Imitation of the New Testament Messiah, the "true martyr" Jesus in his own Passion (Revelations 1:5), was, along with the Old Testament heroism of the Israelites in the Maccabean Wars, the inspiration to early Christian martyrdom. "For to this you have been called, because Christ also suffered for you, leaving you an example, that you should follow in his steps . . ." was written in I Peter 2:21ff. Among early Christian writings, the *Acts of the Martyrs* (*Acta Martyrum*) paint graphic pictures of the intense dangers for the first believers, indicating how the later Roman empire was a real threat to the survival of Christianity. The *Acts* were catalogues, often highly popularized, of episodes of martyrdom which recounted the strength with which Christians, just as their model Jesus, were prepared and willing to die for their beliefs. Believers, faced with the threat of imprisonment, torture, forced labor, burning, or animal mauling, were clearly, with such writings, being encouraged or chastened in the same ways to reflect Jesus' own obedience to death (Phil. 2:8; 2:5).

Modelling themselves after Christ in dying for their beliefs, Christians responded individually to the intense viciousness of the intermittent Roman persecution. Even when persecution did not stem from imperial edicts, as those of Decius (c.250), Valerian (257–60), or Diocletian (c.303–5), it was menacing, for it was frequently orchestrated by popular hatred which the authorities could not or chose not to thwart. By the third decade of the fourth century, however, a fundamental change in the empire's disposition to Christianity was essentially complete. The imperial Edict of Milan (312) had given Christians the right to practice their religion and have direct control over their property for religious or other use. In 330 Constantinople was dedicated by the Emperor Constantine, in thanks to the Christian God for victories in battle, to become the center of the empire (and of the Christian Church). The growth of Christianity, one of the most rapid sweeps in the history of the world's religions, had elicited increasing hostility in the Roman empire on account of the obvious exclusive allegiance of Christians to "their" God and not to the emperor as God. With the sympathy for and conversion to Christianity of many emperors after Constantine, however, imperial power to impose or permit the persecution of Christians for their reluctance to submit to Roman religious practices became relatively unthreatening.

Once the survival of Christianity rested no longer with the martyrs, but with the emperor, the Christian ideal of the martyr underwent changes. As martyrdom ceased to be an active practice, it became a commemorated one. In the spirit of Tertullian's second-century proverb, "the blood of the martyrs is the seed of the Church," martyrs became the center of cults, with their bones authenticated as relics. Willingness to submit oneself to torture became interpreted figuratively as a posture to be adopted "in intention" vis-à-vis spiritual or demonic rather than temporal threats. Even the interpretation of the Eucharist shifted in emphasis. As a lingering vestige of the once highly prominent role of Christ and his followers as martyrs, the celebration of the Eucharist in the practices of the medieval Church of Rome would henceforth emphasize its sacrificial element more than its spiritual or communal aspects. Bishops of the Christian Church would thus appropriate to themselves, as the only ones throughout the Middle Ages who actually reenacted the Last Supper, the glory and suffering of martyrdom in their imitation of Christ's sacrifice.

The anchorite By the third century after Jesus, there were also followers emphasizing overwhelmingly a different part of Jesus' life as *the* way of the Christian: Jesus' withdrawal into the desert. They interpreted his act as a demonstrative retreat from society, an individual confrontation with evil, a testing of the body in asceticism and the soul in meditation. To men such as Anthony in his village along the Nile, Jesus' words and acts took on a very literal meaning as guides to a Christian lifestyle. The sad state of society in the first centuries of the Christian era was to Anthony a symptom of its radical diseases. The rich were preoccupied with their devotion to the delights of luxury, and the poor, with their state of suppression and loss of contact with the goodness of God. Both manifested their failure to seek a way to cure the situation. For Anthony and others, the obvious failure of the Jewish, Roman, and Hellenic societies to acknowledge the social and religious guidance of Jesus of Nazareth, the Messiah divinely sent, was the final sign that a wave of decadence had washed over humanity. Humans had lost sight of God.

A Christian could not truly be a follower of Jesus without understanding how he had met the challenge of the world's distractions. Thus, it was deemed time to relive Jesus' own 40-day stay in the desert. The distinctive lifestyle which men such as Anthony assumed to be that of the devout Christian, though certainly not adopted by all believers, did not go unnoticed, due mostly to a number of writings which emerged by or about the hermits themselves. The meditations and biographies of the desert "Fathers of the Church," as many of them came to be known, reveal that they saw themselves reliving that part of Jesus' earthly life most significant for their time. They were returning "back to God alone," back to the bare essentials of bodily existence, in order to reclaim the freshness, purity, and vitality of the soul beyond the distraction and corruption of their contemporary society.

It was, according to hermits' writings, the need to withdraw from the comforts of the corrupt, to undo the work on one's soul of the ignorant or evil, to pursue life in Christ-like vigor and purity, which led them first and foremost to live in isolation, but also to forgo food and water for days, to sit atop pillars, or to inhabit hyena caves. Although the hermits were often able to continue their ascetic ways throughout their lives, they were rarely able to live for long periods in solitude. Many became very well known and admired as "holy men," and the curious or devout gravitated to them. Some, such as Anthony, found themselves forced to retreat ever farther into the "wilderness" as their followers formed a community. Others, like Pachomius, after failing to find his calling in the solitary life, set about to pursue asceticism in community. Pachomian communities were, in fact, to spell the future. The era of the hermetic as the exemplary lifestyle was relatively short, and although there were numerous isolated instances of individuals, such as Francis of Assisi in the thirteenth century, withdrawing from society in religious fervor, life of the religious in community rapidly came to take the place of life in devout isolation.

A Creation of God

A concept of creation is recognizable in almost every religion which entertains belief in a higher being or god. Christianity is no exception. There are a number of common elements discernible within the writings and practices of the early believers which point to an emerging Christian concept of one god, and a Christian theology. The practice of baptism was joined by other rituals for expressing a belief in the Christian god: the role of life-after-death in determining prescriptions for life-on-earth; the stated authority of the "words of God;" a general explanation of the relationship between God as Christ's father, Christ as God's son, and the Holy Spirit; and the emphasis on the commonness or alikeness of all human beings compared to God. From these elements there began to emerge the Christian concept of man's relation to his god. Thus, in addition to the Christian individual's relationship to the Son of God, or Jesus, Christian thought included also the relationship of the individual believer to God the Father or creator. The concept of creation, meaning the natural world including human beings, became increasingly important within medieval Christianity, and would come under discussion many times as the theological component of the religion grew in strength.

Two works provided a textual basis for medieval discussions of creation, the Bible and Plato's *Timaeus*. The rebirth in Christianity

of the Old Testament, especially in the period following the first full
Latin translation of the orthodox Christian Bible (completed by
Jerome by 420)[2], emphasized the relationship of "creator–created"
in the story of Genesis. On the sixth day, it was recorded in
Genesis, God made human beings to His image (Gen. 1:27). Further
Genesis included the story of the Fall: as Adam and Eve, God's most
prized creations, ate of the fruit of knowledge in the Garden of
Eden, they acted independently of God's will and were thus banished
from Eden. Texts of the New Testament were also connected to the
medieval discussion of creation. The words of the prologue to the
Gospel of John ("And the Word became flesh and dwelt among us;"
"In the beginning was the Word . . . ; all things were made through
him, and without him was not anything made that was made;" John
1:14, 1–3) were interpreted to mean that Jesus was the Word, the
exemplary link between God and His creation in specific time and
place. Creation was affirmed both as a particularized and individual
act and as an offering to redeem the good, a re-creation.

Interpretations of texts which placed emphasis on human beings
as the pinnacle of God's creation would play an important, but not
necessarily unifying, role in Christian theology. The father of one
tradition, Augustine, a prominent bishop of the fourth century,
understood the biblical stories of creation and redemption to illustrate the distance between God and humankind. Only through
God's grace and the sacrifice of His Son could human beings hope
to experience a closeness with their creator. Augustine denied any
connection between divine and human creativity and thus any creative instance or human faculty by which human beings could elevate
themselves to their maker.

Christian thinkers of the twelfth and thirteenth centuries in their
preoccupation with understanding God's essence and creative work
(as well as their own) incorporated the ideas of pagan philosophers
into their writing and began to observe human creativity more
closely. They were especially inspired by the late fourth-century
writer Macrobius, who did not hesitate to compare God's handi-
work to that of the human artist, to formulate a rival tradition. His
belief in the possibility of comparing human capabilities with the
divine was identified during the revival of interest in his work in the
twelfth century with the influence of the *Timaeus* and Plato's
concept of the "creator–created" relationship as one of "modeller–
reproduction." The Platonist's "man as image of the creating
Demiurge" was given Christian temper with the idea that the artist
must earn the ultimate Maker's praise and blessing (Gen. 1:21–2) by
creating with endowed reason and wisdom. As if to assess the

capacity of human reason and wisdom to create, medieval writers observed, listed, and described human activities, categorizing them according to invention and design, or utility and aesthetic component. The parallel between God the creator and His human "likeness" as "creator" in imitation was elaborated. The poet, for example, creates with language as God has with matter. Chrétien de Troyes, a poet of the nobility of the twelfth century, infused but a whisper of modest dependence on his model-creator in describing one of his *estoire* as one "which will always be remembered as long as Christianity shall last."[3]

During the Middle Ages an emerging conscious recognition of the distinctiveness of each human individual was thus due in part to reflections on God's act of creation and his particularized link with humanity. Works in which an autobiographical component was included as more than just a literary device, such as *The History of My Calamities* by Peter Abelard, appeared by the twelfth century. Architects and sculptors signed their works for the first time in the same century. Some historians, such as Auberjonois, have interpreted such signatures, as, for example, "gislebertus made this" as "self-glorification".[4] Indeed, the raising of man as creator into the triad of God's and nature's works, as voiced by William of Conches (following Calcidius, Plato's fourth-century translator)[5], did show an increase in the self-confidence of individuals. It could be argued, however, that the self-confidence was a new perception, elevating the individual more in terms of the "value of the artist or craftsman in intellectual circles"[6] than in terms of vanity.

The Christian Community

Religious communities define themselves by beliefs and practices shared in common. The continued unity of a dispersed religious group depends fundamentally on the ability of its members to communicate with one another. Communication is important both to maintain uniformity in religious traditions and to expand the community. In the modern era, communication has been greatly facilitated with a multitude of technological developments all stemming from the fifteenth-century western invention of printing. In the Middle Ages, however, the transmission of information demanded enormous effort and time. Information was carried primarily by word of mouth, or by the handwritten word. Even well after Christianity was widely adopted in the West, information about Christian beliefs and practices was spread mostly by those travelling as merchants or missionaries. Rome's initial opposition to Christianity added to the obstacles of distance, time, and technique already posed to communication among early Christians, but from the start the exchanges essential to affirming unity and to establishing a sense of identity within the new religion were successfully fostered.

The Importance of Belonging

The early Christians developed signs and practices by which they as followers of Christ were distinguished either to each other or from others. In the earliest decades after Christ's death, Christian rituals were practised in closed community. While the services were probably open, certain components of Christian worship, such as the Lord's Prayer and the baptismal creed, were most likely rehearsed only by believers. Only believers would be baptized or partake of the Eucharist. Should non-believers share in Christian rites, their identity, it was thought, would be revealed by antipathetic effects; for instance, induced illness. The most prominent identifying sign of Christians' faith in their daily life was use of the sign of the cross. By the second century, making the sign of the cross with fingers on the brow "at every forward step and movement, at every going in and out" was an established Christian custom.[7] In the third century Cyril of Jerusalem called it "the sign of the faithful," and contemporary stories, such as that of the Christian quarrymen who because they made the sign of the cross on their tools had fewer broken tools than their co-workers, reflect just how distinguishing a practice it was.

Of what particular importance to early and medieval Christianity were its signs and rituals affirming and communicating identity and belonging? Christian signs and rituals implied to those who understood them that the beliefs of Christianity were shared in common. The process of explaining those beliefs as such would not be necessary for anyone signaling identity. In addition, individuals who would identify themselves as informed and avowed Christians would be acknowledging their strength to respond to new actions and ideas challenging the community either from within or without. Buoyed by their faith and sense of community support, the self-identifying Christians in the early centuries after Jesus' death were fearlessly eager to spread their beliefs. Christian messages were carried by the devout, mostly via the sea along East–West trade routes. Occasionally a particular individual, such as Paul, was invited to visit a community.

During the phase of Christian persecution, identifying signs of adherence to the Christian community were especially important. Missionaries often had to be brought into a community under secrecy which, as it was generally rather risky, necessitated rapid confirmation of a Christian's identity. Of interest in relation to the sociology of early Christianity is the fact that in western Europe, conversions were often sought specifically in the upper strata of society precisely because these strata possessed the wherewithal to shelter believers in safety; of particular interest to intellectual history is the fact that these upper strata had the ability to read, and thus could include written messages among the other signs of belonging to the Christian community. Influence of Christianity in the highest echelons of the western governments of late imperial Rome and the early Middle Ages partly explains how the upper classes became a source from which conversion and manipulation of the peasantry was (sometimes violently) effected.

Within Christianity, the means of communicating identity and belonging were based upon certain rituals and words, which, as has been seen, were symbolic of accounts in the Bible, but also of the experiences of the earliest followers. The widespread and continual use of identifying practices had several lasting effects throughout Christian history, in respect of these sources. In the long run, experiential sources came to be less favored by the official Church, while textual sources were elevated. Along with acceptance of a notion of Christian orthodoxy (correct practice or teaching) came the assumption that there was a written authoritative "source" for Christian rituals. In the ninth century, medieval scholars showed particular zeal searching through the manuscript libraries of Europe for the "foundational" texts of Christian beliefs and rituals to which, with their own copies, they could refer when desired.

In fact, throughout the Middle Ages, connections between the written word and Christian beliefs were eagerly affirmed, and new interpretations were expansively articulated. Christian written works of all kinds were widely sought, and it was thought purposeful to consider all their symbolic and ritualistic aspects. By comparing current practices with the written text, it was believed by many that the most authentic Christian practice could be established for use as the basis of spiritual reflection. Symbolic pre-Christian numerology in the Bible was, for example, emphasized rather than eliminated. Almost any Christian literate in Latin desired access to a copy of the New Testament and the writings of the earliest Christian hermits and patristic writers.

Early transformations in the western Christian liturgy (from

Greek, *leitourgia*, sacred "service") will perhaps provide a good example of one process by which many aims and values for communal expression became incorporated into one set of rituals. Components of Christian service were evolving initially somewhat independently from numerous sources: Jewish rituals, Jesus' words, apostles' experiences, and believers' interpretations. Already by the mid-second century, however, a basic framework of the Mass was clearly described. Although Churchmen, such as Ambrose and Augustine, argued against liturgical uniformity, prescriptive documents appeared from the beginning of the third century, written as if to forestall change and innovation, and to maintain a universal standard of ritual practice in all Christian communities.[8] Contemporary texts note as elements of the liturgy scriptural reading, a sermon, prayers, the Eucharist, and especially the requisite rituals of community acceptance including baptism and the baptismal Eucharist, as well as prayers for ordination to various clerical positions.

Texts and rules were to replace improvisation and changes to liturgical composition. Biblical manuscripts by the fourth century were to contain directives for liturgical use, and *libelli missarum*, books specific to the Mass, began to circulate. Appeal to text meant standardization not only in form but also in language. The Bishop of Rome, Damasus (366–84) Latinized the Mass, until then still conducted in Greek. At the same time, finding inspiration in Roman pagan rites and court practices, he and succeeding bishops would render a simple ceremony lengthy and formal. Scriptural extracts were extended. Prayers were prescribed at specific intervals.

The changes were adopted undeniably at the expense of variety, spontaneity, and regional expression, but at the gain of unity and a sense of common identity among widely scattered Christian communities. The components of the liturgy which had first been the outgrowth of a sense of community became so rigorized that Christian gatherings were dominated by worship rather than fellowship. The transformed proceedings of the Mass actually barred the laity from a sense of participation in the activity at all. Decoration and ceremonious movements, adherence to Latin, and the erecting of screens in front of the altar were all devices to distance the liturgical activity out of the realm of the accessible.

Christianity was not, for all this, reduced to a dependence upon signs and rituals, but these codes did serve as agents of continuity in the practical realm. New groups, once converted to the religion through specific religious individuals and demonstrations, frequently revered their missionaries as saints and commemorated their acts as testimonials of God. It must also be remembered that the sign, second to the spoken word, was of extreme importance in instilling, in a predominantly illiterate community, a sense of belonging. The role of pictorial representations for the illiterate in church wall-paintings and stained glass windows, as well as in manuscripts designated for the literate Christian, was highly important in the intellectual climate of Christianity. The symbols of Christian identity – its signs, its art, and liturgical worship – were, then, far more important in defining Christian identity for the masses of medieval Christians than any of the theology based on the learned study of the Bible and the Church Fathers.

Communities Within

The Church   Hand in hand with the unification and codification of Christian rituals came the formation of an institution in which certain members were responsible for performing those rituals, the acknowledged Church (*ecclesia*) or assembly with its clergy. The power of officiating Christian liturgy entailed the establishing of a hierarchy within the Church. Clergy became distinct from laity, especially as the Old Testament Levitical priesthood with its ritual purity became a strong model for clerical service. Apostles, still seen as the originators of the institution, were thought to have their successors not in the community itself, but in the clergy alone. Within the ranks of the clergy, bishops were designated to preside over the whole of the community and to administer the sacraments. Their official duties comprised the founding and legislating of new churches and the ordaining of clergy, as well as the celebration of the Eucharist. The earlier positions of presbyters and deacons, and those commissioned to minister to the sick and needy or to teach, all came under episcopal administrative care.

The position of bishop quickly became politically important to the Church's survival. The alliance of the emerging Christian Church with regional, civic, or later imperial institutions in order to effect the spread and permeation of Christianity had a great impact on its form. Bishops adopted the Roman *dioecesis* and *civitas* as divisions of their power, ultimately grouping the dioceses into *provinciae* or provinces in full recognition of the Roman administration as the model for Church organization. There was no universal procedure for the ordination of bishops; however, individuals were often chosen to that office for more than their piety. Ambrose, Bishop of Milan, a member of an influential family, was, for example, persuaded to become bishop in 373 despite his not having been previously baptized. He was chosen largely because he had been elected governor of Aemilia-Liguria surrounding Milan, and the people of Milan were faced with an avowed unorthodox Christian bishop as the most prominent contender.

Controversies over the investiture of bishops, such as the renowned friction between Pope Gregory VII and the Emperor of the Germans, Henry IV, which led, until the resolution with the Concordat of Worms in 1122, to the denial by each of the other's power, were not surprising occurrences in the Middle Ages. Secular involvement in the Church increased to more than simply providing an administrative model. After Charlemagne, kings became protectors of the Church, and thus in imitation of Constantine and other favorably disposed Roman emperors, they assumed the title of Holy Roman Emperor. The involvement of the clergy in secular life also increased as bishops administered vast bishoprics and assumed political duties. It was all a bishop could do to turn up for regular services at his cathedral (the church in which the episcopal *cathedra* or chair was located), where his presence and role even within the Mass had become liturgically quite remote.

At first, clergy at all levels were relatively few in number. In all of Gaul in 314, it was reported that there were only 14 clerics. Although the Christian movement was symbolized by a bishop supported by clergy, the sense that the clergy as a whole formed a corporate body was long in coming. Each group of cathedral (or episcopal) canons, chapel clergy, etc. considered itself independent of others. The eighth-century imposition of a "rule" according to which all clergy should live, however, gave identifying uniformity to all ordained priests. Medieval priests were primarily charged with singing the divine office at specific times of the day and night, but with their assuming again in the episcopal Church administrative responsibility at the level of the *parochia* (parish), priests acquired the duties of caring for the physical property and real estate of local churches.

Christianity evolved in such a way as to consider the site of worship almost as important as the ritual of worship. The *ecclesia* (church) denoted the place of assembly or meeting. Edifices were designed and built to reflect the pragmatic and contemplative needs of Christian worshippers. They were thus eventually sited or constructed with chapels to accommodate tombs, relics, and places of veneration for pilgrims, with large porches for weddings, and with raised altars for the rituals of daily worship. Although often in the hands of lay believers, churches did not lose their character as real estate even under clerical ownership. Tithes, offerings, and sworn endowments were used to build and maintain church buildings. With general prosperity the religious edifice became, as exemplified in Gothic architectural creations, an ostentatious expression of wealth and institutional strength as well as a sign of religious piety and welcome to the many medieval poor and those "of various occupations" of high or low station who were reported as rarely going "to church, and rarely to sermons."[9]

The monastery By the sixth century, a new image of the model Christian would emerge. The past role-models of hermit and martyr, adopted during crisis phases in the evolving Christian community, were a highly individualized perception of a solution to the threat to Christianity's survival. With the adoption of Christianity by the Roman empire, the Christian community, whose vitality seemed to have been cut off by isolation and persecution of individuals, could breathe new life. The concept of the Christian as individual needed a new model, and the images provided by the ecclesiastical hierarchy seemed either too sophisticated or too aloof. Often embroiled in worldly power-plays, clerics appeared to be of lax morality, and not worthy of emulation by lay believers.

Monasticism was to derive strength from its contrast to the secularly involved example set by the Church and its clergy. In the eleventh century, monasticism was the reforming alternative to the growing administrative and legal preoccupations of the Church. Most higher religious posts in the Church were becoming secured through means generally dependent upon the social, political, or educational sophistication of the individual, rather than on long spiritual commitment. The popes, bishops of Rome, showed greater interest in secular involvement than in spiritual seclusion, leaving themselves in the long run more vulnerable to criticism for apparently succumbing to the worldly temptations of avarice, venality, and power politics. In the various waves of monastic fervor in the Middle Ages, monasticism as an institution was seen as forceful in part for eliminating the abuses and amorality of which the Church was accused.

In the birth of the monastic movement in the West, attention was focused, however, primarily on individual spirituality. There was seen to be an urgent need to provide a place for the strong personal expression of faith. Its initiators looked back to the conviction of the martyrs and the seclusion of the hermetic desert fathers. The Christian must not be preoccupied with the world and its affairs. The individual ought to be properly oriented toward scripture. Christianity practised in community must be simple and free of distractions. These were among the aims of the monastic movement which represented an alternative to the Church's prominent model of secular involvement. Could not a new model of the individual devout Christian be found, perhaps by returning through the old models to one based on scripture?

The individual emulation of a Christ-like lifestyle which dominated early Christianity was after several centuries still the main inspiration for the dedicated life.[10] The experiences of the hermetic movement seem, however, to have brought several searching believers to recognize realistically the challenge that rigors of withdrawal from the community and physical hardship would pose to any but the most dedicated. The idea that the hermetic life actually depended on a preparatory religious life in community came to be widespread in the West. "It is perfect men who ought to go out into the desert," wrote John Cassian (c.365–433). Benedict of Nursia (c.520) reflected that the era of the hermetic role-model had passed when he described anchorites as monks who had lived in common with other monks before setting out on their own: "Having been well prepared in the army of brothers to be secure for the solitary fight of the hermit, now without the consolation of another, they are able, God helping them, to fight with their own hand or arm against the vices of their flesh or their thoughts."[11]

Could all men and women be monastics? Already in the first phase of the monastic movement, a fundamental awareness of the curious exclusivity of the lifestyle was essentially evident. Ironically the monastic perpetuation of a perceived ideal of early Christianity, that all are equal in Christ, led in large part to its restricted appeal. Monasticism emphasized communal poverty and discouraged privileges, including those of administrative power. Women as well as men were recognized as admissible into the ranks of the initiated. Benedict designed his Rule of Benedictine poverty, chastity, and obedience such that it should "ordain nothing severe and nothing burdensome."[12] The monastic lifestyle was, however, not inviting to all who were religiously inclined. Some regular clergy were frequently quite disdainfully verbal of monasticism. Entry was barred to married women with children.

Lay believers, however, allied themselves fervently with monastics in order to identify themselves with the lifestyle of a true follower. Lay Christians favoring monks as the model Christians were instrumental in bringing about a reform movement in the eleventh century, affecting the institutional Church with their grass-roots pressure. Throughout the Middle Ages, poverty, labor (practised as prayer by monastic workers or *conversi*), and the virginity or celibacy of the monastic were imitated as ideals even by those who did not give themselves completely to a monastery. The opportunity to be fully part of the monastic setting was especially inviting to women in the Middle Ages. When given the opportunity, many women, such as Hilda of Whitby, Hrotswitha of Gandersheim, Radegunde of Poitiers, Hildegard of Bingen, Margery Kempe, whose names are known to us through their pious literary or artistic careers, eagerly accepted this way of expressing their faith. The medieval convent not only afforded women the opportunities of education and independence from the pressures of marriage and childbearing; it also provided them with a setting in which their individuality was exercised and could leave its traces for posterity.

The Christian World

The concept of the Christian's role in the world had its start with the beginnings of the Christian Church. Whereas the concept of the Christian as individual began in the context of role-modelling, the concept of the place of the Christian within the world owed its start to repeated attempts to formulate Christian doctrine and morals and to define the purpose of the individual Christian in the world, according to biblical interpretation. Although some early Christians, such as Augustine, were educated, their concept of the world was not particularly academic. They were focused on themselves, either as they sought isolation or as they gathered together in groups such as church communities or religious retreats. While Jesus seems to have advocated that a specific posture vis-à-vis the world was not of central importance to his message for religious change, the early Christian thinkers showed great interest in establishing a posture, at first a very specific posture. Their programme was in part a social and ethical rejection of the pre- and therefore non-Christian world, in some ways an expression similar to Jewish demands for rejection of the Roman world. Among the principal early Christian thinkers were many who espoused a strong attitude of rejection, an attitude not advanced by Christ, who seems to have regarded rejection as a weak response.

The solidifying of a Christian posture vis-à-vis the world expressed in terms of a role within the world, is thought to coincide with Christianity's establishing its own power base and identifying its leading spokesman as the pope in Rome. The shift in social strength of Christians (initially it derived from martyrs and hermits, subsequently from leaders of religious communities and religious advisers) took place slowly between 60 and 312. The evolution led eventually to the establishing of one individual, the pope, as the ideal of the Christian in the world, with both political power (papal diplomacy) and religious authority (initially doctrinal, and, with Gregory the Great, evangelical). Establishment of a papal see (over which the pope would preside) consolidated the development.

The term "Christianity" referred throughout the Middle Ages in Europe to the religious ideas of the Church led by the papacy. Limited in today's context, this definition predates the sixteenth-century reform movement which led to the development of differing institutional understandings of the teachings of Christ. To label medieval western religious thought as that of "Christianity" implies that it was connected essentially to the teachings of Christ. Indeed it was generally agreed that Christ's ideas, while perhaps adapted subtly by his successors, were the basis of medieval Christianity. The term "Catholic" refers to the all-encompassing (geographical, cultural) and the non-selective (intellectuals, peasants, rulers) embrace of the institution which based itself in Rome upon the orthodox version of its fundamental religious work, *The Bible*, and to official documents of that institution (such as the famous Nicene Creed).

In connection with a discussion of the Christian as part of the world, it should be noted that recognition of the world at large as synonymous with the world of the Christian dates from the fourth century, when in Rome a major change in political attitude toward Christianity took place. Christianity was seriously threatened in the third century with the persecution of practitioners by different Roman emperors. While such conflicts might have damaged the very survival and integrity of Christianity, the Edict of Milan (312) eased the path toward settlement of the question of Christianity's place in the West by recognizing the religion as permitted, a "*religio licita*," and by reallocating property taken from Christians back to them. No provision was made, however, for the treatment of Christians in the future, and the Edict was effectively declared non-existent under the reigns of several later emperors. In 381 and 382, however, decrees favorable to Christianity from Theodosius and Gratian were circulated, indicating that the new faith had regained a political foothold in Rome. This reassuring sign was almost as ephemeral as Constantine's Edict; it was soon undermined by the Roman emperor's loss of power and the battle was on again. The recognition of *religio licita* had become meaningless within the new and increasingly unstable environment of the barbarian conquerors, especially those who saw adherence to *Roman* Christianity as disloyalty. Given the difficulties of early Christians with political authorities, they might consequently have abandoned a worldly role; and there were those who unquestioningly advocated a more neutral, unthreatening posture.

Of the constituents of the medieval Christian's world, it was, however, political authority which was of fundamental importance to well-being. Political tyranny, which figures prominently in the Middle Ages as an actual political tool, was, in relation to the religious and intellectual views of medieval western society, scarcely disguised religious intolerance. For an understanding of the world of the medieval Christian, thus, it is necessary to come to terms with at least some Christian ideas on the political aspects of earthly existence, which reflect social and religious attitudes.

The Social and Religious Context of Christianity

Western Christianity was not strictly speaking an urban phenomenon, but it became increasingly clear to the early western Christians that the survival or disappearance of Christianity was greatly dependent upon the politics and social dictates determined in the seat of government, the city of Rome. In periods of Roman religious intolerance, persecution served as the release-valve. Distance and obscurity were the recipe for Christians' security despite the substantial external threat. Near the end of the third century, Christian individuals in the outlying prefectures of the empire did manage refuge for themselves. The fourth century witnessed, however, renewed presence of Christians in the cities, with their need for a sympathetic and respectful representation in government dramatically acute.

In many respects, the conversion of Emperor Constantine in the early fourth century can be tied to a gradual social change, such that religious and social change in Christianity occurred together. Social change manifest in the growth of Christian communities in size, importance, and most of all, in proximity to Rome caused the ultimate transformation of the Roman empire by early Christianity. It must not be thought that religion usurped the place in society of every other preoccupation of the time. It does, however, seem to have functioned as a critical focus for each. Political, social, economic, and even military factors explain why from the fourth century on, Christianity was to flourish in the West.

As western Christianity flourished in Rome, it evolved toward an identification of "Roman" with "Christian," and toward a greater emphasis on a political dimension for the religion than had been part of the teachings of Christ. Christianity began with the teachings of a single previously unknown individual living in a rural setting under the thumb of a distant emperor. The Church was produced, however, within the urban center of that empire, the great city of Rome. With the encompassing of politics by Christianity, some aspects of medieval Christianity would periodically be at odds with the Roman Church, the most highly politicized institution of the religion in the Middle Ages. The Church sought far more eagerly to gain secure power-bases through bishops in cities, concentrations of the most advanced social, cultural, and economic activities, than through abbots in geographically isolated monasteries.

The bishops of Rome were to launch one strand of Christianity which would throughout the Middle Ages lay emphasis upon guidance and redemption for the *community*. Another strand would tend to stress change and redemption for the *individual*. Christ, through his teaching of "render unto Caesar," gave groups the cue to consider religious ideas separated from secular life. The Roman Church was, however, to maintain the necessity of their integration. Many of the papacy's ideas (especially those concerning "the two powers" or the division of power between Church and State, or papal land claims in Rome, supported by the Donation of Constantine) as well as the ideas of early Christian writers (as, for example, the Christian ruler in Augustine's *The City of God*) were clearly conditioned by the political, economic, and social circumstances of Christianity in Rome.

Christianity evolved within a context not devoid of other religions and metaphysical ideas. It grew up in the midst of Judaism, pagan Roman cults, and Greek philosophy. It was, however, becoming increasingly clear that Christianity countered in particular Judaic beliefs and Platonic philosophy, partly by redefining its use of their ideas, in order to remove grounds for inevitable confusion. Christianity was both a reformation of Judaism and a reaction against Greek and Roman religion and philosophy. The concerns underlying Christianity's self-definition were channelled into Greek or Latin religious expression in "the desert" or in the cities of Rome's empire. A first major Church council, the Council of Nicaea (AD 325) reflected clerical recognition of a much-needed formulation of beliefs in relation to the ethical conduct of clergy and lay individuals, ecclesiastical discipline, religious education, and evangelical activity.

With the arrival on the European continent of the barbarian peoples and their beliefs in Germanic gods and rituals of nature,

Christianity encountered yet other religious ideas. Arabic invaders into Spain in 711 brought with them Islamic religion and culture, which Christians would address with the same seriousness they did Judaism. The manner and degree to which Christianity responded to other religions and philosophies will not be discussed directly in the present study. Non-Christian religious and philosophical ideas periodically received quite xenophobic treatment from medieval Christians. It is, none the less, to be stressed here that medieval thought, however Christian, is undeniably the product of the rich blend of many religious and philosophical ideas within its social context.

Few details of the social context of medieval Christianity can be included in the present study. Christianity played, however, a demonstrable social role; for example, in its conquests for conversion as well as in its education and maintenance of a literate class within society. In fact, examples of Christianity's social impact abound, for the Middle Ages was a period of many social changes, as even the quickest historical sketch reveals. New peoples, traditionally known as the barbarians, migrated into the transalpine plain of Europe, changing unified Roman territory into land dominated regionally by groups with differing languages and cultures. Agriculture far exceeded trade as the foundation of the medieval European economy, and yet for many centuries nothing more than a subsistence living could be derived from it. By the tenth century technological changes, such as the introduction of the plow, began to affect the connection of medieval individuals to the soil. Increased prosperity combined with a second wave of peoples invading Europe to bring about the feudal hierarchical ordering of European society into kings, nobles, knights, and peasants. As economic expansion continued, villages became town centers for mercantile exchanges with new currencies, or cities of political or intellectual importance. The influence of the social context upon numerous medieval religious ideas, and vice versa, is not to be ignored.

Christian Texts

A primary catalyst for an intellectual aspect of Christianity was the belief that the realization and understanding of Christianity could be based most soundly on reference to God's word, as recorded in the scripture of the Old and New Testaments dating from both before and near the beginning of Christianity. Throughout the Middle Ages it was the early period of Christianity which was regarded as having yielded the most valuable written documents, the works of the Church Fathers known as the patristic writings. For medieval Christians the importance of the word of God was summed up in the biblical verse "In the beginning was the Word, and the Word was with God and the Word was God" (John 1:1).[13] What role was the reverence for the word to have in medieval Christianity?

Medieval Christians were recent recipients of the vitality of early Christianity and its texts. Early medieval Christians were ready to affirm that the original *élan* of Christ's message could be sustained. To continue what had begun, however, the New Testament and its earliest interpreters must be kept ever in view. Next to the New Testament as an inspiration was the Old Testament collection of prophecies. As a guide it presented a greater challenge to the medieval Christian intellectuals. It was not to be used to add to Christ's teaching, nor, worse yet, to distort it. It was time to understand all religious texts in light of the revelation of a new Testament. An addition or distortion might reflect the interests of those who saw Christ as the king of the Jews or as one of the line of Old Testament prophets, not the Son of God. The doctrines of hell and payment might be singled out as representing the Old Law, which had played upon sentiments of fear and awe. In adopting a New Testament context for all discussion, Christianity was developing a means of interpreting the Jewish texts in order to incorporate them. In medieval works aimed at explaining the "creator–created" relationship, for example, the "created" was still often designated as Adam or Eve.

Emphasis upon Christ's teaching as the source of inspiration for the medieval vision of the role of the word allows one to grasp why the medieval Christians gave such importance to the Bible and the patristic writers. Even as change and crisis occurred throughout the Middle Ages, there were many who felt that every new age was unfolding just as foretold in the textual sources of Christianity. The carrying out of God's plan, following Christ's presence on earth, was to be found in these writings. There the clues for sustaining Christianity were to be found. Thus, Jerome's translation of the Bible from Hebrew and Greek into Latin, and the conception, by Origen and others, of a methodology of biblical explanation or exegesis, were landmarks in the early attention to Christianity's sources.

By the fifth century both the tome and the tool existed with which the Church would attempt to assure its theological integrity over time. Through the industry of monks in monastic *scriptoria*, the religious writings would eventually become available throughout

Latin Christendom. In this respect the monastic movement was very beneficial to early intellectual Christianity. Providing a locus in western Europe for the reproduction of texts and the study of Latin, and even minimally of Greek and Hebrew, monasteries safeguarded the possibility of direct contact with the most important religious texts, in place of an otherwise widespread exclusive reliance on image, ritual, and sign. In their possessing copies of the essential texts and their fostering acquaintance with philology, the monasteries held the reins of intellectual Christianity following Christ.

For most medieval Christians the library of essential texts consisted of a simple duo: the Bible and the Fathers of the Church, especially St Augustine. What practices and beliefs were to be found in the New Testament and the Church Fathers were seen to comprise all that Christianity needed in order to establish appropriate practices and beliefs for the Church in its age of the Paraclete or Holy Spirit. Small though the basic library of the medieval Christian might seem, it was enhanced by formidable contributions, which shall be explored in the course of this work. Constancy in Christianity which had endured the loss of the earthly presence of its originator captivated the minds of many early medieval Christians with the word as their guide. Western Christianity saw particularly in the life of the apostle Peter prescriptions for the religion's future course. The proper way of carrying out his mission would be the subject of discussion throughout the Middle Ages. One must now step into the fresh stream of early medieval religious thought, if one is to follow the course of these ideas through the long period of the Middle Ages.

For further reading

For general background reading on the Roman empire and the Middle Ages, see:

J. B. Bury et al., eds, *The Cambridge Medieval History* (8 vols: Cambridge, 1911–36).

Edward Gibbon, *The Decline and Fall of the Roman Empire*, ed. J. B. Bury (London, 1909–14).

George Holmes, ed., *The Oxford Illustrated History of Medieval Europe* (Oxford, 1988).

Edward Peters, *Europe and the Middle Ages* (Englewood Cliffs, NJ, 2nd ed., 1989).

R. W. Southern, *The Making of the Middle Ages* (London, 1953).

Brian Tierney and Sidney Painter, *Western Europe in the Middle Ages, 300–1475* (New York, 2nd ed., 1974).

Victoria Ukolova, *The Last of the Romans and European Culture* (Man Through the Ages: Moscow, 1989).

For interesting appraisals of interpretation of the Middle Ages as a historical phenomenon, from the Renaissance to the present day, see:

John van Engen, "The Christian Middle Ages as an Historiographical Problem," *American Historical Review*, 91 (1986), pp. 519–52.
Lambert Marie de Rijk, *La philosophie au moyen age* (Leiden, 1985), pp. 1–81.
Susan Mosher Stuart, "A New Dimension? North American Scholars Contribute Their Perspective," in *Women in Medieval History and Historiography*, ed. Susan Mosher Stuart (Philadelphia, 1987), pp. 81–99.

On the social context of the thought of the Middle Ages, see:

Marc Bloch, *Feudal Society* (Chicago, 1961).
George Duby, *The Chivalrous Society* (Berkeley/Los Angeles, 1977).
Alexander Murray, *Reason and Society in the Middle Ages* (Oxford, 1985).

On the initial impact of Christianity, see:

Timothy D. Barnes, *Constantine and Eusebius* (Cambridge, MA, 1981).
Gerhart B. Ladner, "The Impact of Christianity," in *The Transformation of the Roman World: Gibbon's Problem After Two Centuries*, ed. Lynn White, Jr. (Los Angeles/London, 1966).
Ramsay MacMullen, *Christianizing the Roman Empire. AD 100–400* (New Haven/London, 1984).

2

Early Medieval Religious Thought

The isolation of any historical period, through the designation of all its ideas, techniques, and social structures as original and unique, can greatly hinder a search for synthesis and continuity, essential to an appropriate understanding of history. Fortunately it is no longer seriously debated whether each part of the medieval period provided a backdrop to a succeeding one. Growing emphasis in present scholarship is also now appropriately being placed on the last phase of the Roman period as an important antecedent to the Middle Ages. To link together the end of antiquity with the beginning of the Middle Ages is indeed important. The next three chapters will pursue this emphasis in creating a bridge between medieval intellectual thought and intellectual contributions of classical and late antiquity, through discussions of early Christian thought, pagan literature and learning, and Greek philosophy.

Early Christian thought will be addressed here in light of the process of Christianity's initial intellectualization. The variety of practices and ideas which originally lay behind the early spread of Christianity slowly evolved to acquire the status of rationalized interpretation. Christianity reached a point in the fourth century at which the mere removal of non-Christian practices and abuses was no longer sufficient to keep the reins on a widely extended community. The theologizing of Christianity had led to numerous divergences in exegesis, clerical responsibility, and doctrine. Each was to be regarded as an essential aspect of internal controversies and to pose problems for papal claims to universal authority. Appeal to both tradition and longstanding authenticity as conditions for orthodoxy drove the papacy to seek to adopt a posture to the past.

The Growth of Intellectual Christianity

Older surveys of the Middle Ages tend to present only the later medieval centuries as a period of intellectual activity. In part, this reflects the approbation of certain scholars of the form and context of intellectual expression beginning in the twelfth century. This expression was characterized by probing logical expositions culminating in the scholastic treatise, and cathedral schools evolving into the university. More recent studies, using broader criteria, have recognized that the antecedents to that intellectual activity also deserve examination.[1] Between the first and the seventh centuries alone, at the beginnings of the medieval period, there was already a considerable increase in an intellectual contemplation of Christianity. This intellectual emergence is subtly included as a part of the important study by W. H. C. Frend, *The Rise of Christianity*.[2]

Documents from before and after Roman imperial adoption of Christianity in the fourth century reflect that almost every conceivable aspect of the new religion was undergoing a remarkable intellectual transformation by thinkers in the West and East. During this period, exchanges among Christians, such as epistles or letters, as well as scriptural commentaries, flourished. By the fourth century a wide variety of forms of literary expression (poetry, stories, hymns, and plaques) were being used to proclaim Christian beliefs. The most structured exercise in intellectualizing Christianity took place formally in the Church council. With only a few exceptional gaps, between 49 and 451, Church councils, attended by leading Christians, steadily increased in number. They began to serve the purpose of eliciting a consensus interpretation of Christianity from those present. At best they were debating sessions, where, in principle, decisions would be reached on issues which were to apply universally to all Christians, such as the role of revelation, papal supremacy, religious creeds of belief, and modes of scriptural exegesis. The very convoking of Church councils reflected Christianity's early concerns of authority and interpretation.

The writers of the first six centuries of the Christian era, reflecting an especial interest in establishing Church thought, might be appreciated as the "brainstormers" for a Christian theology. Their strong interest in *doctrina Christiana* led to an intellectualization of the bulk of Christian rituals and beliefs theretofore lacking an abstract formulation. Once undertaken by the institutional Church, the intellectualizing process appears to have been largely restricted to its upper hierarchy. Until the fifth century the laity of the day shows few signs of doctrinal angst.[3] Thus, as the clergy determined *the* interpretation of doctrine without reference to reflections of the laity, the scene was being set, particularly in the *parte occidentalis* of the Roman empire, for the rise of a religious corps as an intellectual elite and its periodic disassociation from the needs of the lay believer.

The notion of the Church as an institution, already noted in chapter 1 as important in early Christian thought, was embodied in the clerical hierarchy and the papacy. Hierarchical clerical structure originated in Christianity neither with Jesus' own teaching nor with the earliest Roman Church. By the early second century, however, most of institutionalized Christianity was connected to a theory of Church organization under bishops. Desire for the permanent local presence of a religious pastor, as opposed to the inspiration of an itinerant teacher, had by then become increasingly important to lay believers. While studies of the origin of the Christian clerical tradition tie it to the model of contemporaneous Palestinian and Hellenistic Jewish synagogues, articulate Christians, such as Irenaeus, were convinced that its roots lay in the succession to the Apostles of certain individuals who had "received, according to the will of the Father, a certain *charisma* [calling] of truth."[4] Indeed, the earliest lay Christians seem to have held their charismatics (prophets, apostles, teachers) in highest regard, but once the celebration of Christian pastoral rituals, such as baptism, liturgical worship, and the Eucharist, had become the exclusive privilege of specific ordained individuals (bishops, presbyters, and deacons), the latter established a definitive supremacy over charismatics.[5] All Christian communities came to be led by a specified ordained Church official. Further hierarchical ordering of privileges gave the highest distinction to bishops.

In the West the Christian Church rapidly underwent yet another transformation, from an institution dominated by episcopal theory, advancing rule by a collective of bishops, to one led by a theory of papal supremacy. There was initially no universal recognition of the need for a "papa" or paternal bishop, and the first drive for supremacy by the Bishop of Rome was really only appreciated among the educated and ruling class of the imperial city. His presence was valued, but more for local political and religious ends than for those of the universal Church. Still, a vigorous campaign for justification of the papacy was undertaken by successive bishops of Rome. The earliest assertion culminated in the fifth-century appeal to Matt. 16:19 and John 21:17, considered by some later medieval thinkers such as Ockham to be doubtful 'supporting literature.'[6] In his Petrine Doctrine, Pope Leo I (440–61) interpreted those biblical texts as providing a foundation for a by then fully developed theory. The pope, he asserted, is the spiritual heir and successor to the first bishop of Rome, the apostle Peter, the "rock" on which Christ chose to build the Church and the follower to whom he had entrusted the "keys." Not all Christian Churches were, however, persuaded of the superior role of Peter among the founding apostles and hence of his see's elevated place in apostolic succession. Papal insistence on the supremacy of the Roman episcopal see was the first significant wedge dividing believers geographically into western and eastern spheres of Christian influence.[7]

By the fourth century the formulation of guidelines and rules of clerical responsibility bear witness to the growing entrenchment of the clerical hierarchy in the Christian Church. Throughout the medieval period necessity for such rules was echoed, accompanied by comments on the misuse of clerical authority and office. Evidence of wariness exists already in the canons ensuing from debates at the Councils of Nicaea (325) and Sardica (Sophia) (342/43). These two early councils addressed the issues of insufficient spiritual preparation and dedication, manifest greed and ambition for higher offices, and celibacy, which would repeatedly be the source of complaints in the medieval Church. Opinions about the clergy during the slow demise of the Roman empire in the first centuries of the Christian era vacillated, as they would throughout the Middle Ages, between the coldly condemnatory and the uncritically reverent.

Counteracting a prevailing impression on the one side that bishops "all are aflame with the fires of greed, and slaves of ambition,"[8] a mythology of the divinely determined worldly role of Christianity was developing among the Apologists concerned with an evolving Gentile Christianity. The Apologists saw this new institution as a divinely chosen successor to imperial Rome, and its members as serving God's plan. The legend blossomed in *The City of God* (*De civitate Dei*), the early fifth-century response of Augustine, Bishop of Hippo, to anti-Christian rhetoric blaming the barbarian invasions of Rome on Christianity. Further evidence suggests that a worldly identity for the Church was being modelled on the universal and orderly identity of the once-powerful Roman empire. In the void left by Rome's fall, bishops and other religious leaders were to become highly valued as administrators, judges, and defenders of the common interests of the new Church and a new society, especially among a devout laity with both fears of the barbarians and the memory of Roman persecutions.

One general comment could be made about the transformation toward intellectualization which took place in the early phase of Christianity. The religion, which was considered by many of its earliest advocates to be a corpus of simple truths expounded by believers and more importantly demonstrated by their actions, came to suffer the confusions and ambiguites thought to be characteristic only of philosophies. What began with the first council in Jerusalem as an exchange of experiences and with the first clerical appointments as the designation of persons responsible for certain accepted rituals quickly became the advocacy of specific ideas and the codification of practice for abstract reasons. Baptism, worship, celebration of the Last Supper, and also the rituals of death had been the first rituals to identify one as a follower of Jesus. In the process of intellectualizing Christianity, the memorial rituals of Jesus' early followers were transformed into something more abstract, into a theology.

The transformation of rituals into an intellectual preoccupation was a distinct phenomenon, as the number of Christian treatises, letters, and councils from the third century onward bear witness. Undeniably many practices of other religions and folkways had antedated Christianization. The integration of some of those, such as the symbolism of the tree into the northern celebration of Christmas, entailed at least in part the importation of their meanings. A concept of life after death, a sort of guaranteed extension for the living as they await the inevitable end of life on earth, held, for example, a popular fascination among believing Christians and pagans alike. None the less, the rationalizing of shared rituals and fascinations was distinctly different from the growing fervor among the Christian elite for a theology.

A rift was definitely to emerge between popular belief and intellectualized Christianity. Initially this was due more to the importance the institution placed on its administration than to the inaccessibility of the ideas which would become its foundation. Once Church administration and intellectualization began, however, to have a collective distancing effect, well underway by the beginning of the Middle Ages, the laity's sense of having a role and understanding of its institution was firmly reduced. To organize smoothly and crystallize abstractly the experiential roots of Christianity meant cohesively elevating its founding practices to a level of "official" belief or teaching, a goal which itself required consensus among believers at the time. As will be seen in the next sections, however, after the late second century there was great confusion in the process of intellectualization. Institutional transformations and pluralistic interpretations of beliefs and conduct prevented a smooth transition to cohesive unity and led to sharp division.

Believers found themselves disagreeing both on proper Christian popular rituals and on their newly asserted theological underpinnings. Later in the Middle Ages, individuals branded as heretics attempted critically to disentangle popular beliefs and rituals from the theology upon which they came ultimately, if preposterously, to rest. To this end, they undertook the education of Christians in the vernacular languages. The virtual failure, however, of this later emphasis on the use of the language of the people in religion as the key to integrating popular practice and an accessible theology sheds light on the difficulties already present in the intellectualization of popular religion in the early Middle Ages. The medieval Church continued sporadically to integrate popular practices into its structure of orthodoxy in such a way that their popular meaning became distorted or lost. Christianized folklore and superstition continued to thrive apart from intellectualized religion.

The Rise of Doctrinal Issues

An early expansion and rapid transformation of institutional Christianity led inevitably to diversity in its intellectualization. Christian expansion transpired during the first millennium after Christ, with episcopal seats and monasteries spreading throughout Europe and in North Africa. As the number of Christians grew, so too did the number of opinions of what Christianity was. Schools of thought formed, usually based upon the espousal of issues by particular thinkers; Augustine of Hippo, for example, was the father of "Augustinianism."

Diversity in schools of thought frequently concerned differing interpretations of doctrine. Three important questions were more than once under heated discussion: How can an individual enter into a relationship with God? What must an individual do if he/she has renounced Christianity under threat of persecution? What is the relation of God, Christ, and the Holy Spirit in the concept of the Trinity? Three different individuals, Pelagius, Donatus, and Arius, addressed each of these questions respectively. The Pelagian, Donatist, and Arian controversies were to evoke wrath among fellow Christians, cause schism in communities, and lead eventually to the calling of Church councils to arbitrate. The questions raised, the ensuing discussions, and the subsequent formulation and defense of the orthodox position are all important facets of the earliest phases of Christianity's intellectualization.

Pelagianism

The articulation and following of the ideas of the fourth-century religious thinker, Pelagius, gave birth to Pelagianism, and fierce reaction against those ideas, especially on the part of Augustine of Hippo, to the Pelagian controversy. Pelagius' ideas, though the product of his lengthy stay in Rome as house chaplain to a wealthy family, were the culmination of interpretations developed from study in relative isolation. From his reading of the Church Fathers Lactantius, Hilary, Ambrose, John Chrysostom, Jerome, and Augustine, and out of his own beliefs, Pelagius determined that God endowed humanity with the resources to attain a state of moral perfection. Human beings had been given the word of God in the scripture, the guidance of Paul, and the assisting power of God's grace to aid them to undertake moral reform. For Pelagius, the sins of Adam and Eve were not visited upon their successors. Infants were born, like Adam, without moral blemish. In the course of a life of temptation, asceticism, renewed moral strength, and humility were some of the means of acquiring God's grace. Salvation of the individual would stem from personal effort and merit, not from grace alone.

Augustine, the Bishop of Hippo in North Africa, had decidedly different views on grace which he had already expressed in the writings with which Pelagius was familiar. Even before Augustine sharpened his quill, Pelagius had seen in the autobiographical *Confessions* (*Confessiones*) Augustine's fatalistic Christian beliefs and sense of the futility of humanity to attempt to redeem itself. As the controversy heated, it provoked from Augustine further development of his doctrines on the Christian understanding of divine grace and justification in *On the Spirit and the Letter* (*De spiritu et littera*) (AD 412/13), *Against Julian* (*Contra Julianum*) (Julian was a disciple of Pelagius) and *On Nature and Grace* (*De natura et gratia*), among his anti-Pelagian writings. For Augustine, humanity had inherited the sin of Adam and Eve and individuals themselves can do nothing to ameliorate it. Receipt of God's grace was the only way that anyone might be saved. Only by virtue of the Holy Spirit and in God's love was humanity lifted up and enabled to obey His law. Augustine believed that God's grace gave humanity "the knowledge of the good, the joy in doing the good, and the capacity to will the good" with the result that through His grace individuals come to be saved.[9] For Pelagius, divine grace had four components: "doctrine and revelation; disclosure of the future, with its rewards and punishments; demonstrations of the snares of the devil; and illumination by the manifold and ineffable gift of heavenly grace."[10]

As part of his theology, Augustine had also developed a doctrine of predestination which he linked to his antiPelagian arguments. Fifth-and sixth-century successors to Pelagius reflected their affiliation to "the remnants of the Pelagian depravity" in their strong rejection of this aspect of Augustine's theology.[11] They objected to Augustine's extension of the role of grace which they interpreted to mean that by divine will an elect group would receive God's grace without *any* efforts and that what God permits is the same as what He wills. By an argument of reductio ad absurdum, Augustine had, with his extended notion of grace, brought the institution of the Church and its sacraments into question.

For Pelagius, the Church was the community most obliged to pursue reform as a model for all men and women. Pelagius thought that educated laypersons should play an important part in the direction of the Church and refused to endorse any exclusive role for the clergy. It was, however, Augustine, not Pelagius, who was undermining the very *raison d'être* of the Church. The practices of both prayer and baptism had traditionally been seen as placing each individual's soul in a receptive, if not beseeching, relation to God and His grace. Now, according to Augustine's predestination theology, the chosen ones might or might not be among the worshippers or baptized.

Accusations of heresy against Pelagius came as early as 415 at synods in Jerusalem and Diosopolis. Although Pelagius was cleared at the earlier gatherings, by 418 Pope Innocent I was asked to anathematize Pelagius at the Council of Carthage. Pelagius was (wrongly) accused of teaching that humanity does not depend on God's grace and was excommunicated. Augustine saw the decision as in his favor, but anticipated that the discussion was not over. He preached in a sermon (Sermon CXXXI) at the time: "In this matter the decisions of two councils [Carthage and Milevis] have been sent to the apostolic see. Letters have come thence as well. The case is finished. Would that the error were finished also!"[12]

Discussion of the "error" continued unbroken into the sixth century, well after the death of both Augustine (d. 430) and Pelagius (d. after 418). The Council of Orange (529) addressed "semi-Pelagians'" criticisms of Augustine's doctrine of grace. Pelagianism was thoroughly condemned, "essential Augustinianism" vindicated. Effectively, this determined the teaching of Augustine, stripped of its predestination theory, as the official doctrine on grace in the Latin Christian Church. Several historians have questioned the wisdom of the early Christian ruling,[13] but that is not at issue here. Instead, of note is that the Pelagian controversy is one example of a highly intellectualized debate concerning very abstract notions (grace, necessity, merit) which would not only establish specific doctrines as normative, but would begin to normalize specific modes of thought, discourse, and decision-making in the Latin Christian intellectual tradition.

Donatism

Division into schools of thought also occurred over a particular aspect of the question of grace. Donatus questioned the state of grace of the individual who had renounced Christianity. He asked how any sinner could come back into a state of grace before God. Donatus was especially concerned with what a priest should do who had succumbed to the threat of persecution and renounced the faith in which he had been ordained. For Donatus, the purity of the sacraments depended on the state of grace of the individual performing them, and he wondered therefore how the renouncing priest could become sufficiently acceptable to God to be able again to perform the sacraments.

Donatists formed an independent Christian sect from the fourth through the seventh centuries, and early declarations of their beliefs coincided with the life of Augustine, as had those of Pelagius. Augustine's theology, in fact, bridged the earlier special-case issues of Donatus, against which he wrote in his *On Baptism against the Donatists* (*De baptismo contra donatum*) (AD 397), to the more general concerns of Pelagius who followed. A doctrine of the significance of clerical ordination, within the larger question of the role of God's grace, was the primary focus of Donatus. Donatus asserted that clerics who had renounced their faith had to be rebaptized before being permitted to administer the sacraments. This controversial position resurfaced periodically throughout the Middle Ages, with the strictest practitioners following in Donatus' footsteps and the Roman Catholic Church leaning toward a more moderate stance.

For Donatus, the individual was obliged to manifest his trust in the Christian God, and not renounce Him under any circumstances. Under threat of persecution of property or person, it was still essential that one hold firm to one's belief in God. Nothing anyone could threaten should be sufficient to break that bond between believer and God. To use instances well known to Donatus, it was those individuals who had tried to deny, hide, or break free from their connection to Christianity under Roman persecution who came to his mind. According to Donatus, individuals must stand firm in the test of their belief, especially because a situation of threat could not be improved by Christians through their submission. Any relief could only come from God. Donatus believed that all individuals, including priests, who lapse or capitulate have entered into a state of personal uncleanliness and sin. They are in need of purification in order to redeem themselves.

Donatus emphasized "purification" to such an extent that he evoked the role of uncompromising believer, already current since the "Novatianists," followers of the outspoken Roman presbyten theologian, Novatian, of the mid-third century. God alone initiated the possibility of defining purity. The integrity of the Church, however, lay in the integrity of its members. "Purity," His gift, is presented at baptism. Entering an initial state of purity is essential for all true believers, and cannot be re-achieved. Only through baptism and even re-baptism could an individual attain a state of purity within the Christian fold. Only then was the administering or partaking of the sacraments appropriate as a reaffirmation of unity and belief.

Donatus emphasized that the rituals of Christianity have theological importance, determined by God himself. They are the mediating instruments of God's grace, and dependent for their purity and efficacy on the moral character of the person who administers them. Priests would lose their capacity to administer God's grace through the sacraments if they had placed themselves in a state of sin. They taint the very sacraments they administer such that recipients of their ministrations are made guilty by association. To avoid such associative guilt, Donatists had turned from the existing organized Church to found their own, in which through adult re-baptism they could rest assured of the purity of their clergy.

Augustine's whole analysis of the question was very different from that of Donatus. Augustine believed that salvation was located within God, not transmitted through sacraments administered by priests. God alone had the power to purify or save men. Therefore, despite the fact that a priest had lapsed from Christianity, by virtue of the fact that he was once ordained a priest he retained the ability to administer the sacraments in all their purity. The personal state of grace of the priest could not jeopardize the purity of the sacraments. Their purity stemmed from God as instances for his transmission of the divine message. As noted earlier in the discussion of the doctrine of predestination, the Christian Church, even within its clerical hierarchy, was for Augustine not necessarily a church of steadfast saints. Augustine made saintliness marginal to the concept of choices made by God so that His plan might be achieved, as evident, for example, in causing the conversion of the Emperor Constantine to Christianity or the invasion of Rome by barbarians. In brief, Augustine's position was "purity by divine designation," whereas Donatus taught "purity by human choice."

The Donatist and Augustinian schools of thought on the issue of the role of the individual human within the Church were quite distinct. Donatus saw humans as weak and subject to lapse, and insisted therefore that individuals must hold themselves strictly to their bond to God through the institution and its rituals. For Augustine, human nature is equally weak, but also impotent; therefore, God merely uses distinct individuals as vehicles for the ultimate salvation of mankind. Men and women live their lives virtually unaided by divine intervention through ritual. For Donatus, purity was a necessarily conscious, active posture, while for Augustine, it was a unstriven-for gift.

One further aspect of the reaction to Donatus needs comment. From Augustine's belief that God gave His grace only to some individuals, it followed for him that it was also determined that the rest should be "forced' to join those whom God has chosen to lead in doctrinal as in political matters. Augustine argued thus against toleration and assumed a posture of coercion. The biblical phrase from Luke (14:23), "compel them to come in," was echoed by Augustine in his publicized position against the Donatists of North Africa for whom from 399 to 412 his offensive was designed to win imperial punishment as heretics. Augustine reflected in this aspect exactly the posture the Donatists anticipated from both within and without the Catholic Church. They saw no reason for optimism in Constantine's conversion, nor reprieves from persecution, but stood ever vigilant, devoted to the cult of martyrs, and prepared to face in turn the martyrdom each anticipated. Donatists' response to their condemnation by orthodox circles was that the true Church is the one which is persecuted, but does not persecute.

Formal resolution of what had become differences between not just schools of thought, but whole Churches, took place at the Council of Carthage in May of 411. Although Augustine had already succeeded in having Donatism officially outlawed by the Emperor Honorius in 405, he further persuaded an imperial tribune to convoke a gathering of both sides. After hearing the debate among 568 representatives in attendance, half from each side, the imperial commissioner recognized the Catholic Church as the only true church in North Africa. By the following January the Donatist Church was banned, its property confiscated, and its adherents heavily fined by imperial edict. Aside from the discussion of abstract issues (purification, guilt by association, the connection between ritual and belief), this controversy demonstrates the extent to which the Roman Church was facing increasing pressure to eliminate all forms of doctrinal difference.

Arianism, Nestorianism, Monophysitism

Discussions of the Christian Trinity, God the Father, Christ the Son, and the Holy Spirit, abound throughout the Middle Ages. In the early Church as later, at issue was frequently the relationship of the Son to the Father. Was the Son equal to the Father? Was the Son created by the Father? Are they of the same nature? These questions were first debated with fervor by the followers of Arius, a learned presbyter in fourth-century Alexandria. Controversy arose as Arians asserted that Christ, if identifiable with the Word or Logos, was, like it, created by God and therefore inferior to Him. Trinitarian controversies were again reawakened a century later by the school of Antioch and the followers of Nestorius. Nestorius advanced that Christ's nature was predominantly human rather than divine. Monophysites in the same century added a further wrinkle to debates on the Trinity. Their teaching insisted on the exclusively divine nature of Christ, countering thereby both the orthodox concepts of the hypostatic union and the already condemned ideas of Nestorians. Although the eastern Church was to be affected far more directly by local Nestorianism and Monophysitism than by Arianism, echoes of these three postures would reverberate in the West well through the Middle Ages.

All these schools focused on understanding the Trinity. They differed, however, quite markedly in their emphasis. Arius, along with such prominent early Christians as Origen and Eusebius, laid great emphasis on the logic of the relationship of creator and created. The created cannot be co-eternal with the creator, for if created, there must have been a time when it did not exist. For Arius, Christ was thus not eternal as was the Father. Arius' followers pushed the conclusion farther still to declare that Christ was not of God's nature or wisdom.

Christological concerns, or those dealing specifically with the nature of Christ more particularly, dominated the schools of Nestorianism and Monophysitism. Both Nestorius, the patriarch of Constantinople in 428, and Eutyches, a monk of Constantinople and the founder of Monophysitism, stressed the contrast between human and divine natures. They did not disagree essentially in their definitions of those natures, but rather in the application of those definitions to the Son of God. Nestorius believed in the conjunction of the two natures. Nestorians considered Christ inseparably connected with the Word, but the connection was not in the form of the hypostatic or essential union of Word with flesh. For Nestorius,

Jesus Christ was distinctly human. He was a man. Eutyches and the Monophysites recognized instead exclusively Christ's divine nature. Christ was of one nature (*mono-physis*). Even His earthly body, like the rest of Him, was believed by later Monophysites not to have suffered pain and not to be corruptible.

Aside from increasing factionalism, these Trinitarian debates had other implications disturbing to the institutional Church. For Arius, the inferiority of Christ as a creation of the Father meant that any institution of His founding was also inferior. Direct expressions of the power of the Father far exceeded the Church and the Christ-inspired sacraments in significance. Christ, who had no more direct contact with or knowledge of God than humans, ought not to be an exalted intermediary in or an object of worship.

Nestorianism posed difficulties to Christian orthodoxy, for it stemmed from a reaction to popular religious beliefs which greatly emphasized the cult of the Virgin Mary. Nestorius refused to acknowledge the Virgin Mary as the Mother of God, *Theotokos*, understanding this to attribute to her the status of goddess. She was for him at most the Mother of Christ, *Christotokos*. The insistence of Nestorians that Mary had given birth to the man, not to the divine Word, was not pleasing to those who insisted it denied proper meaning to the Catholic confession that God "was incarnate and was made man."

The worst doctrinal tensions were dealt with by Church councils and by a strategy of incorporating reminders of Church orthodoxy into the liturgy in the form of creeds of belief. Formal confrontation of Arianism with others' interpretations of the Trinity was scheduled by the Emperor Constantine to take place at the Council of Nicaea in 325. Arianism, or rather Origenism, was debated, and yet, as it was reported, the "parties seemed to be in the dark about the grounds on which they were hurling abuse at each other."[14] Apparently it was Constantine himself who deflected the discussion from the common eternity, immutability, omniscience, etc. of the Trinity to the notion of its co-*substantiality*. The statement of the council which laid down the Church's position that Christ and the Father are of the same substance or essence, *homoousios*, received almost unanimous approval. Its formulation became one of the most long-lived of all doctrinal statements, the Nicene Creed: "We believe in one God ... And whosoever shall say ... that the Son of God is 'of a different substance or essence' or 'created' or 'changeable' or 'alterable,' these the Catholic and Apostolic Church anathematizes."

Refuters of the teaching of Nestorius predominantly appealed to their interpretation of the Nicene Creed. It is not surprising therefore that Nestorianism was condemned at the First Council of Ephesus in 431 for its lack of accord with the declarations of the Council of Nicaea. The Council of Ephesus stated formally that "no one should present, compose or frame a creed different from that of Nicaea," which Nestorius was accused of having done in his interpretation of how God was "made incarnate and was made man." Nestorius was immediately deprived of his clerical status. Further, in 435 and again in 448 the Emperor condemned and ordered the burning of Nestorius' books.

Monophysite teachings were also condemned at a conciliar body, the Council of Chalcedon in 451. The formula of reunion which was issued from the Council was in reaction to Arianism, Nestorianism, and Monophysitism. Christ was declared to be

> of one substance [*homoousios*] with the Father as regards the Godhead, of one substance with us as regards his manhood; like us in all respects apart from sin; as regards his Godhead, begotten of the Father before the ages, but as yet regards his manhood begotten of Mary, the Virgin, the Theotokos, for us and for our salvation; one and the same Christ, Son, Lord, Only-begotten, to be acknowledged in two natures, without confusion, without change, without division, without separation.[15]

Pope Leo I had formulated the essence of the Chalcedonian Definition, and although it did not receive approval from all 500 to 600 representatives of the eastern Church (only two representatives at the Council were from the western Church), it represented the closest a medieval Church council would come to a unified declaration of Christian teaching. Human nature had not been elevated, nor the material world denigrated. As difficult as it had been to find a middle road between advocates of a completely human or completely divine nature for Christ, the contributors to Chalcedon seemed to have recognized the benefits that mapping one might offer.

Orthodoxy and Heresy

Diverse opinions were also expressed on numerous other issues of importance to both religious teaching and worldly activities of the Church. Was any one school of thought, however, to come to be considered the *right* one, and if so, which? Which was to mold most strongly the Church's doctrinal positions? In the early medieval period, already witnessing unprecedented expansion in religious intellectual activity, it was beginning to seem essential that a process or method of *evaluating the correctness* of doctrinal interpretations should be formulated and effected. For reasons that will be explored, only the most pragmatic of evaluations was undertaken. Ideas were slowly coming to be considered universal, by consensus and application, and authentic, by their derivation from the earliest writings of the Christian Fathers.[16] Other ideas were considered to be merely "opinions." To distinguish them from contemporary affirmations of the Church of Rome, they are often referred to by historians as ideas "outside the mainstream" or "on the fringe."

The papacy certainly came to establish itself as the defining body of orthodoxy on all issues it deemed important. In its early days, however, the papacy showed reluctance to define singlehandedly the difference between *doxa* and *opinio*, perhaps recognizing the weakness of its tools of enforcing "true doctrine." Thus despite the existence of the papacy there was, for much of the Middle Ages, a remarkable variety of theological interpretations. It was not always altogether quite clear, therefore, what the orthodox teaching was on any number of matters. A number of the issues which have just been sketched resurfaced throughout the medieval period. Not only was the collective memory of the early medieval Church not infallible, but with the thoroughness of later medieval intellectual movements such as scholasticism, and the organization of Church canons in the form of Roman civil law, such divergent ideas were reawakened and submitted to new scrutiny for the purpose of definitively excluding them by logical arguments or by recording their rebuffs as precedential rulings.

From the longer-term perspective afforded by the twentieth century, the significance of the positions that were being advanced on particular issues throughout the Middle Ages can be more easily evaluated. As the several cases above only begin to bear witness, the degree of nuance in theological ideas even about a single subject is, however, still confounding. To early Christian intellectuals, not to mention to the contemporary institutional Church, almost *all* ideas were thought to be of pivotal importance. Personalities, such as Augustine, Cyril, or Leo I, tended to dictate the priorities for debate, but most recorded opinions attracted at least a little attention. In fact, most issues under discussion proved to be exceptionally important in molding the medieval Church. Ironically, from the very process which was remarkably open to reflection on most issues emerged the notion that certain opinions ought to be treated as heretical or at least ignored.

Among the intellectual roots of medieval thought, doctrinal diversity was an essential one. The pluralism of early medieval thought reflects the fact that the early Christians were still exploring religious ideas in relative freedom. Slowly, however, certain ideas were identified as potential threats to the institution. Among other threats, it was recognized that such a diversity of ideas could not be tolerated if the Church were to secure a cohesive following. The denial of pluralism in the early medieval Church can at its best be seen as a catalyst for intellectualization. It restricted the width of the spectrum of discussion, but within a narrow range the medieval Church strove to express its teachings in a highly abstract intellectual fashion.

A Posture to the Past

The particularly Christian sensitivity to previous non-Christian learning, which was evident in the West from at least the beginning of the fourth century, is of prime significance to the study of the early Middle Ages. Of whom, or of whose writings, ought the Christian take note, especially concerning Christian doctrine? Was the knowledge of anyone who lived before Christ of any value in determining the proper interpretation of scripture? One had to be able to differentiate between helps and hindrances to doctrinal correctness. Witnessing theological activity of extreme vitality led the early western Church to recognize that to distinguish the value of what was said and done, authoritative decisions would have to be made. It was also becoming clear that the decisions would fall to those confident enough in their interpretation of scripture to have their ideas open to discussion and scrutiny. In addition orthodoxy would have to be enforced authoritatively. Ultimately the papacy would need both the confidence for decision-making and the means of persuading (or coercing) those of differing views not to teach them.

Many in the early medieval Church, in the fourth through the sixth centuries, sensed a certain vulnerability within the institution for two main reasons. The first was the constant rethinking and debating of Christian doctrine. As one historian put it, "a clever formula might, in solving an old problem, raise an entirely new one and a compromise meaningful and satisfactory to one generation of fathers was often interpreted in rival ways by the next."[17] The papacy was, however, beginning to assert its own authority, to be affirmed through the Petrine Doctrine and its extensions. The Petrine Doctrine, articulated by Bishop of Rome Leo I (440–61), sought the recognition of the bishop of Rome as "papa" of all

Christendom. It countered the claims of equal authority advanced by the patriarchs of three other apostolic cities, Antioch, Alexandria, and Jerusalem, and especially by the patriarch of Constantinople. Tense vying of the pope in Rome and the patriarch of Constantinople for recognition as highest Church authority continued until 1054, when the Great Schism divided the Church definitively for the Middle Ages into two, a western and an eastern following. Around 1274, passing motions were made to reunite the two again, but no agreement was struck.[18]

Along with making a claim to leadership authority, the papacy had to establish a basis for making judgements in disputes deriving from the historical intellectual evolution of the Church. It was easily resolved that the standard of measure should be scripture, but which interpretation of scripture? Over time, councils would be convoked under the authority of pope or emperor to settle disputes of textual interpretation. No council was, however, convoked to decide between the bishop of Rome or the patriarch of Constantinople as authoritative leader of Christendom. The two leaders themselves conveniently tried to resolve such touchy matters by avoiding the direct confrontation of factions and by choosing strong rhetorical posturing. An institutional practice was being established: powerful rhetoric might hold sway over formal discussion. Any side could use this to its advantage.

Two distinct intellectual strategies for asserting supreme Church authority were developing. One strategy was advanced by those of the opinion that doctrinal authority lay in an understanding of scripture alone. Another was put forward by those who argued that authority resides in the widely informed interpretation of sacred writing. Those who argued that any claim to authoritative interpretation lay in the acquiring of the purest understanding of scripture advocated a strategy of contemplation. In the sixth century, believers such as Benedict of Nursia codified locations, architecture, daily routines, and religious practices all conducive to a life of enlightening contemplation. Benedict felt that the monastic life, as he had organized it in his monastic rule of c.520, was the best strategy for understanding scripture. Failure of monastics, however, to dominate Church structure and decision-making could be regarded as one of the main reasons for Christianity's acknowledgement of past learning.

According to a second strategy, classical learning came to assist the claim for authority. Cenobitic Christians, such as Cassiodorus or Augustine, had already raised the question of whether scripture really could be best understood exclusively by reflection on it alone.

When the question was asked, they looked for means to justify the imposing on scripture of an interpretation, inspired perhaps by secular writings. Rather than using exclusively their understanding of scripture, derived from contemplation, as the standard for its meaning, early medieval Christian thinkers developed many of their theological opinions by questioning the import of scripture itself. The fact that the contemplative (and mystical) lifestyle did not become the model for the authoritative cleric meant that a challenge was posed to anyone, including the pope, who asserted doctrinal authority merely by citing scripture. The addition of the patristic Fathers' works, the least remote complementary sources, as a second strategy in asserting the authority of interpretation led, however, to much doctrinal and theologial confusion in the early medieval period. It was fundamentally unclear with what intellectual tools one could assert religious authority.

The Church was, however, particularly ambivalent about the reception of non-Christian texts precisely because of its sense of vulnerability. The continued presence within Roman Christian culture of secular works was frequently regarded as problematic, especially in light of their demonstrated relevance. The texts were increasingly being drawn into doctrinal and theological discussions in which scripture was ostensibly the basis for interpreting doctrinal orthodoxy. For example, papal edicts and Church conciliar canons had imperial support to suppress unorthodox practices. These means were not adopted without extensive (pagan-inspired) rhetoric. Many early medieval theologians were quite well acquainted with, and focused on, both pagan and spiritual writings. Had either a contemplative authority been recognized or an uncontested intellectual understanding of scripture been available, this would have been the time when pagan influence on Christianity could have been decisively denounced.

The vulnerability of the Church to being swallowed up by theological opinions of its own making and an environment of non-Christian culture made it grope for a unifying sanctioned authority. The papacy, it was asserted by popes as well as others, could respond to the crisis of authority in the early medieval Church. With the rejection of the primacy of contemplative authority, the papacy was forced to confront the need to adopt a posture with regard to pagan authorities of the past. The papacy was slow to advance decisive and determined intellectual responses on contentious issues. (Only two popes, Innocent I and Leo I, were noted in the doctrinal disputes discussed above.) Into the breach came the voices of others, many of whom had already provoked discussion by their infusion of Christianity with pagan philosophical ideas. The reception of pagan writings had taken place, in such a way that even when the Church hierarchy assumed authoritative control, it could not suppress their influence.

For further reading

For useful historical overviews of medieval religious thought, see:

Henry Chadwick, *The Early Church* (Pelican History of the Church, 1: Baltimore, 1967).
Hubert Jedin and John Dolan, *Handbook of Church History* (4 vols: Freiburg/London/New York, 1965–80).
Gordon Leff, *Medieval Thought: St Augustine to Ockham* (London, 1959).
R. W. Southern, *Western Society and the Church in the Middle Ages* (Pelican History of the Church, 2: London, 1970).

For an excellent overview of one respect in which Christianity was rendered intellectual, see:

Jaroslav Pelikan, *The Christian Tradition: A History of the Development of Doctrine* (Vols 1–4 of 5 vols: Chicago/London, 1971–86).

For the impact of doctrinal diversity on medieval Christianity, see:

Stanley Lawrence Greenslade, *Schism in the Early Church* (London, 1953).
Edward Peters, *Heresy and Authority in Medieval Europe* (Philadelphia, 1980).
Henry Ernest William Turner, *The Pattern of Christian Truth: A Study in the Relations between Orthodoxy and Heresy in the Early Church* (London, 1954).

3

Christianity and the Liberal Arts

Together with intellectual developments in Christianity, medieval education in the liberal arts played an extremely important role in the intellectualizing of medieval culture. Although education in the Middle Ages began among a very select group, it provided the catalyst for broad-based intellectual changes. The establishment of secular palace schools in the Carolingian era, of prominent cathedral schools in the eleventh and twelfth centuries, and of the university in the thirteenth century can be paired with the awakenings now frequently referred to as "Medieval Renaissances." In this chapter the methods, ideas, and important players in early medieval education will be discussed, such that their importance to succeeding centuries of the Middle Ages may be understood.

When the term "liberal arts" is used in twentieth-century English, it is usually intended to mean the group of paedagogical subjects which have come to comprise a general undergraduate education, without any necessary connection to Christianity. The "liberal arts" today are seen to be secular, perhaps even areligious, in content. Indeed the liberal arts were theologically neutral when conceived in antiquity. By the early Middle Ages, however, the classical secular education was confronted with religion and religion was to win out over secularism. The medieval liberal arts became remarkably influenced by Christian thought; at the very least, tightly surrounded by Christianity, more frequently, however, permeated with it. Even the term "liberal arts" had a meaning in the late Roman and medieval periods quite different from its meaning today. Few of the liberal arts of the Roman and medieval periods correspond to the modern panoply of undergraduate liberal arts. It is, therefore, in fact best to anticipate retrospectively neither the dynamics nor the content of the medieval liberal arts in order to understand them in their medieval setting.

A clarification about terminology should also be made at the outset of the discussion of Christianity and the liberal arts in the

Middle Ages. Even in English texts, reference will often be made to the Latin terms, *artes liberales*, *trivium*, and *quadrivium*. Respectively, the references are to the liberal arts as a whole numbering seven, and then to their traditional two subdivisions. The *trivium* was comprised of the three "language" arts, grammar, rhetoric, and dialectic (or logic), and the *quadrivium*, of the four "mathematical" arts, arithmetic, geometry, music, and astronomy. This terminology alone begins to make it clear how confusing it would be to assume that the liberal arts of the medieval period were the same as those of today.

The Concept of Education

Today the term "education" designates all varieties and methods of instruction and training. For medieval writers, the term was understood to be much more specifically linked to its "quasi-etymological" Latin roots in "educe," "to lead out."[1] Whence and whither the student was led were important factors in understanding the full meaning of the medieval process of educating. Most important of all was how a student would be led from ignorance to knowledge. The fascination in ancient Greece with education as an epistemological process and in imperial Rome with its functionality for the acquiring of a particular craft or skill were recast into an interesting hybrid of the two cultural legacies. Over the course of the Middle Ages, thinkers began increasingly to see individuals, as creatures who can be changed fundamentally through experience and guided reflection. The responsibility of guiding the individual through the change fell to the medieval teacher, who was admonished to make "a spark flash in the student" and "to know how to use his office to form and not to stifle the spirit of his pupils."[2]

The medieval concept of education fostered new institutions and centers of learning. Medieval concentrations of population differed from those of the classical world. Important political hubs occurred where barbarian groups migrating in the fifth century had settled, near old imperial centers such as Rome and Carthage or at new or previously unimportant sites for habitation, as, for example, Paris, Ravenna, Tours, and Aix-la-Chapelle or Aachen. The spread of learning into centers of secular importance was possible due to its survival within monastic centers. Once teaching extended outside cloistered walls, the development of new institutions and new settings for the learned master (new versions of Plato's Lyceum and Aristotle's Academy) seems to have been almost inevitable. Several historical details might help explain further why particular secular *loci* in Europe, such as Aachen, Chartres, Paris, Oxford, or even Rome should have become cradles nurturing the evolution of medieval education from cathedral school to private masters to the university.

1 In Italy and especially in Rome, discussions of Christian theology, the major catalyst to education throughout the medieval period, flourished with the rise of the papacy. Throughout the Middle Ages Italy continued to produce clergy of intellectual renown, such as Ambrose, Augustine, Gregory the Great, Thomas Aquinas, and Gregory of Rimini. Frequently Italians were sent from Italy's monasteries to fill teaching positions elsewhere. Many of these scholars had careers of intellectual prominence outside Italy. Even as Christianity extended ever farther north, the migration of religious thinkers to and from Rome kept the intellectual influence of that center strong during the whole of the Middle Ages.

2 In political centers throughout Europe and North Africa, a demand for intellectually trained individuals arose, especially during periods of stability. Such individuals were already in demand by the Vandals in Carthage, by Theodoric, King of the Ostrogoths, in Ravenna, at the Visigothic court in Toledo, and later by the Franks Charlemagne and Charles the Bald at the palace at Aachen. It was thus recognized by some enlightened rulers as advantageous to establish centers of study in subjects, including perhaps religion, literature, or the arts as well as law, rhetoric, and political and economic thought, useful for maintaining the strength of a government.

3 In towns, castles, and courts throughout much of Europe, increased economic security from the tenth to the fourteenth century created freedom from manual toil for many and true leisure for a few. The time, and with it the demand, for intellectual stimulation could arise. Devoting oneself to learning and extending patronage for intellectual activity had come to be seen as appropriate uses of time or wealth.[3] The career of Peter Abelard, petty nobleman turned scholar, which began with his teaching in Melun and Corbeil in Brittany exemplifies the extension of teaching even into villages at the beginning of the twelfth century. Even earlier, in 1007, Holy Roman Emperor and King of the Germans Henry II decided to establish an episcopal seat in Bamberg and gave to its church a large library.

4 Cultural centers or groups of learned individuals would occasionally be disrupted, with wars or dispersals causing an exodus of uprooted intellectuals toward another site. In the midst of assassinations and civil war after the death of Theodoric, for instance, Ravenna's intellectuals fled, some founding retreats for study elsewhere, such as that of Cassiodorus in Squilace. In the history of medieval universities, disputes at one institution played an important role in the founding of another. Pisa, for instance, emerged as a conveniently close haven from Bologna, as did Oxford or Angers from Paris and Cambridge from Oxford, resulting in the settling of scholarly emigres to create universities anew in those centers.

The Corpus of the "Liberal Arts"

Although the settings and the concept of medieval education may well have been new, its fundamental curriculum was definitely an inheritance from the classical era. Individual arts were already an object of study for Hellenic Greeks. The Romans thought of their *artes liberales* as the corpus of learning a freeman in Greek culture had needed to be considered educated. Studies have shown that the division of the liberal arts into the trivium and quadrivium was not established until after the writing of Martianus Capella's allegory of the liberal arts, *Marriage of Mercury and Philology* (*De nuptiis Mercuri et Philologiae*), in the early fifth century.[4] None the less, analysis of the components of Greek traditions in logic and of the Roman encyclopedia point to an unquestionable close link between earlier classical education and the medieval composition of the liberal arts corpus.[5]

Defining the liberal arts of the Middle Ages in name, number, and scope is a important task. The concept of a liberal arts education is a medieval legacy still vital today, if little understood in its principles. What was comprised by the medieval use of the term "liberal arts"? Recently, two distinct lines of investigation of the corpus have been pursued. In one, the liberal arts is viewed as a corpus preserving classical learning, predominantly through the language arts. In the other, the liberal arts, most significantly the mathematical arts, are seen to be the vehicle by which the new learning of the Greeks and Arabs was transported into the later Middle Ages. Both interpretations are yielding extremely fruitful results.

Preservation of Classical Scholarship

Without doubt, along with adopting the form of classical education, scholars of the early Middle Ages also attempted to retain some of its content. Yet very few Greek and Roman classical writings survived into the early Middle Ages, and few early medieval scholars could read any language but Latin. None the less, Cassiodorus, Macrobius, and Martianus Capella in Italy, and Isidore of Seville in Spain, inspired by the content and renown of classical texts, laid out in their encyclopedias the early medieval liberal arts paedagogical corpus with lists of ancient works and topics to study. The Carolingians listed Priscian, Ovid, Virgil, Lucan, and Terence in their arts handbooks as works important in the study of specific subjects.

To stop here, however, would be to overlook the issue of *why* the early medievals chose to study at all. Much evidence can be found to indicate that study of the liberal arts in the Middle Ages was seen to be the means to an end, as opposed to the end itself. Understanding of the Bible's literal and figurative meanings was the expressed ultimate end. Medieval scholars claimed to use classical texts as guides to reading, i.e., for inspiration, information, and instruction.[6] Classical knowledge and ancient languages provided the tools to mine scripture for meaning. Writings by early medieval scholars dedicated to interpreting the Bible as a literal or figurative text far outnumbered those dedicated to understanding or emulating classical models.

The "Liberal Arts"

The corpus of the liberal arts encompassed the learning of the post-classical age, which asserted its existence almost in spite of, rather than due to, classical learning. Medieval learning was apparently so essentially religious that while it may have been open to other religious ideas, it consistently deflected any secularizing influences of the third, twelfth, or any other century. The early medieval period is seen as an age which showed interest in classical learning only for the sake of gleaning religious understanding from it, by contrast perhaps to the later medieval period, whose interest in non-Latin learning seems to have flourished for the sole sake of infusing Christianity into the ideas of others. Numerous medieval documents reflect the idea that the liberal education was basically a step into the front lines of the Church. Scholarship meant preparing believers for confronting ideas.[7]

Difficulties can be exposed, however, in the limiting interpretation of the role of the liberal arts in medieval education as exclusively that of a propedeutic or aid to religious training. First, medieval educators appear to have been concerned with the promotion of specific skills which might find a religious application only in higher levels of education. For example, Greek and Latin, or legal scenarios, were used to teach eloquence, while mathematical exercises and the making of astronomical instruments were used to teach the skills of calculation and observation. Any theory concerning the use of education exclusively to inform religion is weakened by the observation that early medievals frequently read Cicero to appreciate (and imitate) his style, or Pliny's *Natural History* (*Historia naturalia*) for his observation of the natural world, rather than completely disdaining them as diversions from religious contemplation.

Early medieval writings reveal further that the medieval liberal arts education was in content and emphasis remarkably heterogeneous. For example, the medieval trivium included everything from the parts of grammar ("lectio" or reading; "ennaratio", history; and geography), to rhetoric, law, and dialectic. The medieval quadrivium might have included medicine as well as the classic four, geometry, arithmetic, astronomy, and music. The various accounts and curricula also show that there was no one set of authors or texts for any one study. The three or four distinct strains in medieval rhetoric observed by Richard McKeon and James J. Murphy[8], or the use, neglect, and subsequent re-use of Boethius in medieval dialectic[9] are only two examples illustrating that the medieval liberal arts education was not homogeneous in content or in organization.

Some early medieval educators of Roman tradition displayed pagan attitudes to education, but others exhibited extreme piety. Some educators were indeed enamored of Roman educational tradition,[10] but others adopted different attitudes to the past. Perhaps even more troublesome to the concept of a Christian education was the preoccupation of some educators with superstition and magic.[11] It has thus become increasingly clear that the early medieval education in the liberal arts lacked a coherent philosophy or purpose. No single paedagogical idea dominated or determined the medieval arts. To speak in terms of "characteristics" of any facet of the Middle Ages risks distortion, but to leave the impression that the expression "medieval education in the liberal arts" is largely meaningless, conveying nothing essential about what was taught or why it was taught, is also inaccurate. A generalized view of education in the Middle Ages will be advanced here.

Before the birth of the university, education in the Middle Ages was envisaged as primarily a procedure of systematic learning according to various recognized categories. To be educated was to be aware first and foremost of the scope of the liberal arts and of those authoritative writers who had contributed to it, and secondarily of the matter of its content or purpose. In its ordered study of language and science, antiquity had provided a model which the Middle Ages could adopt. The educators of the early Middle Ages seem hardly to have been dismayed that there was little content to aid their continuation of the form of classical education. Isidore of Seville very contentedly and systematically increased the content of each of the 20 divisions of learning in his *Etymologies* (*Etymologiae sive origines*) by fabricating etymologies of words under discussion.

In short, early medieval liberal arts education reflected a greater concern that ideas be collected, organized in specific divisions and transmitted, than that the actual content of those ideas be analyzed. An educator might be well read or modestly prepared, but in both cases, the ideas involved would be carried on. The student might be of the Church or a layman. Both individuals could support the classification of knowledge. While one might hope to discover a single purpose central to early medieval education, or a homogeneity in the teaching corpus, far more fundamental appears to have been the way ideas were selected and ordered. It would be excessive to state that the early medieval educators made no original contributions to the content of the liberal arts, but they were primarily paedagogues. Remarkably few early medieval writings were devoted to improving the content of the arts, and their few attempts were quite amateurish. The superficial level of the discussion of ideas in the early medieval liberal arts corpus derives primarily from the fact that saving and transmitting the authoritative expression of those ideas, rather than manipulating it, was of prime importance.

The continuity of thought from the early into the later Middle Ages acquires plausibility in this picture painted of early medieval education. This conception of early liberal arts training allows an understanding to emerge of the relation of the two parts of one long period.

Auctoritates – *The Authoritative Sources*

The paedagogical and cultural program of early medieval liberal arts education can be evoked with one word: *auctoritates*, the authoritative sources. The classical period was over, but its intellectual lights were not meant to shine in that era alone. And even if the works of classical authors were gone, their wisdom could be recorded in collections, organized to contain authoritative ideas on specific topics from any worthy source. The *auctoritates* of Christianity, for example, were the Church Fathers, and foremost, the "authors" of the holy scripture itself.

Auctoritates were the basis for the liberal arts education. It is necessary to recall that the early Middle Ages was an era of destruction and reconstruction. The fourth- and fifth-century arrivals of the barbarians into western Europe and the sixth-century attempt of Byzantium to reunite the two halves of the classical empire resulted in the destruction of much of Roman civilization, and with it much of Roman education. Classical sources had to be "re-membered" as much as re-read to reconstruct the corpus they had composed.

Early medieval scholars thought of themselves as collecting "everything ever known," along the lines of Pliny's efforts in his *Natural History*. Like their model author, they themselves were also gathering, from the past, for the ages and like Pliny as well, they fell short of the mark. The medical writings of Galen (129–200) glowed quite differently in the early medieval light. Cassiodorus' syllabus and that of the school at Ravenna emphasized exclusively his therapeutic works, which provided practical recommendations to generations of scholars who could only hope to understand his theoretical ideas in their own day and age. A lack of completeness and comprehension also existed in the case of the works of the Church Fathers, which could well be attributed to the early medieval absence of linguistic skills noted by the historians Dales and Johnson, among others.[12] Western medieval religious educators were truly fortunate if they had access to a Latin text of the Bible.

Auctoritates was more than a term of flattery. It reflected the absolute dependence on the classical age of those who were caught in the material turmoil of the early Middle Ages. Early medieval educators recognized the erudition of the authors of classical Greece or Rome. Classical texts revealed to them a world of learning, a world which could be regained with such texts as guides. Emphasis on the seven liberal arts in the early Middle Ages opened the way for eventually recapturing the essence, as well as the form, of classical learning. With classical works, the structure of the liberal arts could be filled out with time-tested and detailed content. In its continuity, the Roman educational tradition offered the hope of preservation of some attributes of Rome's culture, perhaps even its moments of peace.

In the night which followed the ascendancy of Rome, the sense of dependence on and reverence for classical learning was almost tangible, a veritable longing for the day past. Objects preserved in the night caught the first light as a new intellectual day dawned. In the writings of Bede, Boethius, and John Scotus Eriugena, Roman secular and Church culture was indeed transferred to a new era (in the guise of new institutions and rulers with the classical authorities as tools). Ninth-century education would flourish to unite and enhance all that had come before.

European Monasticism

Education in the liberal arts was fostered primarily inside religious monasteries, rather than in a secular setting. Thus an appreciation of the place of education within the life of the early medieval monastery is pivotal to a discussion of medieval thought.

European Integration of Eastern Ideals

It appears that at its earliest stages western European monasticism was highly influenced by eastern monasticism. The first monasteries in western Europe had a character decidedly distinct from those of the East; none the less, most of their ideals and practical guidelines had derived initially from eastern monasticism. Travel east, visits west, and manuscripts have been identified as the primary modes of the transmission of ideas from East to West.

1   Western European scholars travelled east to Egypt or the Middle East, perhaps to seek out patristic texts or to meet individuals of holy renown. Having encountered eastern cenobitic communities, they brought the ideas of eastern monasticism back to Europe with them.

2   Individuals of the East visited the West. Cenobitic monasticism entailed establishing monastic communities, and travel was one way of fostering and spreading the ideals of monasticism. Travel from East to West or West to East by those interested in monasticism was considerable. Journeys extended in the West into Gaul and in the East into present-day Russia.

3   Copies of monastic rules or accounts of monastic life originating from eastern sources, such as the *Institutes* (*De institutis coenobiorum*) and *Conferences* (*Collationes*) of John Cassian, came into circulation. The works were recopied or read by westerners, particularly by those who later established monasteries. Some western cenobites, such as Benedict of Nursia, acknowledged by

imitation their indebtedness to eastern models, reflecting thereby their awareness of other monastic practices.

Paedagogical Ideals of European Monasticism

Western European monasticism was dominated by three distinct themes. First, one finds a like concern for "separation from civilization," for removal to remote or forbidding locations symbolizing Jesus' retreat into the desert, as in eastern monasticism. Second, one finds the exercise of individual piety. The Latin expression of *lectio divina*, "reading of scripture," summarizes the sole educational aim of early western monasticism and indicates its meager relationship with classical education associated with the liberal arts. Although early western European monasticism may reflect a new emphasis on "schooling" the individual conscience in confession and penance, with the exception of English and Celtic monasteries, the movement, despite its handy communal setting, did not complement its emphasis on educating the spirit with anything but the most rudimentary education of the mind of the individual. Third, western European monasticism was strongly amaterialistic during its beginnings and repeatedly again at the start of each reform movement, a posture which came to be as much in reaction to the secular Church as to the whole of secular life. Detachment from the material tethers of the earth and material equality among believers were espoused by fervent monastics throughout the Middle Ages, particularly the early members of reform orders (until their orders acquired a taste for prosperity). Distaste for material possessions, including books, was periodically a significant impediment to a monastic posture fostering learning.

Lectio Divina

Since reading the divine text was the only thing a monastic education was initially intended to facilitate, one might do well to ask what the place of *lectio divina* in the monastic life was? Was there a proper way to let scripture stand apart from all other written texts? Three almost contemporary texts on the place of the *lectio divina* in the monk's life, one from the *Institutes* of John Cassian, a second from the anonymous *Rule of the Master* (*Regula magistri*), and a third from the *Rule* (*Regula*) of Benedict of Nursia corroborate the fact that *lectio divina* was given the most "practical" place in a monk's daily and annual life. It was for all intents and purposes relegated to the least labor-intensive part of the agricultural year, winter; and to the beginning or end of the work day, bereft of daylight in the winter months in many European regions. The proper way of reading scripture to the desired effect of permitting "the eyes of the heart" to contemplate its mysteries was directed in some respects beyond practical considerations.[13] The *Rule of the Master* advocated reading out loud to a small group of listeners,[14] while Benedict placed the Lenten obligation (and choice) on the individual to read a whole book in silence.[15] Cassian particularly stressed the contemplative understanding of the Holy Word and shunned the reading of commentaries. The rules reflect differences in emphasis, with each monastic leader expecting his emphasis to apply equally to all monks in the particular community.

Outside the monastic setting, biblical commentaries were thought very early on to play an important role in the proper way of reading scripture. Second-century patristic theologians such as Irenaeus of Lyons began to develop the idea of an approved way of interpreting biblical texts, which he argued went back to the time of the apostles themselves. Scripture should be interpreted neither in a random, nor in a philosophically abstract way; it had to be interpreted within the context of the historical continuity of the Christian Church. Origen in the third century proposed four possible modes of scriptural exegesis: literal, tropological or moral, allegorical or mystical, in which the Old Testament is interpreted as a prefiguring of the New Testament, and an anagogical or revelatory mode, which became the four guidelines for commentary writing throughout the Middle Ages. They were characterized by the following little medieval mnemonic:

> *Littera gesta docet, Quid credas allegoria,*
> *Moralis quid agas, Quo tendas anagogia.*

> The letter shows us what God and our fathers did;
> The allegory shows us where our faith is hid;
> The moral meaning gives us rules of daily life;
> The anagogy shows us where we end our strife.[16]

Already in the sixth century, there were individual monks who also devoted themselves to writing biblical commentarites, the earliest and most well-known being Pope Gregory the Great's commentary on the Book of Job, *Morals* (*Moralia*). By the seventh century, the Benedictine reserve against excessive time devoted to biblical scholarship had clearly faded. Biblical commentaries brought fame to the English monk Bede (673–735) during his lifetime as well as for centuries after. Boniface, a ninth-century missionary monk, wrote to England begging for copies of Bede's commentaries for his monasteries on the Continent. In addition to his commentaries. Bede also wrote teaching manuals in the liberal arts, including, for grammar, a work on metrics, *On the Art of Meter* (*De metrica arte*) and another on the figures of speech in the Bible, *On the Schemes and Tropes of Sacred Scripture* (*De schematibus et tropis sacrae scripturae*). The study of scripture with the assistance of commentators and the liberal arts had come to have a central place for both the secular and cloistered religious in the understanding of the Bible.

Boethius

Among the paedagogues of the early Middle Ages, the one most influential on philosophy and education was Anicius Manlius Severius Boethius.[17] Many specific individuals, including Abo of Fleury, Anselm of Canterbury, John of Salisbury, Peter Abelard, and Robert Kilwardby, to name but a few, were influenced by him, not to mention the numerous unnamed students who learned their logic, arithmetic, music, etc. from his texts. While there is much that could be said in support of the suggestion that Boethius represented early medieval intellectual activity at its best, there are signs that his ideas were but a part of a general positive contemporary tension between Roman and post–Roman emerging medieval cultural visions, between *preserving* and *rendering Christian* the traditional pagan liberal arts education. At the very least, this tension in early medieval thought reflects the fact that Boethius' work cannot be said to represent the full scope of early medieval intellectual activity. Manifestations of the general spectrum of interests can indeed be identified.

1   The interest in aspects of non–Roman classical culture. Boethius was a product of Roman civilization, and considered Latin and Greek the only essential tools for a scholar of his time. To his mind emphasis on non-classical languages, or even on Latin alone, would present preposterous obstacles to his agenda for scholars as transmitters of classical learning. To other intellectuals of approximately the same period, especially Cassiodorus and Gregory the Great, intellectual awareness of the products of other cultures, their language, history, and mores was acknowledged, at least as a matter of diplomatic necessity. Boethius, however, regarded intellectual concern with aspects of non-classical cultures an obstacle to the creation of a sophisticated

neo-Roman era. This may help explain in part his fatal vulnerability to accusations of treason by his Ostrogothic king.

2   The interest in religious belief in relation to the study of the
liberal arts. For Boethius, the life of the mind was not limited by
Christian belief. The adoption of Christianity as the light of the
soul would clarify reasoning concerning such abstract concepts
as fortune, providence, and free will. Boethius saw no division
of intellectual loyalty, as he concentrated on *preserving* the traditional Roman liberal arts, however pagan, while predecessors
and contemporaries, such as Jerome, Augustine, and Gregory
the Great, adamantly used all teaching, including the liberal arts,
as direct instruments of Christianity.

The most popular of Boethius' works was his *On the Consolation of
Philosophy* (*De consolatione philosophiae*).[18] It was, in fact, throughout
the Middle Ages the most widely circulated of all early medieval
writings. It was written in 524, during Boethius' imprisonment
before his execution, but the work had its real impact only with its
appearance in copies executed under Alcuin, probably at the court of
Charlemagne in the late eighth century. It came to be synonymous
with Boethius, apparently undergoing translations into half a dozen
vernacular languages before the thirteenth century. The use of the
Consolation as a source for quotations on all sorts of topics reveals
that the ideas of the author *per se* were not important, nor was
the work as a whole. The *Consolation* became widely read for its
"extractable" ideas, (for example, those on the liberal arts), for its
images (for example, Boethius' tears of misery), or for its model
elegant use of Latin. The success of Boethius' work also ironically
highlights the importance a translation into the vernacular had as a
means of reaching an audience ready for the ideas. Boethius' most
prominent medieval translators, King Alfred of Anglia, Chaucer,
and Jean de Meun, were among those who did not overlook the
importance of the vernacular when propagating their own ideas.

    The *Consolation* developed Boethius' thesis that in keeping one's
sights on the ultimate Good, all other goods become accessible.
Seeking the Good is put forward as the key to real happiness, on the
basis of which one can smile even at fortune's adversities. Boethius
conceived his book as a guide to survival, providing an animated yet
profound exposition of the "consolation" of philosophy. Boethius'
discussion of his philosophy, with its personification Philosophia,
served him as a form of psychotherapy. Guided by philosophy,
Boethius considers fortune, fate, providence, goodness, free will,
and happiness, in order that in his distress he could be free from the

first and open to the last. Philosophia was the "guide of reason," of which, Boethius felt, one ought to make good use. She was the unemotional intellectual guide whom all were called to follow. Boethius' characteristically intellectual emphasis on reason led some to conclude that Philosophia *eliminated* a role for Christianity and provided no motivation for one to turn to God and His Son for solace.[19]

Boethius understood the power of a belief to rest with reason, not with emotion. Emotion is seen as a distraction whose dominance must be suppressed to allow reason to achieve a level of control in the individual. The delegating of any responsibility to emotion would create for it a permanent role of superiority over reason. Also, Boethius' "philosophical approach" presents a "consoling" Christianity with no reference to Christ or the Church; no rituals, clergy, or institutions. Why bother turning for help to an institution, Boethius seems to have asked himself, when you have the resources within to guide you toward the important beliefs? Religion is about an individual's reason and belief is an inward union. Boethius made no reference to the sacraments. Similarly, he did not view the priest or monk as living the most Christian life. Any individual who has released himself or herself from the desire of goods and has desire only for the Good is as devout in his/her belief as any pious monk.

The independent character of the *Consolation* lies in Boethius' suggestion that only reasoned recognition and pursuit of the Good by the lay person leads to the peace of the individual's soul. Institutional Christian guidance, clerical or ecclesiastical, is ignored. Even the study of scripture is not emphasized to bring about self-composure and proper direction of the soul when confronted with the unpredictable and infelicitous whims of fortune on earth.

Boethius had early recognized that the guidance of philosophy might well be necessary for the happy life, and long before writing the *Consolation* had felt responsible for providing a number of major contributions to the cultivation of reason and to the introduction of Greek philosophical ideas into Latin scholarship. First, the mind needed to be trained, in an organized way, through the classical liberal arts. He considered two tools essential to that end, although neither was readily available at the time: access to appropriate texts, and a level of competence in languages sufficient to read the texts.

The difficulty of inadequate access to appropriate texts was to be resolved by Boethius through the project of writing textbooks for each of the arts of the quadrivium, *On Arithmetic (De arithmetica), On Geometry (De geometrica), On Music (De musica),* and *On Astronomy*

(*De astronomia*), dedicated to his father-in-law Symmachus of Rome. Although the textbooks were based on more sophisticated treatments of material written as much as nine centuries earlier, that material (originally from Nichomachus' *Introduction to Arithmetic* (*Arithmetica*), Euclid's *Elements* (*Libri elementorum*), and Ptolemy's *Music* and *Almagest* (*Libri almagesti*)) was not readily available directly from the sources. Boethius' texts were neither a comprehensive nor a sophisticated treatment of each subject. Some important sources were unattainable, and for the works he did have, Boethius had access to copies of questionable accuracy.[20] Of the manuscripts Boethius used, he had both to emend and translate the texts to render them adaptable.

Yet Boethius' textbooks proved to be paedagogical milestones and formed the core of the liberal arts curriculum well through the twelfth century. Not since the heights of classical Rome had educators had the opportunity of using especially designed Latin teaching-tools. Boethius' treatment far exceeded attempts by the encyclopedists, such as Isidore of Seville and Cassiodorus, to preserve many of the important points of classical learning. Having manuals offered the teacher a general sense of confidence in the material he was to teach for each subject, an established curriculum.[21] No longer would a survey of the scope of the liberal arts or a list of book titles for study suffice if one could procure Boethius' textbooks.

Boethius also attempted to circumvent the declining knowledge of classical languages among his contemporaries through his plan to translate into Latin the works of the Greek philosophers Aristotle and Plato, which he began in 514–15. He also set out to demonstrate that the ideas of Plato and Aristotle were not seriously irreconcilable on many points; his translation of their works into Latin was undertaken to establish this. Drawing on commentaries written in the second century AD by Porphyry, Boethius showed that Aristotle's categories in a number of significant respects could be incorporated by those of Platonic persuasion. The three subjects of the liberal arts trivium were in Boethius' day already based on the teachings of both Plato and Aristotle, and virtually all the writings after Porphyry in the dominant Neoplatonic philosophical school were testimonials to previous attempts at finding concord between Plato and Aristotle. Boethius' projects were none the less viewed in general with consternation by critics who considered him arrogant and long-winded. Eventually, however, medieval philosophers would delight in his accomplishments, whose components, a commentary on Porphyry's introduction or *Isagoge* and a translation/

commentary of Aristotle's *Categories* (*Categoriae*) and *On Interpretation* (*De interpretatione*), were later to become known as the *logica vetus* or Old Logic, and would lament his unfulfilled plans to translate the rest of Aristotle and Plato's dialogues as well.

The Carolingians and their Palace Schools

What impact did the liberal arts have on the generations of medieval scholars after Boethius? In order to begin to give a reliable answer, it is necessary to note two successive phases in intellectual development after Boethius: the monastic movement as it took hold in the British Isles under Aldhelm and Bede, and the dynastic presence of the Carolingians in Francia, first under Charlemagne (768–814), and then under Louis the Pious (814–40) and Charles the Bald (840–77). These two phases were very different in profile, although they were intimately interwoven. The Anglo-Saxon and Irish intellectual monastic traditions were well represented on the Carolingian continent in the persons of Wynfrith (rebaptized Boniface), Alcuin of York, and John Scotus Eriugena, and in the ninth-century reforms of the Frankish Church. Both phases adhered to generally the same teaching curriculum (trivium and quadrivium), but the liberals arts were taught in two different institutional settings with correspondingly different student bodies and different specific aims for education. One of the most striking differences between the two phases concerns their different relations to a student population.

The origins of an intellectual "renaissance" during Charlemagne's reign may be traced back to the fourth-century conversion of the British Isles to Christianity, by St Patrick among the Irish, and Augustine of Canterbury among the Anglo-Saxons.[22] Celtic and Anglo-Saxon monks, whose travel and missionary activities had not brought them into contact with any particularly strong Christian monarch, had founded monasteries on the continent at Annegray, Luxeuil, Fontaines, and Corbie before the eighth century. Monasticism in the British Isles was brought closer still to Frankish territory by Willibrord and his successor, Boniface. Anglo-Saxon influences on Frankish monasticism and the Frankish Church in general appear to have been the fostering of a bond between the Frankish ruling nobility and institutional Christianity, and the launching of a reform movement which included the founding of more monasteries such as Fulda, administrative reorganization, reassessing Church tithing and taxation, and changes in liturgy and monastic rule. Many of the clauses in Charlemagne's capitulary, or royal prescriptive, of 779 demonstrate his detailed interest in religious reforms in his kingdom. At the time when confessional and administrative issues seemed to dominate the involvement of most Anglo-Saxon monks on Frankish soil, there are indications that some, such as Alcuin, were also a part of the Carolingian inspiration to establish schools and a literate identity for the Frankish kingdom.

The overall impression gained of Carolingian intellectual life is that of groups of intellectuals based in monastic, cathedral, or palace schools, beginning to develop the vision of cultural transmission, *translatio studii*, to the Franks. The decisive first step in this movement came when Charlemagne, King of the Franks, made two declarations between 780 and 800 that schools should be established by the clergy to cultivate learning in boys from every station in life. From his position as king, Charlemagne had begun to initiate an era of intellectual reawakening based on his perception that kings, like the Old Testament Josias, are to maintain and strengthen Christian society.

Charlemagne invited Alcuin, the learned monk of York, to his court where, from 782 until 796, he served as Charlemagne's private tutor and advisor. The works attributed to Alcuin reflect the particular concerns of early Carolingian paedagogy: orthography, rhetoric, dialectic, grammar, and arithmetic. Louis the Pious was to find his religious guide in Benedict of Aniane in 814, and Charles the Bald in John Scotus Eriugena in 843. Under the three successive kings, great effort was expended to acquire books of all kinds, especially those which would help re-establish correct versions of scripture, and the Roman liturgy and calendar. The later Carolingian rulers showed a more profound interest in encouraging intellectual religious refinement than in advancing learning for all. Louis was extremely interested in the use of Benedictine prescriptions in Frankish monasteries and was greatly influenced and aided by Benedict of Aniane. Charles, his son, was keenly interested in theology and became deeply influenced by John Scotus Eriugena, who continued a project started at Louis' request by Hilduin of St-Denis, the translation of the Christian Neoplatonic works of pseudo-Dionysius the Areopagite.

The following points will illustrate the impact of the Carolingian era of medieval thought.

1   For the Carolingians religion was seen as catalyst to learning. Poor grammar, corrupt texts, and flawed reckoning were considered fundamental impediments to spiritual rectitude.
2   Considerable emphasis was placed upon learning and leader-

ship as the keys to a community's moral regeneration. "The Carolingian renaissance formed part of a program of religious renewal that Carolingian political and clerical leaders sponsored and encouraged in the hope that it would lead to the moral betterment of the Christian people. As a conscious effort to improve man through knowledge of the scriptures, the renaissance emphasized study, books, script, and schools."[23]

3   The relevance of secular enthusiasm for religious learning in particular is primarily one of setting a moral example. Charlemagne adopted Alcuin's idea of the ideal Christian ruler, as best he understood it, and provided a central administration and economy, and cultural and territorial expansion in an effort to lead his people as a Christian monarch ought.

4   The relevance of secular enthusiasm for learning in general was primarily one of patronage and the exchange of ideas. Charlemagne's court was a haven for scholars from all corners of Europe, a veritable melting pot of Lombard, Visigothic, Irish, Anglo-Saxon, and Frankish contemporary culture, and, like it, subsequent medieval institutions would welcome students and masters from all "nations."

5   Certain disciplines, intellectual orientations and authors were singled out by the Carolingians as being of particular importance. For both Louis and Charles the Bald, Neoplatonism and the writings of pseudo-Dionysius were particularly valued. Though Christian scholars would later come back under the influence of Aristotle, the legacy of the Carolingian ninth-century predominant interest in Platonism would last throughout the rest of the Middle Ages.

6   The Carolingian renewal is viewed as a paedagogical revival. A major step had been taken in the establishing of a basic canon of disciplines and authors. Although not prescribed by legislation, the use of Roman grammarians and poets, and commentaries on them revealed, by consensus, a zealous desire to instill classical Latin in students of language. The recognition of the mechanical arts, witnessed, for example, in commentaries on Martianus Capella's *Marriage of Mercury and Philology*, illustrates, however, the breaking away from the Roman idea of the disdained manual *techne* and the elevated liberal arts. Both Alcuin and Scotus Eriugena believed learning in both arts and skills was part of the Christian way of coming to God.

7   Carolingian reforming concerns had an impact on the physical tools of learning, as well as on its content. In many respects Carolingian education was more about texts and books than

about intellectualization *per se*. (The monastic rules Louis the Pious sought to have adopted had existed since Benedict. Manuals for teaching as well as expertise were imported from outside the kingdom. Pseudo-Dionysius' writings were at least as old as the sixth century.) Charlemagne from the start of his reforms seems to have regarded the production and collecting of books as an integral part of cultural revival. Thus he established for three generations a court library, including among others, Augustine's *The City of God*, Pliny's *Natural History*, sacramentary texts, *Dionysio-Hadriana* (a collection of Church law), canons of the Council of Nicaea, the *Rule* of St Benedict, and classical authors such as Horace, Cicero, Cato, and Lucan, and put it at the disposal of court scholars and monastic scribes alike. Not until the reign of St Louis (1226–70) would such a consultative secular library again exist.

To summarize, the Carolingian dynasty gave such recognition to learning and its tools that their renewal was to be an intellectual force of significance for generations. Charlemagne's early program of reform was thoroughly Christian in inspiration, drawing on the expertise honed in the northern monasteries and in the pockets of learning outside the Frankish kingdom. His orchestrated approach to learning as well as the practical and intellectual religiosity of his sons was nothing less than decisive to medieval thought. They demonstrated interest in philosophy and philology which would next be manifest with the Neoplatonism of the cathedral schools and the arrival of Aristotle's texts.

For further reading

On classical education and learning, see:

Aubrey Gwynn, *Roman Education: From Cicero to Quintillian* (Oxford, 1926)
H. I. Marrou, *A History of Education in Antiquity*, tr. George Lamb (New York, 1956).
Elizabeth Rawson, *Intellectual Life in the Late Roman Republic* (Baltimore, 1985).
John Edward Wise, *The Nature of the Liberal Arts* (Milwaukee, WI., 1947).

On education and learning in early medieval Europe, see:

Donna R. Barnes, ed., *For Court, Manor, and Church: Education in Medieval Europe* (Minneapolis, MN, 1971)
Ludwig Bieler, *Ireland, Harbinger of the Middle Ages* (London/New York, 1963).

John J. Contreni, "The Carolingian Renaissance," in *Renaissances Before the Renaissance: Cultural Revivals of Late Antiquity and the Middle Ages*, ed. Warren Treadgold (Stanford, 1984), pp. 59–74.

Margaret Gibson, " The Continuity of Learning circa 850–circa 1050," *Viator* 6 (1975), pp. 1–13.

_____ and Janet Nelson, eds, *Charles the Bald: Court and Kingdom. Papers based on a Colloquium held in London in April 1979* (BAR International Series, 101: Oxford, 1981).

M. L. W. Laistner, *Thought and Letters in Western Europe*, AD 500–900 (Ithaca, NY/London, 1931, re-ed., 1957).

Rosamond McKitterick, *The Carolingians and the Written Word* (Cambridge, 1989).

_____ *The Frankish Kingdoms Under the Carolingians, 751–987* (London, 1983).

J. J. O'Meara, *Eriugena* (Cork, 1969).

W. H. Stahl, *Martianus Capella and the Seven Liberal Arts* (2 vols: New York, 1971, 1977).

David Wagner, ed., *The Seven Liberal Arts in the Middle Ages* (Bloomington, IN, 1986).

On Isidore, Boethius, Cassiodorus, see:

E. Brehaut, *An Encyclopaedist of the Dark Ages: Isidore of Seville* (New York, 1912).

Henry Chadwick, *Boethius: The Consolations of Music, Logic, Theology, and Philosophy* (Oxford, 1981).

Margaret Gibson, ed., *Boethius, His Life, Thought and Influence* (Oxford, 1981).

Michael Masi, ed., *Boethius and the Liberal Arts: A Collection of Essays* (Bern/ Las Vegas, 1981).

James J. O'Donnell, *Cassiodorus* (Berkeley, 1979).

4

The Return to Plato and Aristotle

Most intellectual movements adhere to a specific group of "authoritative" texts, which have permanently determined their scope. For the movements of Platonism and Aristotelianism, the corpus is those texts ascribed to Plato and Aristotle. It is well known that the works of the Greek philosophers are important documents of western civilization, central for their philosophical ideas, and by extension for their influence on learning and culture.[1] Scholars in the Middle Ages attached renewed importance especially to Plato and Aristotle, while adhering to the classical view of the cultural significance of philosophy in general. The principle *philosophia ancilla theologiae* ("philosophy is the handmaiden of theology") became the motto of the medievals attempting to bring the works and ideas of philosophy into partnership with those of the Church. If Christian ideas were the principal subject-matter of the Middle Ages, philosophy came to be their principal mode of expression. If the medievals enthroned the pope, they also invested into office Plato and Aristotle. Almost every part of medieval thought reflects philosophy as the mold by which ideas were formed; yet, for purposes of theology, as shall be seen, non-Christian philosophy proved more difficult than anticipated to cast into the desired shape of "handmaiden." In the present chapter, the medievals' embrace of Plato and Aristotle will be considered in some detail and set in the context of medieval thought in general.

Plato and Aristotle in the Middle Ages

To appreciate classical antiquity as an important influence in the development of ideas in the Middle Ages, and to appreciate the ideas themselves, it is essential to clarify how Greek philosophy was received and treated from the earliest of the medieval periods. In the present section a sketch of the significance attributed in the Middle Ages to Plato and Aristotle will be provided.

The Concept of Authority

For most thinkers throughout the Middle Ages, Plato and Aristotle were *the* sources of classical philosophy. Their works contained almost everything of philosophical importance. There was no real need to look to other classical writers on philosophy for material essential to comprehensive knowledge.[2] There were, however, issues about which Plato and Aristotle had nothing to say, such as, What is the nature of the Trinity? Was Jesus more human than divine? How do specific Christian rituals have their significance? On matters of Christianity, a post-classical religion, medieval thinkers might well have felt at total liberty to formulate answers based exclusively on scripture, rather than speculate, as they did, on what Plato or Aristotle might have said. The purest of medieval theological judgements was to be colored by philosophy, which came to be regarded in importance as at the immediate right hand of scripture.

From the beginning of the Middle Ages, Plato and Aristotle were adopted as classical *auctoritates*. The concept of authority came to be of great importance in the incorporation of classical philosophy into the interpretation of scripture. In their discussions of the influence of Plato and Aristotle, Markus and Lohr have helpfully alluded each to one of the two distinct medieval understandings of the concept of authority which were consciously in use. They are designated here "Authority 1" and "Authority 2."[3]

Some of the earliest medieval Christian writers set the agenda for scholars in the later Middle Ages by turning to classical philosophers for Christian understanding. Augustine, writing in the fourth century, emphasized the consciousness of his foray into classical learning: "If those who are called philosophers, especially the Platonists, have said those things which are indeed true and are well accommodated to our faith, they should not be feared; rather, what they have said should be taken from them as from unjust possessors and converted to our use."[4]

In response, however, to doctrinal controversy and especially to the ideas of Gnosticism, the aid of classical philosophers in a methodical interpretation of scripture was not embraced by all in the early Church. Early Christians, such as Tertullian (died c.220) and Arnobius (died c.330), only begrudgingly acknowledged the notion of the authority of the pagans Plato and Aristotle. Each registered that the philosophers dated from well before the arrival of Christ. Their authority, like that of any other recognized thinker, was seen as historically fixed and "given"; it was passed down, unsubstantiated, as it were, from one generation to another within a cultural group. This understanding of the philosophers' authority is the concept of "Authority 1": the inherited assessment of someone as an esteemed thinker.

A tradition of recognizing scholars as authorities "in their own sphere" is, however, distinct from the respectful honoring of the scholar's ideas as "authoritative." In the second respect, authority is understood to pertain to the time-honored and distinguished ideas of the individual, as well as to the historical persona in question. According to this notion, a thinker would be considered an authority not only as a product of history, but also based on the transmission in writing of the individual's ideas of timeless value. In the Middle Ages, this slightly different meaning of authority was also at work. Authority in this sense is identified as "Authority 2."

The impact of the two concepts of authority can be quite different. Authority 1 is based on a single source of deserved reputation. Reputation in based on tradition, and authority refers to the persona, historically assessed as authoritative. Authority 1 thus means recognition by virtue only of contributions in a biographical context. It left medieval scholars the possibility of acknowledging a pre-Christian thinker as an authority and yet remaining unthreathened by that designation.

Authority 2, however, steps outside the bounds of historically determined authority and demands recognition for the timeless value of the ideas a thinker expressed. It claims a double source for deserved reputation. The "authority's" written words are esteemed as well as the non-textually documented biographical tradition. Most inclined, in the Middle Ages, to the concept of Authority 2 were those who felt Christianity could not be understood in an entirely insular way and that its ideas had to be interpreted within the context of all historical contributions to intellectual ideas and beliefs. They believed that Christian ideas had to be discussed within the community of all authoritative ideas, including those of Plato and Aristotle. On the one hand this was thought to be a positive encounter, for even the most authoritative writings, which were undeniably silent on a number of issues, could find their deficiencies supplemented by another "authoritative" source. On the other hand, it proved to be threatening, for an assertion which was not to be found in scripture might on the basis of Authority 2 be considered worthy of adoption. As will be seen, it was principally Authority 2, the double-source concept of reputation, that was to dictate the impact of classical philosophy in the Middle Ages.

The Textual Presence of Plato and Aristotle

When a medievalist refers to the writings of Plato or Aristotle, what is almost invariably meant is the corpus of works accessible in the Middle Ages, which included both the authentic works of Plato or Aristotle and those attributed to each at the time. The terms "pseudo-Platonic" or "pseudo-Aristotelian" were not in general use in the Middle Ages. "Pseudo-" is a modern qualification, used now to distinguish specific works which, while considered in the Middle Ages to have been written by Plato or Aristotle, are not today deemed to be authentic.[5] The works of Plato and Aristotle were by no means inherited by the Middle Ages in their entirety, nor via a single Greek version, but rather with omissions to differing degrees, and in a number of forms varying considerably from one to another.[6] Scholars in the earlier Middle Ages, as evidenced by writers from Augustine through Boethius, appear to have had access, in more than one Greek version, to only the *Meno* and *Timaeus* of Plato and some logical works of Aristotle. It was not until the eleventh and twelfth centuries that exposure to the classical philosophers would be broadened with a wave of translations of their Greek texts, often through Arabic intermediaries, into Latin. By that time most medievals could not read Greek and hence Latin versions were a necessity.

Over time it became clear to medieval readers that there was no "standard" Greek text of any of Plato's and Aristotle's works. Desire to acquire a more definitive understanding of the philosophers' meanings fostered interest in learning Greek, but especially in acquiring new translations especially from Greek as well as Arabic. As medieval Christian scholars began to acknowledge the reputations of Plato and Aristotle in light of Authority 2 and to grapply with their ideas, they seem to have begun to realize that the use of different versions of the corpus of each would inevitably result in problematic variations in understanding the philosophers. An apparent desire for standardization led first to the coalescence of the joint efforts of numerous translators into a "corpus," such as the *corpus vestustius* of Aristotle's natural philosophical works. Later, individual ventures were also undertaken, seemingly with standardization in sight, such as William of Moerbeke's, whose new translations of Aristotle's natural philosophical works from Greek texts yielded the *corpus recentius*.

Speculation by intellectuals at the universities in the thirteenth and fourteenth centuries also appears to have played a large role in thrashing out the "true" meaning of certain passages from Plato or Aristotle. These discussions often resulted, however, far less in standardizing interpretations than in inflaming disputes of extreme hostility. University centers, such as Paris and Oxford, were recognized as leading the study of classical Greek writings, but with particularly focused interests, as, for example, in metaphysics or natural philosophy. An inevitable result of specialization was that a predominating interpretation of Plato or Aristotle became normative within that university context.

Medieval scholars, honoring Plato and Aristotle in terms of Authority 2, linked by circumstance the philosophers' reputations to faulty and incomplete translations of their works. Plato was identified predominantly with a very truncated translation of a flawed version of his *Timaeus*. Aristotle was identified with numerous, often confusing versions of his authentic works and with spurious works riddled with Neoplatonic philosophy not easily reconcilable with the rest of his corpus. Only in the present century, with the editions of the Latin medieval texts of Plato and Aristotle exposing systematically the discrepancies between the available versions, can the extent to which medieval scholars were prisoners of the texts at their disposal be fully appreciated.[7]

Medieval Versions of Plato and Aristotle

Medieval Latin versions of Plato stemmed only from Greek texts. They comprised only the translations from Greek into Latin by Chalcidius (fourth century) of almost half of the *Timaeus* (17A–53B) and by Henry Aristippus (fl. 1150–65) of the *Meno* and *Phaedo*. Aristippus' little-circulated translations are the only ones of Plato known to have been executed in medieval Latin. The scarcely known translations by two Roman scholars, Cicero's *Timaeus* and fragmentary *Protagoras* and Apuleius' *Phaedo* and *Republic* (and a book of proverbs, possibly Platonic) were the only other direct medieval sources of Plato in Latin until the translations of Plato's *Dialogues* and *Letters* by Marsilio Ficino from Greek manuscripts "rescued" from Constantinople as it fell to the Turks in 1453. During the whole medieval period, Neoplatonic writings, the Greek writings of Plotinus (204/5–70) and his followers through the fifth century, extended medieval contact with the thought of Plato through their close references to his many other works and their interpretations of the whole of Platonic philosophy.

During the Middle Ages, many more of the works of Aristotle than of Plato became available. In fact, Aristotle's works became accessible in multiple versions from two fairly distinct groups of medieval Latin translations. Although it was once thought that medieval translation activity had occurred in two waves, each at a distinct time and in a distinct place, it is now recognized that the medieval flurry of interest in non-Latin texts can not be so neatly categorized in time or place.[8] Medieval translating continued vigorously from the mid-twelfth through the thirteenth centuries and took place in centers as far apart as Constantinople, Antioch, and Nicaea in the East, and Anagni, Viterbo, Sicily, Toledo, and Lincoln in the West.

None the less, the translations do divide into two groups distinguishable in one important respect, language of text translated. One group of texts comprised translations into Latin from the pool of Greek texts directly from the Greek; the other group was of translations into Latin from the pool of Arabic texts, either texts originally written in Arabic, or Greek texts transmitted via Arabic intermediate translations. All in all the medieval Latin corpus of Aristotelian texts comprised about 55 different works. Most of the works received more than one translation. At least 17 translators of Aristotle are identifiable by name. For some of the more prolific, such as Gerard of Cremona, John of Seville, Alfred of Sareshel, Michael Scot, Robert Grosseteste, and William of Moerbeke, translating works by Aristotle comprised but a part of their achievements. A vivid example of the confusing abundance of translations from the two different language-pools is provided by the medieval versions of Aristotle's *Metaphysics* (*Metaphysica*). There was only one version ("*nova*") translated from Arabic. Executed by Michael Scot (c.1220–35) in Toledo, it comprised Books II, I.5–10, III–X, XII.1–10. Four different translations of Aristotle's *Metaphysics* were made from Greek. One by James of Venice between 1125 and 1150, comprising Books I–IV.4, has come to be called the "*vetustissima.*" Another anonymous twelfth-century version, the "*media,*" is extant, complete except for Book XI. The third known translation, completed between 1220 and 1230, is also of anonymous execution, but is a revision of the "*vetus*" translation of James of Venice. Finally, William of Moerbeke translated the whole of the *Metaphysics* sometime before 1272 to yield the "*nova translatio.*"[9]

The initial motivation for the translation of the works of Plato and Aristotle was partly spiritual anxiety, partly intellectual curiosity. It was spiritual in that the Latin Christians were concerned by the challenge of "pagan authorities," and intellectual in that the renown of Plato and Aristotle had preceded their words and whetted a desire to know more about them. The retranslation of certain works was motivated slightly differently. The wish for standardization, clarification of unclear passages, and fuller texts all played a part. A notable result of multiple versions of a single work was that scholars, with texts for comparison, were quickly enabled to detect very subtle differences between translations and their sources.

No return to "better" translations from the philosophers' original language, would, however, determine the path of Platonic and Aristotelian philosophy in the Middle Ages, and stimulating though the different versions were, their importance must not be exaggerated. Each version was simply a facet of the works attributed to Plato or Aristotle. It is, in fact, the attribution itself of the work which is proving to have been far more significant to the medieval understanding of Platonic and Aristotelian philosophy than the actual version of the translation. Evaluation of translations set only one part of the agenda for discussion. The absorption of Plato and Aristotle into medieval thought would be primarily determined through the application of schemata of philosophical classification and abstract theological deliberations well after the work of the translators in Toledo or Sicily had come to an end.

The Medieval Role of Platonic and Aristotelian Doctrines

The history of medieval thought concerns the consequences of contact both with Christianity and with classical learning. Medieval interest in Plato and Aristotle, it might be noted, was not organized or even fostered by the Church. Despite the overwhelming involvement of ecclesiastical figures in the universities, study of the philosophers was an academic venture. (While the texts of Plato and Aristotle underwent interpretation to yield medieval Platonism and Aristotelianism, Christianity was also transformed through its own "ism's": Albertianism, Thomism, Bonaverturism, etc., the interpretations of which have partly survived into present-day Catholicism.) Since, however, the authority of the text was not thought to guarantee the authority of the interpretation, no one medieval interpreter was considered as the representative of his time, either as a new authority or as a stipulator of the norms.

During the whole of the Middle Ages, increasing emphasis came to be placed on the role of philosophy for understanding anything, and the commentator of a philosophical text was considered to be under its guidance. As will be seen, there was a great deal of confusion and disagreement over the nature and import of authoritative texts throughout the later medieval period, such that it was far from clear at the time who ought to be considered to have the 'authentic' interpretation of Plato or Aristotle. John Blund? William of Auvergne? Robert Grosseteste? Roger Bacon? Albertus Magnus? Thomas Aquinas? Siger of Brabant? Boethius of Dacia? John Duns Scotus? The Merton School *Calculatores*? William of Ockham? Nicholas of Cusa? Many another master or doctor of arts or theology at the university? In practice, the scholars of the hour seem to have been those holding the Chairs of University Regent Master to whom some authority gravitated, particularly in the tradition of the regent master's semi-annual plenary lecture, the *quodlibetum*, on topics of his choosing. There was, however, sufficient discussion in the Middle Ages that pluralistic views flourished and frequently remained unresolved into any one interpretation.

Platonic Inspiration

It has already been noted how little of Plato's work was available for study throughout the Middle Ages. Plato's own *Timaeus* and the writings of Augustine of Hippo and pseudo-Dionysius were the sources of two very different approaches to Plato's thought. Augustine became an indirect source of Plato's ideas with his enthusiastic embrace of him as an authority in the Authority 2 sense. As Thomas Aquinas wrote, "Whenever Augustine, who was imbued with the doctrines of the Platonists, found in their writings anything consistent with the faith, he adopted it; and whatever he found contrary to the faith, he amended."[10]

It might be interesting to see what particular aspects of Plato, such as his ethics, were adopted by the Church Fathers, and which ideas, such as Platonic cosmology, were integrated into the teaching of the early medieval schools. Among others the following aspects of Plato contributed to a number of important issues in medieval Christian thought.

1 Plato's great emphasis upon the need to transcend the material world established the priority of the immaterial over the natural world, which became a particularly strong sentiment in the earlier medieval period. According to some medieval Platonists, the material world was to be rejected (Gnostic position) or at most considered symbolically through a "theological" system of significants (Augustinianism). For others, serious observation of quantitative aspects of the phenomena of nature provided a

channel for transcendence, as found, for example, in the work of Robert Grosseteste.

2   Plato's theory of ideas was for most of the Middle Ages to be read creatively into a monotheistic context, rather than abandoned to pagan classical antiquity. Sustained interest in Plato, despite the lack of texts of his own works, was fostered by the initial efforts of Augustine of Hippo and those who followed to fuse the Platonic realm of Ideas with the divine sphere of the Christian God. To do so, the Ideas, through which created things are fashioned as images, were to be considered as not really distinct from God, except in the way human beings conceive and name them. Ideas were described as being in the divine mind or contained in Christ the Word, the Image Himself of the Father. By further extension, the Platonic distinction between shadows, man-made creations, and the super-humanly produced creations of nature (an essential hierarchical distinction in Plato's metaphysics and epistemology) became a Christian triad for the Fransciscan Bonaventure: confused representations (mortal bodies), distinct representations (human beings of fallible free will), and close representations (human souls). The last phase of medieval Platonism emphasized the Platonic conception of the divine itself. God is unity and goodness, and is the source of being, as opposed to being itself.

3   Platonism encompassed two essential tools whose use was required for any of the medieval transformations of classical methods of study to have occurred. First, it presented the concept of causality in multiple aspects. Plato's principle in the *Timaeus* that everything which comes into being owes its being to a cause gave his twelfth-century readers a direct route to the concept of efficient causality. Platonic forms with existence in the realm of the Ideas provided the inspiration to formal causality. The classical four elements incorporated into the cosmology of the *Timaeus* offered material causality. Plato had described final causality or purpose as the desire of the maker of the universe that all things should be good like himself. Second, the Platonic teaching of the *Timaeus* made philosophically accessible the notion of creation and a hierarchy of being, whose story twelfth-century Christian scholars could easily reconcile with the biblical creation story of Genesis. The work of Thierry of Chartres, *On the Labours of the Six Days of Creation* (*De sex dierum operibus*) is an excellent example of the Christian transformation of ideas of Plato. Twelfth-century commentaries on Boethius were also a common context for Platonic discussion: Gilbert of

Poitiers and Clarenbaud of Arras each produced commentaries on Boethius' *On the Seven Days of Creation* (*De hebdomadibus*); William of Conches wrote a gloss of the *Consolation of Philosophy*; Thierry of Chartres and Clarenbaud of Arras each produced masterly commentaries on Boethius' *On the Trinity* (*De trinitate*).[11]

4 The medieval philosophical movement developed logical techniques capable of weighing in detail the arguments of the ancients. These techniques were first to be developed by Boethius, for example, to discuss the validity of the concept of universals. After Boethius it would become almost impossible to avoid discussion of the philosophical positions of Plato or Aristotle on the existence of universals, which had crept into the lime-light in Boethius' commentary on Porphyry's *Isagoge*. Boethius was to present to his successors Platonic partisanship in asserting that universals are not fictitious, for they have existence as separate entities in the mental process of understanding. Plato, Boethius reminded his readers, maintained still further that universals such as genus and species exist not only in the mind but also in reality. This strongly realist position was certainly adopted by some medieval Platonists, but not as frequently as more moderate positions such as that of Boethius. None the less, the issue became an important litmus-test for Platonic influence. Many, like Peter Abelard, would rise to Aristotle's challenge that universals exist only in sensible things. Christian doctrine, however, often triumphed over philosophical discord, for, as will be seen, even Plato's Ideas or Forms, universals with "real" existence, independent of the sensible world, were often considered to be abstract concepts in the mind of God.[12]

5 Medieval Platonists tended to regard the soul as the mediator between the sensible body and the spiritual would, with whose faculties the link could be made through the appropriate methods. Occasionally the Augustinian Platonic notion of the individual's being identifiable exclusively with the soul, which uses the body, would be included in this conception. The soul acts as a mediator by guiding the body simultaneously in the ethical practice of virtue and the intellectual pursuit of wisdom. Via mathematics, that study of eternal, immutable truths, the soul (having an arithmetic principle) could lead an individual from the study of the visible world to a true understanding of the purely intelligible world of ideas. Hence, both for early and later medieval Platonists, like Macrobius and Nicholas of Cusa respectively, mathematics was to be studied with spiritual dedica-

tion. It has been asserted that the periodic medieval excitement for scientific investigation was a by-product of the periodically resurging interest in Platonic ideas.

6   In his *On the Trinity*, which became like his many other works enormously influential throughout the Middle Ages, Augustine of Hippo argued that knowledge is not due to the soul's remembering ideas known in a previous state of existence. Instead, divine illumination of the human mind was the key to human knowledge. Both memory and conscious effort to learn were marginalized by Augustine. In Plato, however, lay more than these ingredients for what would become Augustine's prominent conception of the discovery of truth and especially the knowledge of God. Platonic views, such as that of the divinity as the source of light in the intelligible world, continued to have wide circulation among Christian Platonists, as did a purer form of Platonic reminiscence-theory espoused by Boethius: indeed the soul was once aware of its intuitive knowledge of immaterial reality, but confined to the body and senses, it was now reduced to making use of reason. These views unquestionable emphasized learning as a path pursuable only by reason and thought and inaccessible to the senses. Although Augustine had adopted an epistemological approach to truth which contrasted in some respects with Plato's reminiscence-theory, Augustinianism is regarded as having sustained a role for Platonism within Christianity.

Aristotelian Ideas

It has already been noted that about 55 different works attributed to Aristotle were available for study in the Latin West from the early thirteenth century. The logical works of Aristotle were circulated as the core of the "New Logic" corpus. Aristotle's *Book of Six Principles* (*Liber de sex principiis*), *Categories* (*Categoriae*), *Topics* (*Topica*), *On Sophistical Refutations* (*De sophisticis elenchis*), *On Interpretation* (*De interpretatione*), *Prior Analytics* (*Analytica priora*), and *Posterior Analytics* (*Analytica posteriora*) were joined by Porphyry's *Isagoge* and Boethius' *On Division* (*De divisione*).[13] The early thirteenth-century Latin collection of his natural philosophical works, the *"corpus vestutius,"* included in a representative manuscript the following translations (pseudo-Aristotelian works are identified by an asterisk): *Book of Causes* (*Liber de causis*, Gerard of Cremona)*, *Metaphysics* (*Metaphysica*, James of Venice revised and *Metaphysica*, Michael Scot), *Meteorology* (*Meteorologica*, Gerard of Cremona and Henricus Aristippus), *On the Difference between the Spirit and the Soul* (*De differentia* *spiritus et animae,* John of Seville or anonymous)*, *On Generation and Corruption* (*De generatione et corruptione,* anonymous), *On the Heavens* (*De caelo,* Gerard of Cremona), *On Length* (*De longitudine,* James of Venice), *On Memory* (*De memoria,* James of Venice), *On Plants* (*De plantis,* Alfred of Sarashel)*, *On Sense Perception* (*De sensu,* anonymous), *On Sleep* (*De somno,* anonymous), *On the Soul* (*De anima,* James of Venice), *Physics* (*Physica,* James of Venice).[14] The late thirteenth-century natural philosophical collection, the *"corpus recentius,"* translated by William of Moerbeke, comprised in the most comprehensive manuscripts of the corpus, many, if not most, of the following works: *Book of Causes* (*Liber de causis*)*, *Letter to Alexander* (*Epistula ad Alexandrum*)*, *Life of Aristotle* (*Vita Aristotelis*)*, *Metaphysics* (*Metaphysica*), *Meteorology* (*Meteorologica*), *On the Apple* (*De pomo*)*, *On Breathing* (*De respiratione*), *On Colors* (*De coloris*)*, *On Death* (*De morte*), *On the Difference between the Spirit and the Soul* (*De differentia spiritus et animae*)*, *On Generation and Corruption* (*De generatione et corruptione*), *On Good Fortune* (*De bona fortuna*)*, *On the Heavens* (*De caelo*), *On Intelligence* (*De intelligentia*), *On Indivisible Lines* (*De lineis indivisibilibus*)*, *On Length* (*De longitudine*), *On Memory* (*De memoria*), *On the Motion of Animals* (*De motu animalium*), *On Nothing* (*De nilo*), *On Plants* (*De plantis*)*, *On the Progressive Movement of Animals* (*De progressu animalium*), *On Properties* (*De proprietatibus*)*, *On Sense Perception* (*De sensu*), *On the Soul* (*De anima*), *On the World* (*De mundo*)*, *On Youth* (*De iuventute*)*, *Physics* (*Physica*), *Physionomia*.[15] Apart from the three corpora, there were more than two translations of almost every known work, and hence the sources for medieval ideas on Aristotle were not only abundant but often confusing.

From the beginning of the thirteenth century, enthusiasm for understanding Aristotle could not be quelled even by ecclesiastical prohibitions. Amidst the dozens of medieval commentators on Aristotle, no one scholar was able to impose his interpretation of the philosopher's ideas. There were, however, several individuals whose reflections drew a great deal of attention and whose focus determined in large degree the aspects of Aristotle which came under closest analysis. The new paedagogical institution of the medieval university was instrumental as the locus of this analysis and the hotbed of contentious disagreement. Together, the scholars and the institution produced an era intellectually dominated by Aristotelian thought in a number of important respects.

1 During the Middle Ages Aristotle was usually read in Latin, even by those most eager to understand his ideas. Arabic and Greek were not widely known or taught in the thirteenth

century, a fact which scholars, such as Roger Bacon, highly deplored. Thus it was only through the translations of Aristotle into Latin that his works exercised such influence.

2   The great emphasis on Aristotle's works did lead, however, to the recognition of another language and culture: the mediating Arabic/Islamic culture of Spain. The realization of what was hidden in the Arabic texts established the learning of the Arabic language as a priority among a small but eager group of translators. The translations of commentaries by Averroes and Avicenna along with the words of Aristotle meant that in many cases Aristotle entered the Latin West through Islamic interpretation, much of which filtered in initially unnoticed.

3   The reasons for the importance attached to Aristotelian philosophy in the thirteenth century are not absolutely clear. His star certainly rose with access to and a growing interest in the body of learning under discussion in Arabic Spain, including works on Arabic philosophy, alchemy, mathematics, and medicine. Also, philosophy had acquired an exonerated position in medieval Latin thought since the twelfth century and the exemplary use of reason in theology by Abelard and Anselm, among others. Further, as requests by students of their masters reveal, the thirteenth-century scholarly ideal was to absorb and understand all of the new learning. For those familiar with Aristotle's scheme for classifying knowledge, an appealing rationale for the organization of the new learning was provided.

4   Scholasticism, or the methodological school of the university scholars, sought to understand Aristotle by approaching the texts through the aid of previous thinkers. Objections to commentaries and glosses *per se* in the process of learning had disappeared centuries earlier with the use of biblical exegesis. The texts of Aristotle were not only received interlaced with commentary, but would be further interpreted by all forms of the commentator's art, epitomizing the heights of philosophical exegesis.

5   Aristotle's works provided an irresistible collection of texts to the medieval university, such that their incorporation would permanently alter the scope of education. The availability of six Aristotelian works on logic elevated the role of dialectic well above the arts of grammar and rhetoric. The abundance of works on natural philosophy transformed the prestige and scope of the quadrivium: astronomy, for instance, on the one hand, yielded its time-honored place to the divisions of Aristotelian natural philosophy, such as terrestrial and celestial physics, and

biology, while on the other hand, with the aid of Aristotelian commentators such as Albertus Magnus and Thomas Aquinas, astronomy as well as music found a new place within the *scientiae mediae* of optics, mechanics, and perspective (the middle sciences, between the physical and the mathematical sciences). Ethics and metaphysics also became subjects in their own right, with Aristotle's works as their textbooks. The liberal arts education became one of preparation for the "arts and sciences" courses of the university.

6 Aristotle's *Posterior Analytics* set out two tools which would be deemed obligatory to the practice of medieval science: the complementary ones of induction and deduction, and the demonstrative syllogism. Interest in Aristotle heightened the epistemological importance of empirical observation in all areas of learning, especially the sciences. Aristotle's analysis of objects as composed of qualitative and quantitative properties limited, however, the application of mathematics among strict Aristotelians to only the quantitative properties of things, their spatial dimension and number.

7 In his *Physics*, which became one of the first influential works of the Aristotelian corpus to arouse major controversy, Aristotle had demonstrated the existence of the Prime Mover according to natural philosophical principles of motion and substance. This type of demonstration and the words of scripture were to epitomize the medieval distinction between philosophical and theological truth. A methodological and epistemological distinction, it encouraged thirteenth-century theologians to devise in innovative fashion argument by analogy and the hypothetical construct, in order to "save" both truths.

The Authorities Meet

It might seem awkward to speak of "the medieval return to Plato *and* Aristotle" in one chapter and in many instances in the same sentence, for the ideas and works of the two philosophers filtered into medieval culture at different times and through different mediators. Some of Plato's work had already made its way directly into Latin by the fourth century with the partial translation of the *Timaeus* by Chalcidius; then again not much more of his work was ever to reach medieval Europe. The *Timaeus* and Neoplatonic texts, Plato's main vehicles of influence, were, however, in early circulation, and Plato did affect medieval Latin culture before Aristotle.

Not until the fifth century did Aristotle surface, in two logical works translated by Boethius (along with their Neoplatonic commentaries). Does it represent events accurately to set the reception of the two philosophers only a century apart?

In fact Plato's ideas had not only an initial but a long medieval predominance over Aristotelian philosophy, as reflected in the interest shown in the works of the Neoplatonist pseudo-Dionysius beginning in the ninth century and the appeal of the *Timaeus* well through the twelfth century. Plotinian, Boethian, and Eriugenian reflections on the relation of creator to the created come under lively discussion in the twelfth century. In the same century numerous commentaries inspired by the *Timaeus* – for example, the commentary on Genesis by Thierry of Chartres, *Cosmography* (*Cosmographia*) by Bernard Silvestris, *On Essences* (*De essentiis*) by Herman of Carinthia, and Gundisalinus' *On the Process of the World* (*De processione mundi*), as well as literary works, such as the poems of Alan de Lille – bear witness to the captivating influence of Plato's cosmology based on the Greek doctrine of the four elements, the mathematical harmony of the cosmos, and the living world-soul. The medieval Platonism of the twelfth-century European scholars has also been deemed the catalyst for the first translations and eager reception of scientific works from the Arabic culture. With their emphasis on a doctrine of creation, order, and links between the intelligible and the sensible realms, Arabic ideas could find accommodation in European Platonism, just as Arabic scholars themselves had integrated many Neoplatonic ideas earlier.

By the thirteenth century it was becoming evident that the ideas of Aristotle encompassed far more scope and detail than the early translations of a few of his logical works could ever have revealed. The excitement over the volume of his work discovered in Arabic libraries cannot be exaggerated. Without question, the translation, absorption, and analysis of Aristotle dominated the thirteenth and fourteenth centuries. In the fifteenth century, however, perhaps genuinely for the first time, both Plato and Aristotle could boast simultaneously an envigorated following. A banquet to honour Plato's birthday, at which the text of Plato's *Banquet* was read, took place again after 1200 years, at Careggio in 1447. As well as new texts of Plato, the fifteenth century ushered in a third wave of translations of and commentaries on Aristotle, with his metaphysics, logical works, ethics, poetics, and attributed mechanics serving as numerous *foci* to the last phase of medieval Aristotelianism.

Meeting Each Other

Although the history of their reception differs, Plato and Aristotle were from the beginning of the Middle Ages both known and interest in their work was sustained throughout the period. Plato and Aristotle were both considered philosophers with whose ideas any scholar would have to reckon. The medieval consensus on the status of Plato and Aristotle was that the two philosophers were not only renowned as authorities, but that their ideas merited that recognition: that is, they were both in the class of Authority 2. Despite the lack of texts of their work, it was thought by virtually every generation of medieval scholars that along with their reputations the whole of their works, even if not yet uncovered, had been preserved, and that eventually it would be rendered fully accessible.

Understanding them posed an undeniable challenge, however. Three responses to that challenge can be observed during the Middle Ages. One response was to use the philosophers, in effect, to explain each other. Boethius was the first in the Middle Ages to attempt to grapple with Plato and his pupil Aristotle. Undertaken in the conviction that the philosophical schemes of Plato and Aristotle could be reconciled, his attempt reflects the approach of coming to understand the philosophers through their similarities.

The notion that Plato and Aristotle were essentially in concord had been a mainstay of the late Roman Neoplatonic school. While this early Neoplatonic conviction was influential in Boethius' reading of Porphyry's *Isagoge* or Introduction to Aristotle's *Categories*, it was also transmitted into medieval culture by another route: Arabic philosophers reflected this perspective in their incorporation of the works of the two philosophers into their own culture. The only extant remnants of Porphyry's work, *Concerning the Agreement between Plato and Aristotle*, are in fact found in an Arabic tenth-century treatise by Al-'Amiri, who had collected citations from each philosopher to illustrate their agreement. The Arabic philosopher Al-Fārābī also wrote of the harmony of thought between Plato and Aristotle: "Both have given us an account of philosophy, but not without giving us also an account of the ways to it and of the ways to reestablish it when it becomes confused or extinct."[16] The medieval historian Pierre Duhem has collected numerous reflections by medieval Latin scholars which illustrate that they too perceived extensive harmony in the ideas of Plato and Aristotle.[17] Among the more unusual comments of the kind are the authority in alchemy attributed to both Plato and Aristotle by the fifteenth-century writer, Hugh of England, and their common

medical expertise concerning regional influences on the combination
of bodily humors noted by Peter of Abano in the late thirteenth
century.

A second medieval response to the philosophies of Plato and
Aristotle was to consider each as a specialist in specific respects or
on specific subjects. Again it is among the Neoplatonists that this
modified form of symbiosis is first found. Syrianus, the teacher of
Proclus, speaks of having read the corpus of Aristotle as "'small
mysteries' in preparation for the greater mysteries of Plato."[18]
Among the Latin medievals, Albertus Magnus exemplified this way
of approaching the work of Plato and Aristotle: "One can be a
perfect philosopher only if one knows both Plato and Aristotle; if
we consider the soul in itself, we follow Plato; if we consider it as
the animating principle of the body, we agree with Aristotle."[19]
Thomas Aquinas, Albertus' student, also represents this approach,
as David Knowles has noted,

> Indeed Aquinas makes so much use of ways of thought that are
> ultimately Platonic that it may almost be said of him that he
> achieves that fusion of the [Platonic] Academy and the [Aristotel-
> ian] Lyceum that so many of his predecessors and contemporaries
> were attempting. He accomplishes this, however, not by a
> synthesis, but by using elements from Platonism mainly in the
> higher levels of metaphysics. . . . In this way he adds all that is
> true in Plato's idealism, other-worldliness and spirit of love to the
> common-sense, rationalistic empiricism of Aristotle.[20]

To depict Plato and Aristotle as distinct philosophical antagonists,
the third medieval tactic for understanding and explaining their
ideas, was, as might be expected, the most popular. Plato and
Aristotle were portrayed as disagreeing on a multitude of subjects,
including the nature and location of the human soul, the process of
intellection and aspects of sense perception, human reproduction
and the use of mathematics. The medieval author, after having
described the different opinions of Plato and Aristotle, would most
frequently opt for the wisdom of one or the other. Statements
by self-confident medieval authors were as derogatory as "Plato
(or Aristotle) erred (*peccavit*, sinned)," "Plato (or Aristotle) does
not speak the truth here," or announcing that a position leads to
"absurd" consequences. These same medieval authors frequently
justified their commitment to the view of one philosopher or the
other with reasons, citing experience or observation, (the persuasive-
ness of) the other writer, or the principles or premises of the area of

study. Although many medieval intellectuals found themselves at one time or another obliged to prefer one philosopher's opinions, most were not consistent followers of either Plato or Aristotle, and hence any mention of medieval Platonic or Aristotelian schools ought not to bring to mind a pure form of either philosopher's position.

Meeting Other Authorities

Plato and Aristotle were not the only authors of antiquity to be known in the Middle Ages. Even before the thirteenth-century wave of translations, there were other non-Christian thinkers whose renown had survived, and the works of certain classical authors were known well enough to be considered sources of wisdom. Hippocratic and Galenic medical writings were, for example, part of an early Latin corpus preserving the remnants of ancient scientific thought. By the later Middle Ages the list of revered writers included those of Greek origin, Euclid, Apollonius of Perga, Archimedes, and Diocles on mathematics and scientific ideas, and Ptolemy on astronomy, as well as many Arabic thinkers, such as Al-Khwārizmī on mathematics, Geber or Jābir ibn Hayyān and Rhazes on alchemistry, Alkindī and Ibn al-Haytham on optics, Thābit ibn Qurra, Al-Bitrūgī, and Abū Ma'shar and Costa ben Luca on astronomy and astrology, and Avicenna and Averroes and the Spanish Jew Maimonides, commentators on Aristotle. These new authors were frequently received with great relief, for they supplied new works and ideas, many of which filled gaps in the Aristotelian scheme of classified knowledge.

On many occasions, classical or Arabic writers were integrated as commentators, elucidators, or followers of either Plato or Aristotle. Pythagoras was directly connected to Plato by Clarembald of Arras, Bernardus, and William of Conches in the twelfth century, as part of the tradition teaching that the relationship of God and matter is that of unity and multiplicity. William of Conches joined the name of the eleventh-century North African adaptor of Arabic medical works, Constantine, with that of Plato, stating that Constantine's theory of the elements did not conflict with that of the philosopher. There were, however, also medieval writers who recognized a distinct difference between the older classical heritage and the works more newly received. Adelard of Bath, writing at the beginning of the twelfth century, juxtaposed the teaching and doctrines of the "Gallic schools" to those of the Arabs. In ascribing to the Arabs reason and to the Latins a disparaging adherence to authority,

Adelard was voicing an opinion widely shared by the translators of Arabic works, if little echoed among the scholars absorbing them.

Discrepancies between classical authorities on the subject of astronomy actually caused, however, more than a little dismay. Thirteenth-century theologians Albertus Magnus and Thomas Aquinas, among others, noted some difficulty in reconciling the mathematical astronomy of Ptolemy and the physical astronomy of Aristotle. Ignoring the problem of the use of eccentrics in a system based on priniciples of regular motion about a physical center, Albertus Magnus believed that Aristotle in his *On the Heavens* had "consented to the opinions" of the Babylonians and Egyptians, of which he made Ptolemy a follower. Thomas Aquinas sought a solution to the problem by giving greater weight to metaphysical principles and their "absolute certainty" than to observation. Experimental verification of a hypothesis does not, he asserted, demonstrate the necessity of the hypothesis, while, from metaphysical principles, necessary conclusions must follow: "in astronomy a system of eccentrics and epicycles is posited because this assumption enables the sensible phenomena of the celestial motions to be accounted for. But this is not a sufficient proof, because possibly another hypothesis might also be able to account for them."[21]

Meeting Christianity

The contradictions among pagan authorities were, however, to arouse far less controversy than discrepancies between the words of the philosophers and of scripture. Caught to some extent by their own affirmation of the authority of Plato and Aristotle, medieval scholars decided that Aristotle or Plato were speaking figuratively, allegorically, or hypothetically when they differed from scripture. Such explanations were not, however, satisfying to everyone. Siger of Brabant (1240–84), master of arts at the University of Paris, objected strongly to such attempts at *concordia discordantium*. On the other hand, he did not believe that the opinions of the philosophers ought immediately to be rejected either. For him, while the philosophers had no claim to unerring wisdom and might indeed make assertions in conflict with faith, an understanding of the principles underlying their conclusions would be of great assistance in the purpose of philosophy, the search for knowledge. The ultimate "truth," according to Siger, probably lay somewhere between the theological and philosophical assertions to date, and those that remained as yet unknown.

Statements such as those of Siger were methodological challenges to administrative ecclesiastical attempts, such as the Parisian declaration in 1272, to forbid the masters of the faculties of arts, the "philosophers," from discussing theological matters. Boethius of Dacia's subsequent rejection of constraints on philosophical discussions was, however, far more outspoken. Boethius believed that there was a place for both faith and reason in human life, but that they could never be reconciled, and would remain forever separate. There might well be eternal contradiction between them. While Boethius of Dacia did not posit the so-called Averroistic "double truth," one for philosophy and one for theology, of which he was accused, he did claim that both pursuits had different routes to different goals.

As advocates of a philosophy/theology dichotomy grew more vociferous, ecclesiastical figures in Paris decided they must act. Both the claim for complete liberty in philosophical discussions and the consequences in terms of troublesome teachings were addressed in the thirteenth century. In 1270, Giles of Rome wrote a work entitled *On the Errors of the Philosophers* (*Errores philosophorum*), including in his list the errors of Aristotle, Averroes, Avicenna, Algazel, Alkindī, and Maimonides. In the same year, Etienne Tempier, Bishop of Paris, issued a formal condemnation of 13 propositions being voiced at the Faculty of Arts at the University of Paris. In 1277, he drew up a much more extensive list of teachings, comprising the earlier 13 and adding 206 more articles. It condemned such teachings as "the world is eternal" [uncreated by God]," or "a natural philosopher ought to deny absolutely the newness [that is, the creation] or the world because he depends on natural causes and natural reasons. The faithful, however, can deny the eternity of the world because they depend upon supernatural causes."[22] The medieval Church could not tolerate the belief that philosophy and theology were irreconcilable; nor was this a position advanced frequently in the Middle Ages. Far more common were resourceful attempts to understand Plato and Aristotle in terms of Christianity.

The Interpretation of the Philosophers by the Word

"Scripture is the only true authority for Christians." This oft-repeated conviction of the medieval scholar summarizes more than just the earliest medieval centuries' attitude to sources of learning. Although this view of the role of scripture did not go unchallenged, throughout the Middle Ages the supremacy of the Bible as the authoritative text was staunchly maintained. With the condemnations of specific university teachings in the thirteenth century, it was reaffirmed that all ideas for paedagogical and general intellectual stimulation in both lay and religious settings were required to be grounded in scripture. The foundation of Christian learning was unwaveringly the written word of God. This view reflects the remarkably important role designated for the Bible by the scholars of the Middle Ages.

Medieval scholars grounded the paedagogical supremacy of the Bible in its relation to Truth. That relation was absolute identity for most. The Bible *was* Truth. For some, however, the relation was slightly more circuitous: the Bible *contained* the Truth. Nevertheless, there was a consensus that the Bible was to be read as if it were God himself who was speaking its words. The value of the Bible was, in part, specifically grounded in the fact that it was a written text, *scriptura*. As McKitterick stresses, for the Carolingians, "the Book represented the gift of the written law of God in the Old and New Testaments . . . possession and use of writing were, for the Franks, the keys to faith. . . ."[23] It was asserted throughout the Middle Ages that the Bible could stand on its own, able to speak as God, to meet challenges and assertions opposing its time-cast but eternally true statements. Scripture was able both to pass judgement upon any other written text (and find it in error) and also to provide the foundation for the reception of the "new learning" which would "stand on its shoulders" from the thirteenth century on.

Two main points will bring out the principles of that role for Holy Writ. First, medieval theologians insisted vociferously that the authority of any other written (or spoken) ideas was subordinate to that of the Bible. This was not necessarily to say that they had *no* authority. Medieval theological scholars allowed other writings, even those of the pagans Plato and Aristotle, a genuine authority, occasionally even in matters of doctrine. It was, however, to say that such authority was determined or measured by scripture, and was thus subordinate to it. The influence of the Aristotelian concept of science had, by the thirteenth century, rendered theology a speculative science, an endeavor much more encompassing than strict exegesis. Dominic, the founder of the Dominican Order of Preachers, was described by his contemporary biographer as embracing speculative theology: "God added unto him the grace of science; he became not only apt for the milk of Scripture; with the understanding of a lowly heart he probed the secrets of difficult questions, and swallowed the meat of inquiry with sufficient ease."[24] The Franciscan Bonaventure staunchly defended the role for scripture within speculative theology. Although he welcomed considering the opinions of the philosophers, he cautioned: "Let the [university] masters beware, then, not to commend or appreciate too highly the sayings of the philosophers, lest the people take it as a pretext to return to Egypt [the godless land], or dismiss because of their example the waters of Siloe [waters the Lord has made to flow gently, cf. Isaiah 8:6–7] in which is supreme perfection, and go to the waters of the philosophers in which there is eternal deceit."[25]

Second, medieval theologians were to argue that the authority of the paedagogues of theology or of any other discipline did not derive from their status as university masters, but from the Word of God which they taught. Before the rise of the universities all teaching tended to be undertaken by clergy, and their traditional role had been to train young men in the rudiments of understanding scripture, reading, writing, and basic reckoning. Paedagogical deviation from the goal of understanding scripture, let alone from the text itself, was very slight in the early Middle Ages. Already, however, with the emphasis on a full liberal arts curriculum in the cathedral schools, but even more so with the arrival of the Aristotelian corpus, the list of "propaedeutics" or aids to scriptural understanding had begun to grow, as well as the amount of time devoted to their mastery. Eventually, as a university master, a medieval paedagogue might actually never be engaged himself in lecturing on any part of the Bible,[26] and the principle of the paedagogical role, to permit the understanding of scripture, would have shifted in large part away from the individual *per se* to the institution of the university at large. The authority of the university master thus resided no longer in the fact that he was teaching scripture or direct aids to its understanding, but rather in the fact that he was teaching nothing *contrary* to the truth of scripture. With that and only that, the traditional role of the cleric as teacher was preserved, and thence derived the adamancy of concerned bishops about what the professors were teaching.

For further reading

For an introduction to the place of Plato and Aristotle in philosophy and especially in western European thought, see:

A. H. Armstrong, *An Introduction to Ancient Philosophy* (London, 4th ed., 1970).

Michael Haren, *Medieval Thought: The Western Intellectual Tradition from Antiquity to the Thirteenth Century* (New Studies in Medieval History; London, 1985) pp. 7–35.

For studies illustrating the role of philosophy in the medieval period, see:

E. Gilson, *History of Christian Philosophy in the Middle Ages* (London, 1955).
A. Maurer, *Medieval Philosophy* (New York, 1962 rpt. Toronto, 1982).

For the role of Plato and Aristotle in Middle Ages, see:

A. H. Armstrong, ed, *The Cambridge History of Later Greek and Early Medieval Philosophy* (Cambridge, 1967).*
D. A. Callus, "Introduction of Aristotelian Learning to Oxford," *Proceedings of the British Academy* 29 (1943), pp. 229–81.
Tullio Gregory, "The Platonic Inheritance," in *A History of Twelfth-Century Philosophy*, ed. Peter Dronke (Cambridge, 1988), pp. 54–80.
Norman Kretzmann et al., eds, *The Cambridge History of Later Medieval Philosophy: From the Rediscovery of Aristotle to the Disintegration of Scholasticism 1100–1600* (Cambridge, 1982).*
D. J. O'Meara, ed., *Neoplatonism and Christian Thought* (Albany, NY, 1982).
F. van Steenberghen, *Aristotle in the West: the Origins of Latin Aristotelianism*, tr. L. Johnston (Louvain, 1955, 2nd ed., 1970).

*The relationship of the volumes' content to one another is well explained in the Introduction to Kretzmanns' *Later Medieval Philosophy*, pp. 1–8.

Of especial interest is the role assigned to philosophy in medieval religious teaching. Claims of philosophical breaches of orthodoxy are conveniently brought together, in English translation, in the following texts:

E. L. Fortin and P. D. O'Neill, trs, "The Condemnations of 1277," in *Medieval Political Philosophy: A Sourcebook*, eds Ralph Lerner and Muhsin Mahdi (New York, 1963).
Giles of Rome, *On the Errors of the Philosophers* in *Medieval Philosophy*, ed. H. Shapiro (New York, 1964), pp. 386–413.
Michael Haren, tr., "The Condemnations of 1270," in *Medieval Thought: The Western Intellectual Tradition from Antiquity to the Thirteenth Century* (New Studies in Medieval History: London, 1985), pp. 198–9.
Lynn Thorndike, tr., "The Condemnation of 1210," "Expurgation of 1231," and "Curtailing Statute of 1272," in *University Records and Life in the Middle Ages*, tr. and ed. Lynn Thorndike (New York, 1944), pp. 26–7, 39–40, 85–6.

See also:

F. van Steenberghen, *Thomas Aquinas and Radical Aristotelianism* (Washington, DC, 1980).
J. F. Wippel, "The Condemnations of 1270 and 1277 at Paris," *The Journal of Medieval and Renaissance Studies* 7 (1977), pp. 169–201.

5

The Vernacular Breakthrough

Vernacular (regional, native, or indigenous) languages are one of the most important contributions of the Middle Ages. They figure prominently not only in linguistic history, but also in the social, political, and religious history of medieval Europe, especially in the evolution of national cultures in the British Isles, France, Germany, Scandinavia, Spain, Italy, and Russia. In many respects, the barbarian tongues appear as the victors over Rome's Latin, with remarkable strengths, yet noteworthy flaws. Indeed with individual self-assurance and courage, they achieved a far-from-unified advance on the classical linguistic traditions in artistic expression, politics, and religion over the course of the Middle Ages. It was, however, popular use of a "vulgar" Latin which presented itself as the first direct challenge to the hold of classical Latin culture. There were both laments for and condemnations of the "classicalness" of Latin, such as those of Gregory of Tours, who hoped that faith would compensate for his ignorance of classical Latin, and of Pope Gregory the Great who found it outrageous that he should have to make the prophetic words from heaven conform to the grammar of Donatus. Both indicate that already by the seventh century, linguistic deviation from the classical path was definitely being acknowledged.

The role that vernacular languages themselves were to play on the medieval stage was due in large part to a shift in values and power. So all-pervasive was Latin at the height of Rome's power that writers of the early Middle Ages were still convinced that the language of cultivated Rome, with its style and universality, was the one to fill all but the most localized of post-classical linguistic needs. For some, however, like Pope Gregory in the late sixth century, it seemed necessary to reassess the suitability of classical Latin to individual, or parochial, expression, and having done so, to recognize the use of its more "vulgar" forms. Others later, while attempting to adopt the content and scope of Latin, would choose different languages to play its role. With the fading of imperial power, Roman linguistic ideals of senatorial style and universal communication were to give way to medieval linguistic values of individuality and self-expression.

To perceive this shift clearly, it would certainly help to be able to pinpoint a single vernacular breakthrough, and yet no one such event can be isolated. For each emerging language the course of assertion was different, and there were many steps. Some steps, such as the so-called renaissance of the twelfth century, were of common importance, but others were completely unique. None the less, the catalyst behind the strength of each linguistic group was ultimately the same, the growing need of individuals to experience *through language* their personal connection to their God, their ruler, and their imagination. Within the dominant context of the medieval Roman Catholic Church, it is perhaps not immediately obvious what form linguistic individuality and self-expression could take, and it therefore becomes important to explain them and their significance. Thus, in appreciation of the enormous impact on medieval intellectual life of the changes brought about by European vernacular languages, they will be considered here in some detail.

The Latin Presence

In its days of imperial greatness, Rome's unifying use of Latin seemed to have eliminated the need for any other linguistic expressions of culture within its geographic area. Even with its fading ability to maintain political geographic unity, the Christian Church, the religious institution Rome had adopted, was to perpetuate linguistic and territorial dominance. The Greek of the early Church gave way to Latin in the *parte occidentalis* of the fading empire. All western Christian documents, including the Bible, would be written in Latin, and Latin alone. Was there any role for the vernacular languages of Europe, particularly written vernaculars, in such a homogenized Christian context?

Latin has been thought to have been the conservative tongue of the Middle Ages.[1] More appropriately perhaps, it ought to be seen as the "conserved" tongue.[2] Among the major languages to have emerged from the Middle Ages, representing four evolutionary groups (Romance languages, Germanic languages, languages of the British Isles, and Slavonic languages), those of the Romance language group actually preserved Latin. In the case of the geographic areas of present-day Italy, France, Spain, and Portugal, Vulgar Latin was persistent enough first to be adopted as a functional second language even for the unlettered, and then to offer Romance linguistic features to the evolving regional languages. During the three to four centuries of Roman occupation in these areas, pre-Latin languages apparently had succumbed to Latin in all communication except the most colloquial. Even the numerous hostile peoples invading the Roman empire from the fourth through the sixth centuries, the Alemanni, Goths, Franks, Burgundians, Huns, Vandals, and Lombards, did not with their Germanic tongues make any lasting linguistic impact on Vulgar Latin. Limited in their numbers, these so-called barbaric tribes became assimilated.[3] Only traces of their languages survived into the Romance languages: a few words derived from Germanic roots, and some place names.

In areas under only temporary Roman political and cultural influence, contact with Roman Latin was notably less significant. The roots of the British and Germanic languages are independent of Latin influence, and it was only through Christianity that both were to come significantly within the Latin cultural sphere. The earliest Britons had actually suffered Roman occupation, during which time, despite the arrival of Latin, they had tenaciously maintained an independent spoken tongue in everyday discourse and in entertainment or the recording of history. Until the sixth century, a squirearchy of native British Celts learned Latin, holding local political strength through bilingualism: Latin for the Roman occupiers, vernacular for the tenants. The Anglo-Saxons, who next occupied southeastern parts of the British Isles, caused, with their displacement of the upper classes, the virtual disappearance of Latin. The Anglo-Saxon and the Viking conquerors after them were only affected by Latin through Christianity. To the Anglo-Saxons and Scandinavians, Latin offered a useful alphabet as well as some subtler influences in the form of vocabulary and literary forms. Through contact with Christianized Anglo-Saxons, Germanic peoples on the continent in turn also incorporated the Latin alphabet into their language, which evolved from Old Saxon to Old High German to Middle High German without much Latin influence.

When groups of Europeans ceased in the Middle Ages to speak Latin, its conservation depended not so much on the adoption of its alphabet, but rather on addressing the difficulties of preserving its written form. A divorce between the written and spoken versions of Latin had existed even in the classical era, such that to some historians, as for example J. Cremona,[4] spoken or Vulgar Latin already qualified as a vernacular or native language by the first century AD, and it is certainly true that the different rhythms and modes of its transformation in different areas reflect an assertion of regional identity. What is therefore all the more striking is that literary Latin survived throughout the Middle Ages with some prestige and active use. Some of the reasons for its survival also shed light on its ultimate slip from power.

(1)   Latin emerged strong from a falling Rome. In the fourth century it was experiencing a veritable renaissance. The first signs of this reawakening were to be seen in Gaul, where schools which had been patronized by Emperor Constantius I, the father of Constantine, were flourishing. By the middle of the fourth century, Rome too was revitalizing Latin in the work of the Christians, Jerome and Augustine, and the Roman teachers, Donatus and Marius Victorinus, continuing later with Macrobius and Boethius. It would be the literary tastes of this fourth-century revival which would pass on to the Middle Ages.

None the less, with the disappearance of the Roman imperial court and its patronage, the virtual demise of Roman culture intervened from the mid-sixth until the mid-eighth century, during which time the greatest quantity of Latin literature ever to be lost vanished. The fact that spoken and written Latin had become distinct began to tell, and while Vulgar Latin was still in wide use, there were few who attained any competence in writing classical Latin. For example, Gregory of Tours' poignant explanation for his own poor Latin grammar was lack of guidance. His father, who was also his teacher, died when he was eight.[5] Interest on the part of wealthy or powerful individuals in their edification, amusement, or education was critical in sustaining, in the secular world, some degree of Latin literacy.[6]

Early medieval secular interest in Latin was too tenuous and sporadic to function effectively as its conserver (without relying on the Church). The degeneration of classical Latin was inevitable, and the evolution of vernacular languages became accelerated. By the twelfth century the interest of noble families in literacy had decisively shifted to the eager enjoyment of the new vernacular writing. By the thirteenth and fourteenth centuries many people were literate, but in their vernacular, not in Latin. Most late medieval secular patronage of Latin, including the twelfth-century flourish of Latin Goliardic poetry written mostly by clerics (at least in name), was effected through the Church or university. Signs of this trend reversing itself to yield the secular excitement for the classics which would be manifest in the Renaissance are not evident until the fifteenth century in Italy, with the growing distinction between the clerical vocation and scholarship and some noted secular patronage, such as that of the famed de Medici's.

(2)   Once it became institutionalized in Rome, Christianity in the West adopted Latin, and it would remain the language of the institution and its faith throughout the Middle Ages. Christian writers such as Avitius were an active part of a vital late-classical Latin culture. The fourth-century Vulgar Latin of Jerome's translation of the Bible would become the standard for Latin teaching throughout the Middle Ages. In the fifth century, with the barbarian invasions into Europe the Church received an infusion of a number of strong partisans of Rome, like Sidonius Appolinaire, who turned to it as a way to continue to serve Roman culture. None the less, the Church was not immune to a loss of sophistication in its Latin during the following several centuries. A missionary movement to England in the seventh century, however, sowed the seeds of a religious Latin revival, and from Northumbria Anglo-Saxon missionaries brought Latin learning to the monasteries they founded throughout the continent.[7]

As literate Christianity expanded, more religious texts, spiritual and scholarly, were needed, and monasteries dedicated whole rooms called *scriptoria* to manuscript production. Liturgies, biblical commentaries, and Church histories, such as the *Ecclesiastical History of the English People* (*Historia ecclesiastica gentis Anglorum*) of the Venerable Bede, were written and reproduced in numerous copies, all in Latin. Monks would conserve Latin learning well through the remaining centuries of the Middle Ages, in both their scholarship and their missionary activity. In the case of British and Germanic culture, introduction of Latin by the Church was more to counter many of the pagan vernacular practices, such as trial by ordeal, than to eliminate the presence of the vernacular *per se*. Despite Latinization, many such practices, so integral a part of pagan culture, continued to be executed in the vernacular.

The next resurgence of the vitality of Latin in the religious sphere would be in the newest of medieval teaching institutions, the cathedral schools, and then the universities. Cathedral schools placed their greatest emphasis on the trivium, or arts for using language – that is, on Latin. New form and content would be added to medieval Latin discourse in the university scholastic approach to logic, philosophy, and theology. Philosophy and theology will be discussed in the next two chapters. It is of note here, however, that with the conservation of Latin in its new academic role came the gains of enrichment, as well as the costs of rarification. An enrichment of Latin was fostered by the twelfth- and thirteenth-century activity of scholars translating texts newly available to Latin culture at points of contact with Greek and Arabic learning in Spain, Sicily, and Constantinople. The "new learning," with its subjects varying from astronomy and alchemy to zoology, demanded an expanded lexicon in Latin. To meet the need of an expansion in language, new Latin words were created by transliteration as well as transformation. In the thirteenth century, Latin also became more sophisticated and less accessible. This rarification of Latin transpired with the use of the scholastic commentary form and its dissection of the newly available texts into philosophical minutiae.[8]

Many academics of the late Middle Ages became absorbed with the state of Latin grammar, but with a sentiment quite opposite to the frustration of Gregory the Great with Donatus. The late scholastic philosophers turned with new zeal to Latin grammar and logic as the keys to natural language and human thought. These speculative grammarians, or Modistae, as they are known, investigated the function of language through its abstract forms and relations, as reflections of modes of understanding and signifying. For the most part they carried out their investigation unwittingly using categories they had detected in only one language, Latin. Academia, like the institution of the Church, played a role in the conservation of Latin as the universal language.

(3)   Throughout the Middle Ages, Latin signified human civilization, culture, and history. There were those who at the time of the barbarian migrations appreciated the invaders as being more just than the Romans, but ironically they showed their respect by grafting the laws, customs, and history of the new culture onto those of Rome, in Latin! It is hard to say when the concept of *translatio studii*, which saw Rome as the successor to Greece in the transmission of human culture, began to affect medieval self-perception, but even the earliest new arrivals to the Roman empire in Europe desired to be a part of continuing what was once the glory of Rome. There is no doubt more than a grain of truth in Orosius' story of King Athaulf, who when he appraised the relative strengths of his Visigoths and the Romans, turned his arms to the restoration and power of Rome.[9] The barbarians who settled seem generally to have desired to diminish tensions between cultures, and to have wanted themselves and their important traditions immortalized in Latin. Cassiodorus was, after all, commissioned by Theodoric to write in Latin a history of the Goths which, using the Romans as the standard, aimed to show that the Goths were an equally ancient and

august people. Works such as the *Law of the Visigoths* (*Lex wisigothorum*, 654), *Salic Law* (*Lex Salica*), or *Volksrechte*, codes of common tribal law, were all compiled in Latin, between 400 and 800. Charlemagne, king of the Franks, is supposed to have spoken Latin as well as, if less often than, he did his mother tongue.

Many medieval histories, as, for example, those of the Crusades by William of Tyre, Raymund of Agiles, and Foucher, successfully conserved the use of Latin. This legacy of Latin as the language of recording culture would survive to fuel the post-medieval Renaissance. In fact, histories in the vernacular do not appear until the late Middle Ages, when prose narratives begin to find "vulgar" expression. As for the official documents of a culture (law codes, treaties, correspondence, etc.), at times the quality of their Latin left something to be desired. Those who aspired to Latin culture often fostered it only superficially, and at some points there was simply no one capable of providing a credible linguistic veneer. The first dynasty of kings of the unified Franks, the Merovingians, employed court scribes of Latin training and although it was an artifice, the kings themselves learned the rudiments of reading and writing in Latin. By the seventh century, however, the only scholars the Lombard king Rotharis could find to set down his code of laws, the Edict of Rotharis (*Edictus Rothari*), produced the document in a Latin incomprehensible in passages for its many errors.

In the written documents of governments and courts of law, vernacular languages rapidly began to usurp the role of Latin. It is worthy of note that the very earliest document extant in the French and German vernaculars was a formal treaty agreed upon at Strasbourg in 842 by Charles the Bald and Louis the German, the grandsons of Charlemagne. To reconcile territorial disputes, it was apparently determined that an oath had to be exchanged which was understandable to both armies. Since the armies did not understand Latin, the oath had to be composed in the two vernaculars, even though each army was ignorant of the adversary's vernacular. As the example serves to illustrate, the audience rather than the seriousness of the content seems predominantly to have dictated the legal and political languages of medieval Europe.[10]

Until the end of the twelfth century most vernacular literature was designed for the military and the courts or for the clergy. Charters, notarial documents, and inventories are extant in numerous Romance languages and in Old English already by the ninth century. In Middle High German of the eleventh century, legal documents concerning ceremonies, marriages, swearing-in of Jews, and trials by ordeal begin to appear, not to mention the *Sachenspiegel*, a comprehensive code of Saxon law, written by Eike von Repgow in the thirteenth century. *The Customs of the Beauvaisis* (*Les Coutumes des Beauvaisis*) by Philippe de Beaumanoir (before 1296) and Bracton's English statutes and treatise (before 1268) are interpretations of feudal law in the vernacular. Through the reign of Charlemagne such documents would have been written in Latin, but by the thirteenth century the fact that they were destined to a local readership significantly determined their language of composition. The late thirteenth century seems to have been a linguistic watershed in the realm of political culture where communication among people of all classes at the local level acquired such importance as to make choosing the vernacular inevitable.

(4)   Latin was considered the vehicle of certain literary genres. In some instances it is not the influence of the Latin language *per se* which assured its conservation, but rather the literary genres in which it was employed. Among medieval writers, Latin held on to such an aura of prestige in literature that it continued throughout the Middle Ages to be deemed the only language, in their command, suitable for "serious" genres. Even by the late Middle Ages, the general notion of the appropriateness of a specific language for a specific genre had not disappeared. Latin remained the language of choice for most genres, sharing its exonerated status, according to Dante, famed poet of the fourteenth century, only with Provençal, the best-suited language for lyric poetry, and French, suited for narratives.

Translations or adaptations of Latin works into the vernacular were, of course, produced before the thirteenth century. In some instances (there are notable canticles in Old High German), the vernacular text corresponds so closely to the Latin word-order that it is virtually incomprehensible without the accompanying Latin. In others, a work's rendering into the vernacular opened a whole new chapter of its influence. The *Book of Beasts* or *Physiologus, Reda umbe diu tier* in Middle High German prose, started, for example, an interest in zoology reverberating in numerous eleventh-century versions of the work. A few translations, particularly those of Old English, reveal through their own prefaces and elsewhere a high level of sophistication in prose, although it was not to be exhibited in an any freer manner until the late Middle Ages.

Independent vernacular expression was limited until the thirteenth century primarily to genres most closely connected to the spoken word: the heroic epic and the lyrical or alliterated poem. There are examples to be found in each emerging vernacular, frequently using a language of exclusively poetic meaning. The following works might come to mind: for the heroic epic in French, *The Song of Roland* (*Chanson de Roland*), in Spanish, *The Poem of el Cid* (*Poema de mio Cid*), in German, *Song of Roland* (*Rolandslied*), *King Rother* (*König Rother*), *The Legend of Duke Ernst* (*Herzog Ernst*), and *The Fall of the Nibelungs* (*Nibelungenlied*), in English, the Christian *Dream of the Rood*, and *Beowulf*; for lyric verse, in early German *Incantations of the Merzeburge* (*Merzeburger Zaubersprüche*) and the *Song of Hildebrand* (*Hildebrandslied*), the *Owl and the Nightingale* in English. Except for religious homilies (again a spoken genre), the only significant independent vernacular works were technical or medical writings in the Germanic and English tongues.

It is in the written forms of both the spoken epic and lyric that most medieval vernaculars reached a peak of refinement. French particularly led the way in transforming each genre into a vehicle of the theme of courtly love. The heroic epic, or *chanson de geste*, becomes the courtly epic or romance with the Anglo-French *Tristan* and the *Perceval* by Chrétien de Troyes, influencing Hartman von Aue's *Erec*, Gottfried von Strassburg's *Tristan*, and Wolfram von Eschenbach's *Parzival* in German. The lyric was tailored to a courtly love poem in Provençal by Jaufre Rudel of Blaye and Bernart de Ventadorn, becoming the *Minnesang* of Walther von der Vogelweide. German, however, added the political *Spruch*, or single-stanza didactic or satirical poem, to the poet's repertoire, and the highly literary *Meistergesang*, abstract and allegorical poetry of the thirteenth century. Guides to the composition of such specific genres in the vernacular begin to appear in the early thirteenth century, the first being the work of the Catalan poet Raimon Vidal, *Rules of Lyric Poetry* (*Razos* [*Reglas*] *de trobar*) on the writing of poetry in Provençal.[11]

While it yielded to all forms of vernacular verse, in all but the English sphere Latin retained its hold on literary prose until quite late in the Middle Ages. Influenced perhaps by the role of the Arabic and Hebrew languages within Spanish culture, Castilian writers of the late thirteenth and early fourteenth centuries seem to have been the first to break away from Latin in the prose narrative. The prose adaptation of narrative poetry, *dérimage* (de-rhyming) was underway in French by the thirteenth century. The realization, expressed by Heinrich von Wittenweiler in his *Ring*, that "*Kluge Sach will Reimens nicht*" (wise words need no rhyming), had, however, little effect in German until the end of the fourteenth century. As noted, English is really the only exception to this slow evolution of the use of the vernacular for prose works. The realization of English as an adept language for prose writing came remarkably early, in the late tenth century.[12]

Discovery of One's Own Tongue

Most surviving vernacular developments took place within the Middle Ages, and it is, therefore, not surprising that Latin is spoken of as the older language which the medievals took upon themselves to conserve. As successors to Rome's culture and religion, through Latin they could maintain a linguistic connection to the glory of Rome, and the see of St Peter. It is hardly surprising that Latin appealed to political and religious authorities as a generally more universal language. Indeed, some traditional uses of Latin, in legal and religious declarations, were retained well beyond the Middle Ages. The medieval institutions of both Church and Crown were painfully aware of the difficulties of linguistic regionalism, and their authorities attempted for a long time to forestall the influence of localization, in part by placing emphasis upon the use of Latin in official documents.

It is inaccurate to suggest that all advocates of vernacular languages elevated them above and to the exclusion of Latin, or that they all welcomed the descent into political regionalism. It was unquestionably true of some, just as a radical adherence to Latin was true of opponents. A great deal of variation can be detected within the vernacular breakthrough on this point. Some advocates of the vernacular simultaneously espoused a role for Latin, particularly a religious role. Others were prepared to abandon the concept of Latin as the only vehicle of God's or the monarch's word, in favor of what was considered a heretical or base alternative.

Was not the answer to favor a "universal" vernacular language, a language somewhat aparochial, but also not a totally native language, a refined version perhaps of a powerful vernacular? In particular situations the answer was decidedly yes. Of *langue d'oc* dialects, Provençal was widely accepted as the instrument of courtly poetic expression by native speakers of Catalan and Italian as well as by many poets born into other dialects of French. Both Anglo-Saxon and also later Anglo-Norman, for example, became adopted as the political language of a wide region. For the Normans, the role of their language was wedded to their presence and thus grounded in their military and political show of force. The Norman tongue was, none the less, in England fused to the local vernacular to serve, like Latin, as a politically normative instrument.

One of the main reasons why particular vernacular languages grew to be highly regarded over the course of the Middle Ages was that they came to be accepted as the expression of the people. Applications of the vernacular in the political sphere in the Middle Ages would mean that those literate in both Latin and the vernacular or even non-literate in Latin could more readily assume significant political roles in new spheres than had their predecessors. It would also mean that, once in positions of influence, they would accept the vernacular as the generally more appropriate language of exchange. The proponents of political vernacular writings, such as histories, were often also the very ones who were trying to develop the whole culture they represented, primarily with the strength of their language.

The vernaculars were, however, valued more broadly as both gauges of self-survival and vehicles of self-expression. The Florentine Brunetto Latini, for example, emphasized in the mid-thirteenth-century their affective cultural significance, even over their political importance. The new literary, religious, and political roles for the vernacular would include uses as various as feast-day plays, peace treaties, and love poetry, and those who had begun such multi-purpose use of the vernacular would be loath to accept Latin in its stead. Cultural development was precisely what further use of the vernacular would achieve. None the less, the increasing regard for local vernacular expression of one's culture would give a strong bias toward what was actually, and perhaps continues to be, the most de-unifying aspect of pan-European culture, regional languages.

In terms of their historical development, the vernacular languages cannot be considered a unity. Each followed its own course. Here, medieval English, French, German, and Italian will be briefly traced in their distinct yet representative evolutions to becoming dominant languages of European civilization.[13]

English

Successive invasions brought about the presence of three distinct languages on English soil: Old English or Anglo-Saxon, Old Norse, and Anglo-Norman. The earliest arrival was Old English or Anglo-Saxon, a Germanic dialect. The English spoken by the Anglo-Saxons had a vigorous tradition, with several regional variants and a vernacular literature. After the founding of the abbey of Whitby in 657 the first known poet in vernacular English, Caedmon, came to the fore. Patronized by Whitby's founding abbess St Hilda, he produced

Old English poems on religious topics. Somewhat later, beginning in 887, Alfred, the extremely literate king of Wessex, translated a number of works for the clergy from Latin into Anglo-Saxon, including the *Book of Pastoral Care* (*Regula pastoralis*) of Gregory the Great and Boethius' *Consolation of Philosophy*, as well as numerous extracts from the Church Fathers, Augustine, Jerome, and Gregory the Great.

With the invasion and occupation of England by the Vikings, Old Norse dialects of Danish and Norwegian source would dominate during the ninth and again in the eleventh century. The major blow to Old English came, however, with the arrival of Norman, a dialect of *langue d'oïl* brought by Duke William of Normandy and his men in their invasion of England in 1066. English vernacular literature was to suffer a certain discontinuity. Norman French acquired importance among the ruling classes of both Church and State following the Norman Conquest. English never ceased to be spoken by the populace, however, and proved as resistant to Norman as the Normans did to adopting it.

A standard written form of English did not resurface again until the late fourteenth century, and then in the form of the so-called Middle English. Traces of local literary dialects are extant from the thirteenth century, but no texts of note reflect any standardization. The language of the most famous of late medieval English poets, Geoffrey Chaucer (c.1340–1400), captured, however, many features of what became by the fifteenth century the standard Chancery Middle English. The language was based on the urban dialect of London enriched by the Midlands dialects brought by immigrants in the wool trade coming into the capital. English emerged from the Middle Ages a viable standardized language, used in literature, politics, and religion.

French

Already by the ninth-century Carolingian era, the concern that certain traditional vernacular oral recitations ought to be preserved in writing can be noted. Einhard wrote that the Emperor Charlemagne commissioned a written collection of traditional songs and poems. The first extant example of the written Frankish vernaculars is, however, the document of the Oath of Strasbourg of 842 between the troops of Charles the Bald and Louis the German, recorded by the chronicler Nithard in Old High German and Old French. The Carolingian rulers perpetuated past Frankish unity in their ability to understand the vernaculars of the former eastern and western halves of Charlemagne's empire. Hugh Capet, the father of the succeeding Capetian Dynasty, was, however, to understand only his own western dialect, not the Germanic counterpart. The weakness of the Capetian monarchy was, in fact, reflected in the relative slowness of the dialect of the Capetians on the Ile de France to dominate French culture.

At the end of the ninth century, manuscripts of poems in Romance language began to appear. The cantilene of St Eulaie is only the most well known. No Romance language had much literary import, however, until the middle of the eleventh century. West Frankia became two linguistic regions: that of *langue d'oïl* in the north and *langue d'oc* in the south. There were numerous dialects of *langue d'oïl*, predominantly Norman, but also Français, Picard, and Champenois. *Langue d'oc* was composed of even more dialects, including Limousin, Gascon, and Catalan.[14]

The French vernacular is said to have achieved early maturity, reflected in an early homogeneity despite the multiplicity of its dialects. From the eleventh century, the *chansons de geste* flourished in a limited range of northern Old French dialects. The troubadours of the *langue d'oc* area in the south were especially instrumental in creating a "common language" of Provençal, as they suppressed the most local attributes of their individual dialects. Medieval versions of French, especially Provençal, dominated European vernacular literature from the twelfth through the fourteenth century. French translations from Latin and other vernaculars of a striking variety of works were in circulation in this period, as, for example, the *On Things Military* (*De re militari*) of Vegetius, Boethius' *Consolation of Philosophy*, the letters of Abelard and Heloise, Aelred of Rievaulx's *Spiritual Friendship* (*De spirituali amicitia*), and Gerald of Wales' *History and Topography of Ireland* (*Topographia hibernica*) as well as numerous scientific and technical works of other authors.

Few early writers in the French vernaculars had a secure enough literary command of their "native" language, its grammar or its potential for rhetorical flourish or poetic manipulation, to mold the conventions of their genre to reflect individuality. Most troubadour poems suffer from relative stylistic uniformity. The prosaic and poetic accounts inspired by the first Crusade, *Anonymous History of the First Crusade* (*Histoire anonyme de la première croisade*) and *Song of Antioch* (*Chanson d'Antioche*), provide an interesting contrast in this vein. The first was an eye-witness account by a knight in the company of the Norman prince Bohémond, replete with emotion but also full of stereotypical conventions. The second, by the northern troubadour or *trouvère*, Richard the Pilgrim, was more original, filled with notations of the feelings of the crowd and the poor in the first Crusade.

Not until the vernacular romances of Chrétien de Troyes, his *Perceval, Eric and Enid*, and *Lancelot, Knight of the Cart*, does one find work of uncontested originality. The tone and style of Chrétien's works were those of the aristocratic circles and of Latin convention. His choice of language, however, was not. He actually created a language to suit his use of the romance genre to express underlying ethical values allegorically. He demonstrated exceptional artistic mastery in extending the vernacular to the stylistic and conceptual sophistication of his subject matter and his audience. Like the troubadours, Chrétien freed himself from his own dialect, Champenois, but he was able at the same time to retain his ties to a direct, spontaneous expression of emotions.

Another prominent original work in the French vernacular was *The Romance of the Rose (Roman de la Rose)* (1225–37 and c.1275). The poem which began as an allegorical courtly romance unfinished by William of Lorris received its most popular completion by Jean de Meun 40 years later. The poem incorporates elements of both the Provençal troubadours' art and northern French lyric traditions. Differences in language between the two poets are far less pronounced than their differences in style and message. William's allegorical treatment of romantic love withdrawn became, under the quill of Jean de Meun, a digression on women, using personifications and caricatures to describe all sides of love before concluding the story with an assault on the garden's Ivory Tower to reach the rose.

For his completion of *The Romance of the Rose* Jean de Meun had been inspired in part by the *fabliau*, or short ribald tale, which was a trademark of the medieval French vernacular. Of these stories, told in verse of eight-syllable rhymed couplets, 160 are still extant. Many of the names of their authors are known, such as Jean Bodel of Arras or Jean de Condé (d.1346) and though the *fabliaux* were designed for elite audiences, it is thought by some historians that they may have had a following even among the bourgeoisie they mercilessly ridiculed.[15] Despite their popularity, the middle of the fourteenth century marked the virtual end of the genre as distinct.[16] This correlated, in fact, with the general passing of the literary dominance of the French vernacular in Europe and with the interest among French intellectuals to assess their language in terms of its strengths vis-à-vis Latin (e.g. was its grammar fit to express what Latin could?).[17] Standardization of French throughout the whole of the French nation was a post-medieval realization.

German

Even in the centuries of Rome's strength, the territory of Germania was never completely dominated by Rome. Islands of Latinity, such as Treves, were established, but the indigenous or incoming barbarian peoples continued to speak their own languages, all "unsettling tongues" to the Roman ear. Dependent upon the size of a particular group, Germanic dialects were imposing themselves quite clearly by the ninth century. The area affected by languages of German origin extended in the north from the mouth of the Somme, in the west from Lille and Tournai, in the southeast from the banks of the Sambre and Meuse, and in the south across the Vosges, from the borders of Bourgogne and the high valley of the Rhone eastward into Pannonia. Although this is known as the period of Old High German, there was little linguistic unity binding all the dialects the region encompassed. Works survive in the Bavarian, Saxon, and Francique dialects.

The gains in Germanic tongues were certainly losses in the Romance Latin and French dialects. Whole areas including England, and on the continent from the left bank of the Rhine around to all the land between the Danube and the southern Alps, were by the ninth century effectively immune to strong Romance influences. The Frankish Austrasian aristocracy, the ruling elite of the eastern half of the earlier Carolingian empire, was of Germanic tongue. With no linguistic affinity to their own language, Latin was artificially learned via the study of grammar and without any intermediary of a Romance native language. It was necessary for the Germanic Franks to learn Latin from the very rudiments and to forge grammatical tools for the teaching of their own vernacular. A monk of ninth-century St Gall, Notker the Stammerer, recognized the need and wrote a treatise on rhetoric explaining the technical terms in German.

Without any linguistic intermediary between Latin and the Germanic vernaculars, a very early separation of the spoken languages from literary Latin took effect. Translation into the vernacular rather than education in Latin became the preferred way to avail oneself of the Roman culture. Notker, who was among the first to consider insistence upon the acquisition of Latin to be linguistic pedantry, used German as the language of instruction at St Gall. None the less, he valued Latin learning, and aside from original works in the vernacular, he completed many translations, of Boethius' *Consolation of Philosophy* and *On the Trinity*, the *Distichs* (*Disticha*) of Cato, Virgil's *Eclogues* (*Bucolica*), Terence's *Andria*, the

Marriage of Mercury and Philology by Martianus Capella, Aristotle's *Categories* and *On Interpretation*, an anonymous work on arithmetic, a commentary on the Psalms accompanied by his own commentary, part of the Book of Job, and Gregory the Great's commentary on Job, *Morals*. His translations were criticized, but not because they were novice ones, strongly influenced by the idiom and structure of Latin, or because they were often paraphrases adopting Latin words. Objection stemmed from an episcopal view that translations into the vernacular were dangerous and unworthy innovations. In response to Bishop Hugo of Sion, Notker said, "you will soon excel in reading them [the classical texts he translated] and will recognize how quickly we can understand by means of our mother tongue what can be understood only with difficulty or not at all in a foreign language."[18]

By the time German vernacular literature began to develop rapidly in the twelfth century, its authors, as for example, the *Minnesänger*, Wolfram von Eschenbach, Walther von der Vogel-weide, Hartmann von Aue, and Gottfried von Strassburg, had made full use of a language "elevated" above regional dialects, Middle High German. Standardization of the German language would entail two more steps: the integration of the features of High German as written in all parts of the Germanic kingdom, and the use of German as the language of preference in prose as well as poetry. The German vernacular faced literary decline during the thirteenth and fourteenth centuries. None the less, sermons, legal and medical treatises, as well as the code of common and feudal law, had wide circulation in the vernacular. Ultimately the German of a single work, the Bible in the translation of Martin Luther, would by its tremendous circulation be acknowledged as the "best form" of the German language.

Italian

Latin had never been totally uniform from its written to its spoken form. Indices of a spoken, less universal form of Latin were already extant in inscriptions and sermons of bishops and early Christian preachers. Like most popular languages, spoken Latin was a simpli-fied version of the written form in terms of vocabulary and syntax. St Augustine reflected a Roman dialect in his sermons, where, for example, word order, and not inflection as in classical Latin, carried the burden of meaning. The richest specimen of the early changes in written Latin is found in the account by the Spanish nun, Aetheria (or Egeria), who travelled to Jerusalem in the late fourth century.

She clearly infused her native tongue into her written Latin, giving an interesting taste of literary Latin becoming vulgar.

There are a few noteworthy signposts on the way to Italian's distinguishing itself definitively from Latin. The differences between many Italian dialects and Latin was still not large by the tenth century, when the monk Gunzo of Novara defended his slips in Latin to monks at St Gall by pointing to the close similarity between his native "Italian" tongue and Latin, which made it all too easy to confuse the two. Of Italian dialects, Sicilian was the first one to assert itself as a literary language of vernacular Italian. Its comparatively rapid evolution is not surprising, given the political and administrative unity of the island after the tenth century. The first Italian lyric poetry was written, however, in Umbrian, by Franciscans, Francis of Assisi between 1224 and 1226 and Jacopone da Todi (1236–1306). Francis' *Canticle of the Sun* (*Cantico de lo fratre sole*), reminiscent of a psalm, gave Umbrian quite wide circulation; but neither Sicilian nor Umbrian would become the predominant dialect.

Tuscan became the leading literary language of the Italian peninsula. The central location of Tuscany gave its speakers and writers the practical advantages of lying between the areas of northern and southern dialects and of being understood by all. The Italian vernaculars were generally quite late in developing as a literary vehicle. The remarkable thirteenth-century literary contributions of Dante, Petrarch, and Boccaccio, all of Florence, were both to cement dramatically the dominance of Tuscan within Italy and to give prestige to the Italian vernacular north of the Alps. Dante, in his *On the Eloquence of the Vernacular* (*De vulgari eloquentia*), makes it very clear that the Italian literary vernacular ought not simply to be spoken Tuscan in writing, but rather an "ideal" language, a refinement of Italian dialects above the crudity or regionality of any one. A confirmation, as it were, of Dante's theory, the idealized form of Tuscan used by Dante himself in the *Divine Comedy* (*La divina commedia*), by Petrarch in his *Songs* or *Canzionere*, and by Boccaccio in the *Decameron* (*Decamerone*), brought to the literary Italian at the end of the Middle Ages a standard for imitation and improvement.

The Social Context and Consequences of the Discovery

The difficulty of a theory which posits a conscious discovery of the use of a language appears increasingly clear as one looks at the evolution of language. What does it mean to discover the use of a language? What change takes place in the use of the language to reveal that one is conscious of that use? To assume a notion of conscious discovery implies that one could detect without any undue difficulty a culture's demonstrating this revelation. Indeed that event might be determined to occur when the language was first used to reflect the oral insights of a group's forefathers in their language; it might be argued that at this point a people have become so trapped in a particular language that they cannot extricate themselves except at the price of a loss of self-expression and collective memory.

Medieval writers can be interpreted as having spoken to the "discovery." French Waldensians, English barons, troubadour poets all relate how they are part of a traditional group, (faithful Christian believers, feudal lords, or entertainers) which has tried with all its abilities to express what was desired in Latin. They are that part of the group which finds itself more and more convinced, however, that expression in Latin is no longer effective. It seems that for them Latin could not meet the conditions of self-expression, and could therefore not continue to be used as the means of written expression. Believers could not feel close to God; political figures could not debate with one another; artists could not express their feelings, except through the vernacular languages.

Evidence for a "discovery theory" of the use of medieval vernacular languages would be appropriately sought in or around a phase of particularly vital use of the vernacular and in the areas of a group's culture most affected by that use. The twelfth century has been identified by medieval historians as the most dynamic in intellectual changes and it will be examined here in light of the rise of the vernacular. The medieval religious and political contexts were both dramatically affected by use of the vernacular, and they too will be analyzed here for evidence of this discovery.

The Twelfth Century – A Dynamic Period of Medieval Culture

The twelfth century, considered in the context of other medieval intellectual revivals, was the ultimate medieval triumph of intellectual and artistic endeavors over the material environment of the Middle Ages and the problems it posed to human survival.[19] Remarks that it had "all the characteristics of a true renaissance" and was "the most important turning point in the intellectual history of the middle ages" summarize the importance medieval historians have attributed to the activities of the eleventh and twelfth centuries in the course of medieval thought.[20] Major developments have been identified in the education, religion, thought, and art of the period, which are regarded by some historians, such as Christopher Brooke, as a reflection of an increase in the variety and sophistication of medieval culture; by others, such as Richard Southern and Colin Morris, as a sign of pre-Renaissance humanism or the discovery of the individual.[21] Stephen C. Ferruolo has very carefully pointed out the distortions and perversions that either the contribution of the twelfth century or the notion of "renaissance," or both, have undergone in order for the century and this idea to be paired.[22] For the purposes of this discussion, only one specific point needs to be addressed.

The writers and thinkers of the eleventh and twelfth centuries were not participating primarily in a fervent effort to recover the ideas and writings of antiquity and thus not focusing exclusively on Latin. The twelfth century may indeed have been a period of revival and dynamism, but it was not a rebirth of classical influences such as Italy was to experience in the fourteenth- and fifteenth-century Renaissance. For Urban T. Holmes, it was "a vigorous reawakening of cultural enthusiasm in which dialectic, theology, legal studies, *vernacular literature* of a worldly type, decorative art, and Latin poetry rose to new heights" (emphasis added).[23] The emphasis imposed here on vernacular literature is not meant to be subtle, for the mention of it by Holmes distinguishes him from any number of writers on the achievements of the twelfth century. Many of the latter, by omission, such as Charles Haskins, or by commission, such as Ferruolo,[24] seem to view Latin as the victor over its opponent, the vernacular, in this period. This is to deny any connection between the "general quickening of spirit" in the Latin sphere and the fact that English, French, and German were all reaching the height of their medieval literary contribution.[25]

Indeed, one may need, as Ferruolo recommends, to see the twelfth century "as a diverse and yet integrated cultural revival", and not fail "to realize that the second half of the twelfth century was as active and creative as the first half"[26] to include the proponents of Middle English, *langue d'oc, langue d'oïl,* and Middle High German, as well as those literate in medieval Spanish and Italian, as participants in, rather than obstructions to, intellectual vitality in the eleventh and twelfth centuries. For some historians, this has not been a difficult task. John C. Moore in *Love in Twelfth-Century France* has examined both Latin religious and vernacular secular culture together in the whole period.[27] Colin Morris, author of *The Discovery of the Individual, 1050–1200,* reports evidence in both vernacular and Latin documents for his thesis that the "self" found expression in this period.[28] It is for some, then, neither compromise nor failure to assert that at the same time as twelfth-century scholars were making considerable effort to improve their written and spoken Latin, twelfth-century writers were also demonstrating a intellectual verve in the vernacular. Nor do all historians of the twelfth-century revival determine its end to have come with a lessening preoccupation mid-century with the reading of Cicero or Ovid or with the monopoly on Latin by scholastic theologians. One could argue, along with Ferruolo, that throughout the whole of the century there was a constancy of interest in vernacular expression and of cultural motivations and objectives.[29]

Was the twelfth century the time of the "discovery of the vernacular"? It was undeniably a period of discovery. Irnerius (1088–1125) brought the "discovery" of the Codex of Roman law compiled in 534 by the eastern Roman Emperor Justinian to light in Bologna. Peter Lombard revealed his "discovery" of systematic theology in his work, *The Four Sentences* (*Quatuor libri sententiarum*), in which extracts from scripture and the Church Fathers are organized topically to address theological issues. In discussing the written use of vernacular languages, the term discovery might also be considered appropriate. There is "a sheer abundance of testimonies" that love-language had discovered a new home in the vernacular and that new images of love were being drawn from older sources.[30] The genre of literary fiction was "discovered" in the 1170's by vernacular writers, along with the consciously creative author's role which fiction entails.[31] However, as the brief sketches of vernacular use above reveal, since in practically every medieval century a vernacular "discovery" or two can be found, the twelfth century must be seen as one phase of the continuous breakthrough vernacular languages were making during the Middle Ages.

Religion in the Vernacular

The Church's imposing use of Latin in the medieval period would seem to have allocated no role whatsoever to any of the vernacular languages in religious expression. Encounters between Latin and the vernacular languages did, however, take place in the religious sphere, and that interaction might be characterized under three different ideas: rivalry, dominance, and ceremony. Each of these addressed one of the three main concerns of the Church throughout the Middle Ages: to establish and guarantee orthodoxy, to maintain supremacy over other religions and factions, and to inspire believers to reverence and awe.

At first, the idea of religion meeting the vernacular in the Middle Ages might seem surprising. Did the Church not adhere to its rejection of the vernaculars, in favor of the use of Latin alone? In fact, it was only in 813 with the Council of Tours that Latin was recommended for use in sermons to lay parishioners. The notion that a particular language would play a significant role in expressing the truth or eliminating the possibility of non-orthodox beliefs or distortions to orthodoxy was to become more and more a point of insistence. The idea of a vernacular "interpretation" of scripture was in principle perfectly acceptable to the Church, although it became increasingly the belief that the vernacular interpretation could not be orthodox. Translations of parts of the Bible into the vernacular had been available in the earliest Germanic tongues and also in Anglo-Saxon.

The only wing of the Church to apply the Latin-only practice consistently was the papacy. No pope took as his the right to represent the Church in a language not shared by all; in one restricted to a specific region or people. The pontiffs rejected for themselves the use of the vernacular (to which many a preaching bishop became committed) as barring the access of some to the community of all. There was no explicit rhetorical reference to scriptural texts to support this practice, but Latin clearly raised the individual above the sectarian limitations of his local tongue. Most local saints and regional religious festivals were also rejected as resting upon events inadequately universal. Use of the vernacular by the Church was presented as limiting the access of the individual to the universal institution. It was ironically seen as a recipe for exclusion, and as the history of the Catholic Church of Rome both during and after the Middle Ages demonstrates, many voluntarily chose the vernacular for purposes of self-exclusion.

Christianity had from its beginnings espoused the idea that all human beings can have a one-to-one relationship with their God. This idea was considered an integral part of the Christian doctrines of individual moral responsibility, salvation, and redemption. As has already been discussed in the first chapter, in the Middle Ages a number of different expressions of the idea flourished, taking the form, for example, of the hermetic and monastic lifestyles, of the confession of sins, of the giving of one's worldly goods to the Church, of tending to the sick and needy, and of striving for a personal understanding of scripture. In the case of the last, language was thought to be a potential barrier to contact with God, since many could not comprehend the Latin of the sacred texts through which communication or understanding was made possible. Outspoken individuals in the twelfth and thirteenth centuries began whole movements advocating that fundamental Christian texts and teaching be accessible in the vernacular.

The Latin of the Church began to experience rivalry with the vernacular. From the ninth century, Latin was the clerical language. Claim to clerical status, not to mention to the right to own books of scripture, depended on proof of ability to read and write Latin. By the eleventh century, religious ideas were rarely treated in the vernacular despite its otherwise increasing use; from the twelfth century, use of the vernacular for religious purposes had become highly suspect. Certain fringe groups of believers, such as the Waldensians in the twelfth century, held to the necessity of making the Christian message available in the vernacular through biblical translation and sermons in local dialects. The Church itself tried to deflate the rivalry between the vernaculars and Latin in specific areas of practice. Spiritual guides, such as religious poems and sermons, again appeared in the vernacular. The Church embraced whole new orders, the Franciscans and the Dominicans, for whom use of the vernacular was an important element. The human side of Christ, His birth of Mary and His Passion, were allowed to become important affective responses to a religion which was remote linguistically as well as in other ways.

The Church had limits, however, to what it could tolerate in the use of the vernacular. The Church had very early developed its strategies for dealing with the unorthodox written word – the banning and burning of texts. For centuries, the Church had encouraged that the Christian message be passed on to believers in a visual and oral manner, and when expedient, it could assert that no religious texts need be in lay hands. Responding to unauthorized uses of the vernacular was a relatively small part of the medieval Church's response to heresy, and it was a partial response to circumstance, rather than to the issue in question. The majority of the medieval lay population was illiterate; thus, whatever the sympathies of the populus, it was mostly only their leaders, such as Peter Waldo of Lyons or Peter de Bruis, who were liable to accusations of heretical unauthorized use of the vernacular. The exertion of Latin linguistic dominance over the vernacular took the same form as the dominance of orthodoxy over heretical beliefs. Vernacular texts were banned and burned, and those in whose possession they were found were tried for heresy. One additional detail is of linguistic significance: the inquisitional process was conducted in Latin, to the distinct disadvantage of the illiterate laity accused.

The reluctance with which the Roman Catholic Church abandoned the use of Latin in the Mass in the twentieth century demonstrates to what extent the Latin language played an integral part in more than just its orthodox texts. Part of the significant aura of the religious ceremony was thought to depend on Latin. The connection between Latin and western Catholic ceremonies which had begun with Pope Damasus (366–84) would be strongly adhered to throughout the Middle Ages.

Political Role of the Vernacular

It is perhaps not so difficult to imagine that, as in the case of medieval religion, the vernacular would play an equally important role in the medieval political arena. Historians of medieval political theory, such as Walter Ullmann and John B. Morrall,[32] have conservatively noted in passing a two-fold effect of vernacular languages on medieval political thought and action. For the most part, medieval political issues rested on philosophical and theological foundations, which themselves determined the use of the vernacular. Of significance was, however, that legal texts in the vernacular made judicial and political theory accessible to a wider audience. Further, use of the vernacular reflected recognition of individuality and self-expression, both important components of medieval populism.

Discussion of particular vernacular languages has already revealed that legal texts had been translated into the vernacular or actually formulated in the vernacular from the early Middle Ages. Latin was also a significant political presence, however, and its law codes and procedures were models even in a vernacular context. Those using Latin perceived its universality as politically important in exceeding regional linguistic boundaries and combating the interests of particular pockets. Latin could reflect and safeguard the interests of the large group and perhaps even allow it to function as a "nation."[33] Vernacular advocates argued, however, that Latin permitted particular interests to be represented over those of the group and that local interests were not even represented. Indeed, vernacular form seems to have followed local content in the French vernacular work of Beaumanoir, *The Customs of the Beauvaisis*, where "each baron is sovereign in his own barony."[34]

The notion of a political unity was, however, defined by medieval intellectuals in different terms than by use of the vernacular. The *gubernatio* or government was defined by the common code of law. *Regnum* or kingdom was defined by the person of the monarch or perhaps his "personal" territory. The *natio* or state was the com-

munity of citizens. Thus, although linguistic historians have observed
that the growth of national consciousness has been closely linked
with the passage from dialect to national language, Thomas Aquinas
and most other political theorists of the Middle Ages did not consider even theoretically that the vernacular could have such a
dramatic effect.

By extension of various medieval political theories, use of the
vernacular could, none the less, have been contemplated for its
political effect. In addition to making the law and processes of
politics accessible, use of the vernacular reflected recognition of
individuality and individual expression. The medieval definition of a
state as a community of citizens, which derived from Aristotle, also
entailed that recognition. Medieval populism or any medieval
theory of the popular derivation of authority was based on the
recognition of man as an individual, not as a class of individuals.
Corresponding to the abstract notion of individual was the practical
concept of citizen. Thomas Aquinas considered the individual as far
more than a mere transitory portion of the institution of the state.
As leader, the citizen could effect change. One of his tools might
very well have been deemed to be the vernacular.

The most definitive political impact of use of the vernacular was
its accentuation of regionality. As the most outspoken of vernacular
advocates dismissed all need of Latin with their new enthusiasm for
a role for the vernacular, they adopted a recipe for the political and
religious disintegration of pan-Europeanism which, although not
truly a medieval phenomenon, eventually came to pass.

For further reading

For an introduction to the variety of medieval vernacular languages, see:

David Daiches and Anthony Thorlby, eds, *The Mediaeval World* (Literature
and Western Civilization, vol. 2: London, 1973).
W. B. Lockwood, *A Panorama of Indo-European Languages* (London, 1972).
Philippe Wolff, *Western Languages, AD 100–1500* (New York, 1971).

On the history of particular vernacular languages, see:

James Carney, *Medieval Irish Lyrics: Selected and Translated* (Dublin/
Berkeley, 1967).
Eduard Hartl, "Die deutsche Literatur des Mittelaters," in *Verfasserlexikon*,
eds W. Stammler and K. Langosch (Berlin, 1933–55), vol. IV, col. 1067.
K. Jackson, *Language and History in Early Britain* (Edinburgh, 1953).
Mary Dominica Legge, *Anglo-Norman Literature and its Background* (Oxford,
1963).

Peter Rickard, *A History of the French Language* (London: rev. ed., 1989).
Gerhard Rohlfs, *From Vulgar Latin to Old French* (Detroit, 1970).
Arthur Terry, *Catalan Literature* (A Literary History of Spain: London, 1972), pp. 1–60.
R. M. Wilson, *Early Middle English Literature* (London, 1939; 3rd ed., 1968).
C. L. Wrenn, *A Study of Old English Literature* (London, 1967).
S. Zenkovsky, ed., *Medieval Russia's Epics, Chronicles, and Tales* (New York, 1963).

For introductions to writing and works in the European vernaculars, see:

H. M. and K. N. Chadwick, *The Growth of Literature*, vol. 1: *The Ancient Literatures of Europe* (Cambridge, 1932).
H. J. Chaytor, *From Script to Print: An Introduction to Medieval Vernacular Literature* (Cambridge, 1945).
E. R. Curtius, *European Literature and the Latin Middle Ages*, tr. W. R. Trask (New York, 1953; rpt Princeton, NJ, 1973).
Peter Dronke, *The Medieval Lyric* (London, 1968).

For detailed analysis of facets of the vernacular breakthrough, see:

P. Bourgain, "L'emploi de la langue vulgaire dans la littérature au temps de Philippe Auguste," in *La France de Philippe Auguste, le temps des mutations*, ed. R. H. Bautier (Paris, 1982), pp. 765–83.
J. Cremona, "Dante's Views on Language," in *The Mind of Dante*, ed. U. Limentani (Cambridge, 1965).
A. G. Jongkees, "*Translatio studii*: les avatars d'un thème médiéval," in *Miscellanea Mediaevalia in memoriam Jan Frederick Niermeyer* (Groningen, 1967), pp. 41–51.
Gottfried Wilhelm Leibniz, "Unvorgreifliche Gedanken, betreffend die Ausübung und Verbesserung der deutschen Sprache" (1687), in *Handbuch deutscher Prosa*, ed. K. E. Ph. Wackernagel (Berlin, 1837).
Serge Luisignan, *Parler vulgairement: les intellectuels et la langue française aux XIIIe et XIVe siècles* (Paris, 1987).
K. Malone, "When Did Middle English Begin?," in *Curme Volume of Linguistic Studies*, ed. J. T. Hatfield (Baltimore, 1930), pp. 110–17.

For excellent accounts of the social role of the vernacular, see:

E. Auerbach, *Literary Language and its Public in Late Latin Antiquity and in the Middle Ages* (London, 1965).
Brian Stock, *The Implications of Literacy: Written Language and Models of Interpretation in the Eleventh and Twelfth Centuries* (Princeton, NJ, 1983).

For interesting accounts of the religious role of the vernacular, see:

Rosalind B. Brooke, *The Coming of the Friars* (London, 1975).
M. D. Lambert, *Medieval Heresy* (London, 1977).

Emmanuel Le Roy Ladurie, *Montaillou* (London, 1978).

R. I. Moore, *The Birth of Popular Heresy* (London, 1975).

—— *The Origins of European Dissent* (London, 1977).

Edward Peters, *Heresy and Authority in Medieval Europe* (Philadelphia, 1980).

W. L. Wakefield, *Heresy, Crusade and Inquisition in Southern France, 1100–1250* (Berkeley, 1975).

For reflections on the political role of the vernacular, see:

R. W. and A. J. Carlyle, *Medieval Political Theory in the West* (6 vols: London, 1903–36).

T. Gilby, *Principality and Polity: Aquinas and the Rise of State Theory in the West* (London, 1958).

J. K. Hyde, *Society and Politics in Medieval Italy, 1000–1300* (New York, 1969).

G. de Lagarde, *La naissance de l'ésprit laïque au déclin du moyen âge* (5 vols: Louvain 1956–70).

Archibald R. Lewis, *The Development of Southern French and Catalan Society, 715–1050* (Austin, TX, 1965).

P. S. Lewis, *Later Medieval France: The Polity* (New York, 1968).

6

Scholasticism

The preoccupations of scholasticism seem to have made it among the least understood of intellectual movements. Indeed, amidst the topics which were debated by the "schoolmen" or scholastics can be found such puzzling questions as: Is one body, through a miracle, able to be in several places at the same time? Is "age" substance or accident? Does the will move itself? While none of these questions could alone dispel the impression that the movement was one absorbed in indulgent, futile pondering, no study of medieval scholasticism can avoid their discussion. Instead the attention they attract ought rightly to be diffused, as in this chapter's description of the broad intellectual context of scholastic activity, e.g., in philosophy, theology, law, and architecture. It will here thus be shown that all scholastic questions had an important, far from futile, place in the critical step in medieval intellectualization which was scholasticism.

The primary institutional context of scholasticism was the university. University intellectuals until well beyond the end of the Middle Ages were indeed engaged in a variety of hair-splitting discussions whose main focus of interest was theology. Since, however, philosophy rather than exegesis was their intellectual route to theological concerns, ontological and epistemological questions also attracted their attention. From its height in the thirteenth century, scholasticism, however, was no longer to be contained within discussions of orthodox theology and Christian philosophy; its influence began to test orthodoxy and to be felt in other fields, for example, in architecture, medicine, and politics. Scholasticism became thus a part of a wider intellectual context than simply that of the university. This discussion will begin with a definition of scholasticism, and then a description will be offered of the movement which so dominated intellectual life in the later Middle Ages.

Scholasticism Outlined

Works on medieval philosophy or thought offer differing definitions of the intellectual movement known as scholasticism. To define any intellectual movement requires noting common features according to which certain ideas and thinkers can be considered to belong to one group. The features identified as common for scholasticism and scholastics often seem elusive, or too trivial to carry the weight of a complex intellectual movement. The scope of the present study already limits its definition somewhat, geographically to western Europe, and chronologically to the later Middle Ages. There are those who argue that scholastic ideas can be discovered throughout the East and West and both before and after as well as during the medieval period.[1]

In its most detectable phase, between 1250 and 1500, scholasticism was located in the intellectual centers of the universities. These institutions were fundamentally extensions of the earlier western European educational system of the Church, initiated and fostered first in monasteries and then in cathedral schools in the growing towns. The late eleventh-century diversion of violent feudal activity toward the Holy Lands had mitigated political turmoil within Europe and had permitted the establishment of institutions of higher learning which needed to be able to draw students from a wide geographic area. Most universities, whose cartulary origins date from the early thirteenth century, such as the University of Paris, were located in urban centers and intimately connected with, and housed in, the urban religious institutions. There was, however, also direct intellectual stimulus for the new institutions: the entry of Plato and Aristotle in Latin into western Europe. By the thirteenth century, their combined style and scope were stimulating learned reaction to each of their ideas.

Scholasticism was essentially a movement which attempted a methodological and philosophical demonstration of Christian theology as inherently rational and consistent. The desire to render Christian theology systematic and the intellectual concern with the distinction between theological understanding through reason and theological belief through faith had already begun to dominate medieval religious thought, in the eleventh century with, for example, Anselm of Canterbury and Peter Abelard, and in the twelfth century with Peter Lombard. It was, however, the integration of Aristotle's ideas into the framework of Christianity which posed the major challenge for scholastics. The focus on giving a place to the Aristotelian corpus in the scholarship of the Latin West has become for historians, in fact, one of the three most frequently noted trademarks of unity in the scholastic movement. The other two trademarks of the movement's cohesion were intimately connected to this first one: the passionate embrace of reason as the route to knowledge, and the use of the *scholium* or textual commentary as the method for integrating and understanding texts.[2]

Scholastics vigorously exploited the basic methodological tool of the *scholium*, or textual commentary. The works of Aristotle had begun to be adopted as official textbooks, by the University of Paris, for instance, in 1255. The scholastic commentary took a variety of forms to meet the fundamental challenge of understanding these new texts. Commentaries were as short as a few words (a *glossa*) or as long as several pages. They were organized to follow the text (as in the commentary *ad literam*), or ordered around topics (as in *questiones*).

For the first time since Boethius, medieval intellectuals of the thirteenth century tried following Aristotle to embrace the whole of human knowledge.[3] Following his model they both analyzed the principles overriding the specifics of their work in logic or metaphysics and theology, and wrote all-encompassing expositions. The (encyclopedic) *summa* or the *tractatus*, the lecture (*lectio*, or expounding of the text), and the disputation in the form of *questiones* or *sophismata* were all adopted or developed by the scholastics as equally important literary or paedagogical methods to echo Aristotle (and Plato) in a systematic exposition of ideas. Such were the steps and methods by which medieval scholasticism intended to demonstrate the complete harmony of Christian theology with the rest of human thought and opinion by a minute re-examination of every aspect of Christian theology in light of philosophy.[4]

Scholasticism in Academia

Scholasticism was especially dominant in academic institutions: in France at the Universities of Paris and Toulouse, in England at Oxford University, in Germany at the Universities of Cologne and Erfurt, and in Italy at the University of Padua. It had a profound effect on the formal techniques of education (evident, for example, in the commentary exposition, the choosing and ranking of Aristotle's texts for study, the training of students in debating), as well as on the language and content of discussion. Its influence was undeniably most prominent and lasting on the mode of presenting arguments dialectically.

In fact the overwhelming application of scholastic dialectical method and Aristotelian ideas in the universities, even to theology, resulted during the thirteenth century in confrontation between the Church and the university.[5] For example, the University of Paris, instumental to the development of scholastic thought, witnessed in 1277 a most violent ecclesiastical outrage against the effects of Aristotelian scholasticism, with an episcopal condemnation of 219 unorthodox alleged teachings. None the less, both scholasticism and Aristotelian philosophy survived the assault. Aristotle's sustained influence is reflected in the close dialectical scrutiny given to the wide range of ideas in late medieval scholastic ethics, politics, ecclesiology, logic (as a subject, no longer simply as a tool), and applied mathematics. Amidst the conflicting opinions concerning its value, scholasticism continued to play a role within academic strongholds through the fourteenth century and beyond. As late as the sixteenth century, for example, Galileo was trained scholastically, and Martin Luther was reacting to its dictates.

Differences between various strains of scholasticism need not be denied to emphasize the quite similar intellectual context in which they all thrived, the university. A university received official acknowledgement of its existence as a *studium generale* (school offering many subjects) or an *universitas societas magistrorum discipulorumque* (corporation or guild of teachers and students) from the pope (or a bishop), the emperor, or the king. The universities' faculties of arts and their higher faculties of theology, canon law, civil law, and medicine, were all to adopt a scholastic approach to learning. Scholasticism which began in the universities as a new way of organizing knowledge and absorbing new learning, particularly the ideas of Aristotle, into an intellectual setting (already well-defined as Christian), later degenerated, as will be seen in the next chapter, into an instrument of conflict between vested theological and political interests. Initially the ostensible scholastic goal, a greater understanding both of Christian doctrine and of classical, Arabic, and Judaic philosophies, yielded to the undisguised advocacy of certain prescriptions for both thought and action.

The Variety in Scholasticism

Many works on medieval philosophy testify to the fact that simplification of the philosophical ideas under discussion in the Middle Ages is difficult. Any absorption with detailed explanations, which may appear to be pedantry, will perhaps go some way toward underlining the fact that grappling with language was as much at the heart of scholasticism as grappling with ideas. The distinctiveness of schools of scholastic thought, as well as their similarities, lay embedded in intricate reasonings, and the vehicle of expression was language. For an initial understanding of scholasticism, some of its vocabulary and the scope of its views must at least be introduced. This shall be tackled in terms of three basic *foci* of medieval thought: ontology, epistemology, and theology.

In Positions of Ontology

Ontology merits consideration as the first most significant dimension of scholasticism, if only because ontological issues are the oldest concerns of Christian philosophy and theology. Ontology immediately suggests the difficult notion of metaphysical being. Well before the intense discussions of medieval schoolmen, classical philosophers had already had ontological debates, focused on the distinction between the use of the verb "to be" and the actual existence of the objects described. Medieval ontological issues were considered in the metaphysical terms of essence and existence, reification and de-reification, potentiality and actuality, and the individual, plural and universal. Medieval ontology encompassed the discussion of the meaning, structure, and principles of whatever is, and inasmuch as it is or exists.

As traditionally contemplated by Christian theologians, the concept of "existence" had fundamental importance when applied either to God (as in "the characteristics of God's existence, such as His eternalness," or as in "the states in which He was revealed to humankind") or to human beings (as in "their two phases of existence, first in the material world, then in the life hereafter"). Within the Bible, the theme of existence is especially associated with the Old Testament stories of creation and reflections on existence, or the New Testament stories of Jesus' birth and resurrection. One of the earliest writers to develop a comprehensive Christian concept of existence, divine and human, was Augustine of Hippo, of the late fourth century. His version of the concept of being was the highly influential Neoplatonic notion of Plotinus, that which is unchangingly itself which Augustine made refer to the Christian God. By the eleventh century there was again definite interest in the notion of existence, demonstrated both in scriptural exegesis and in works of a more topical nature, such as Anselm's *Proslogion* and *Monologion* and Abelard's *Yes and No* (*Sic et Non*).

The most fundamental question raised by scholastics was ontological: Does God exist? It is unlikely that any medieval writer seriously doubted the appropriate theological answer. As witnessed by Anselm of Canterbury's "I believe in order to understand," the question was philosophical, stemming from a new interest in language, the logic of linguistic expression, and the connection between reason and faith. Early scholastic discussions of the existence of God, such as those of Anselm of Canterbury and Peter Abelard, broke from exegetical tradition as they laid the burden on persuasion on the logic of language and ideas, without reference to the authority of scripture, the source of revealed truth. Anselm, for example, set out to establish logically first that God exists, according to his definition of God as "that than which nothing greater can be thought" and secondly that God, so defined, must exist by necessity.

Anselm argued first that whether or not one grants the existence of God, if the concept of God as "that than which nothing greater can be thought" is granted, then it follows logically to grant His potential existence. Anselm stated the premise that it is greater to exist both in reality and as a thought in the mind than simply as a thought in the mind, as, for example, the centaur. Thus, if God, as "that than which nothing greater can be thought," were to exist only as a thought in the mind, it would in fact be possible to conceive of a being greater still existing also in reality. That being would, however, by the definition of God, be God. As a second part of his argument, Anselm chose to qualify his statement concerning God's existence as a logical assertion of necessity, rather than possibility. "That than which nothing greater can be thought" was for Anselm the only being which cannot be thought not to exist, for "what cannot be thought not to exist" is greater than "that which can be thought not to exist." "That than which nothing greater can be thought" is thus "that which cannot be thought not to exist": therefore God must exist.

Anselm's application of a modal argument of possibility and necessity to the question of the existence of God drew much subsequent attention to the logical challenge of proving God's existence. Numerous medieval scholars attempted to devise their own proofs through new logical approaches. They were inspired by both Platonic and Aristotelian ideas and methods of induction and deduction. By the thirteenth century, the existence of God was affirmed in refined scholastic tradition in the *Summa theologiae* by Thomas Aquinas, the most noted of all medieval theologians. While Anselm had devised his proof wholly deductively, Aquinas arrived at his conclusions both deductively and inductively, from such evidence as the existence of motion. Later medieval and Renaissance thinkers, such as Duns Scotus and Francis Suarez, rejected the inductive use of sensible and empirical facts (such as the existence of motion) as the foundation for their proofs for the existence of God.

They started instead from metaphysical premises, such as "things can be brought into existence," or "individuality comes from outside nature." Throughout scholasticism, interest in the question of God's existence and its affirmative answer were constants; there were, however, notable differences in argumentation stemming from different uses of the deductive and inductive methods.

Other issues of ontology, not tied quite so obviously to theological concepts, figured prominently in a wide variety of scholastic questions. Notions of individuality and plurality, essence and existence, and permanence and change were among the most widely discussed.

Universals One particularly controversial ontological issue in the Middle Ages, the existence of universals, was related to the distinctions between the philosophical postures of "realism" and "nominalism."[6] In the early scholastic period, various interpretations of realism, deriving ultimately from Platonism, were dominant, giving way to nominalist ideas around the mid-fourteenth century. Realism and nominalism both addressed the issue of whether "universals" (concepts applying to more than one thing or universally) really exist, or whether they are simply conceptions in the mind. For the extreme realist, any universal, say "book," exists prior to and independent of any particular book. It also exists completely within each individual which derives from it. For the extreme nominalist, only the individual thing has existence. There are no universals which exist over and above the individuals; hence a common name, such as "book," denotes only the similarity of like things. By extension of these positions, further philosophical questions also arose. For the realist, if universals do exist outside the mind, how do individual things come to exist; what is the principle of individuation of numerically individual things? For the nominalist, if universals do not exist outside the mind, what then inspires the collectivizing concepts so frequent in speech; how are they related to existing things?

Scholasticism accommodated the extremes of both realism and nominalism, located at opposing ends of a spectrum, as well as moderate stances in each. In the twelfth century John of Salisbury in his *Metalogicon* recorded a list of nuanced positions that irritated him even to note: one (John Roscelin) holds that "universals are mere word sounds [*voces*]"; another (Abelard) that "universals are word concepts;" another influenced by Boethius "says that genera and species" (universals) are "acts of the [intuitive] understanding;" another (Walter of Mortagne) reasons "that either the universal is numerically one, or it is non-existent;" still another (Bernard of Chartres) says "genus and species are nothing more nor less than" Platonic ideas; another (Gilbert of Poitiers) "places universality in 'native' forms" [or copies of an original]; still another (Joscelin of Soisson) "attributes universality to collections of things, while denying it to things as individuals," and finally "there are some who fix their attention on the status of things. . . ."[7] Of all these relatively early positions, Abelard's was the most influential and moderate one, asserting that while (on the nominalist side) universals exist only in the human understanding as "word concepts," they none the less (on the realist side) signify real things, that is to say, the particulars in which they are known to be present.

The discussion of universals persisted on an Abelardian path until well into the later thirteenth century, when the issue of individuation intensified. The moderate realist Duns Scotus would, for example, assert that although individual things exist, the mind can affirm the existence only of universals. Since individuals without observably differing features ("accidents") cannot be distinguished from one another except in number, their individuality (what Duns Scotus called their "thisness" (*haecceitas*)), must be hidden unknowably within themselves. In reply, there was nominalist ontology, voiced in the scholasticism of William of Ockham, Gabriel Biel, Gregory of Rimini, and Hugolino of Orvieto. While strongly asserting the distinctness of the individual, to affirm the reasons for that distinctness their nominalism had to go well beyond "nameism," whereby things are thought to have only a name in common. It had to acknowledge the predominant commonality of attributes among groups of similar things. For these late medieval nominalists – though no more confident than their realist counterparts in the conclusions to be drawn from observation – the individual was thought to exist as one, separate and distinct, by virtue of the one or more attributes that it (perceptibly) does not share inherently with a group of like things.

Essence and existence   Another hotly debated topic in scholastic philosophy was the ontological distinction between "essence" (*quod est*, that which is) and "existence" (*quo est*, that by which a thing is). Its formulation was a product of the late twelfth and thirteenth centuries, when the works of Aristotle and his Arabic commentators, most notably here Avicenna, were beginning to cause a stir. The issue derived from the analysis of things which exist, by asking of what they are necessarily composed. Essence refers to the thing that exists. Existence refers to the act or state of the essence in the realm of existing things. Avicenna became the source in Latin scholasticism for the doctrine that all things are composites of essence and existence,[8] and most scholastics from the thirteenth century on admitted an effective distinction between essence and existence.

The catalyst to the discussion of essence and existence may well have been the logical distinctions made by Aristotle between the concept of "what a thing is" (*quid est*) and the fact "that a thing is" (*quod est*), and by Boethius between "that a thing is" (*quod est*) and "that which makes a thing what it is" (*quo est*). Avicenna had been inspired to make essence ontologically distinct from existence (existence is a non-essential property, an accident of essence), and to reason that essence could take on different modes of existence in reality and in the mind (individual or universal). Thomas Aquinas vigorously considered an essence–existence distinction as reflecting conceptually the composition of things, elevating, however, existence, his "act of being" (*esse*), to a superior position as "the actuality of all acts and the perfection of all perfections." The discussion following Thomas turned on the ontological status of essence and existence, with some of his successors, such as Giles of Rome, conceiving the two as real separable things, and others, such as Henry of Ghent, describing the existence of a thing's "essence" as a concept of possible being (*esse essentiae*) and its "existence" as the actual existing thing (*esse existentiae*). Still others, such as Duns Scotus, saw essence and existence as composed, existence being a mode of essence.

Change   As a third ontological issue, the scholastics addressed the notion of *kinesis* in Greek, or *motus*, in Latin, which terms can both be translated as either change or motion. This issue encompassed virtually all thirteenth- and fourteenth-century scholastic "scientific" thought, that is, intellectual endeavors emphasizing the study of nature and adhering strictly to a logical method of investigation. Scattered individual scholastics, such as Urso of Calabria, Robert Grosseteste, Roger Bacon, Albertus Magnus, and John Buridan, and others working at specific university centers, such as Thomas Bradwardine and the *Calculatores* of Merton College, Oxford, approached the task of analyzing change with great verve. All forms of change in nature visible to the naked eye came under scrutiny: changes in land formations, in weather, in light and color, in planetary positions, in minerals, and in plants and animals, including human beings (growing, moving from place to place, becoming ill, etc.).[9] The central issues were to *describe* change (what is it?) and to *explain* change (why does change exist? what causes change?).

For the scholastics, change was alteration, in the non-static but ordered material world, of the existing state of things, either in respect of the components of individual things, form and matter, or in respect of the distribution of things in the universe as a whole. A state of "becoming" (*in fieri*) was distinguished from the state of "having become" (*in facto esse*) and a "potency" (*potentia*) for change was distinguished from the "actuality" (*actus*) of the change's taking place. To render the concepts more concrete, consider, for example, a house. A house, like all material things, was thought by the scholastics, following Aristotle, to be composed of both matter (its construction materials) and form (its ultimate size, shape, etc.). Bricks and mortar readied for construction have the potential or potency of being used to build the house. When no more than a two-meter high circumference of bricks and mortar, the house is in the process of being made or of coming into existence. As construction continues, the potency of the bricks and mortar to build a house is being actualized. When the house is finished being constructed, the house "has become" a house.

Describing change thusly was one direction taken by the scholastics. For them most changes fell within the Aristotelian category of quality, i.e., change in which a thing would be altered in respect of its temperature, color, velocity, etc. Along with modest contemporary improvements in practical instruments of mensuration, the scholastics' efforts to apply mathematics theoretically to the description of qualitative change were among the most innovative of medieval scientific contributions. Jordanus de Nemore and his followers did so for statics, as Bradwardine and the Merton College *Calculatores*, Richard Swineshead, William Heytesbury, and John Dumbleton did for dynamics. The *Calculatores* developed mathematical descriptions specifically of motions continually accelerating at the same rate (uniformly) by correctly relating their elapsed time to the distance traversed, and by a "mean speed" theorem, according to which the velocity reached at the mid-point is equal to the average velocity of the entire movement. They also introduced primitive graphs as descriptive devices to relate velocity and distance. Graphic techniques to visualize increase and decrease (or intension and remission) were to be applied subsequently to all varieties of qualitative change, color, texture, or degrees of sickness or wellness.

Scholastics divided into two groups according to the ontology underlying their quantified descriptions of qualitative change. One group, represented by Walter Burley, adhered to a "succession theory," according to which, as a quality (for example, heat) becomes more or less intense, each current degree of the quality is destroyed and replaced by a new greater or lesser degree. Each degree was thus conceived as a discrete, indivisible, realized state of a thing's "having become" what it was "becoming," and quantification was deemed possible by analogy to numerical increments. An opposing group of scholastics, fathered by Duns Scotus, advanced an "addition theory," whereby any quality is made more or less intense in the combining of a new part of the form with the old part by addition, or in the separating of a part of the old form from it by subtraction. The earlier form did not continue to exist as such, but a part of the new form was equal within or without the old. For this group, quantification of the changing parts was deemed possible by analogy to line segments.

Explaining change was yet another challenge scholastics took in stride. Their starting point was Aristotle's theory of the four causes of change: change by an effecter of change, or *efficient* causality, change according to matter, or *material* causality, change according to form, or *formal* causality, and change toward the actualization of a potency, or the teleological *final* causality. The Aristotelian cosmological order of the universe, with the spherical earth at the center surrounded most closely by spheres of the three other classical Greek elements, water, air, and fire, and more remotely by spheres carrying the planets, lent the conceptual framework. Almost undisputed in the Middle Ages was the Aristotelian idea that each change has a proximate cause in contact with it, but that the ultimate cause of all change must derive from a being or realm which is itself unchanging. For Aristotle the ultimate cause was *the* efficient cause, the eternal, unchanging, and unchanged Prime Mover located at the eternal perimeter of the universe.

Aside from transforming Aristotle's Prime Mover into the Christian God, the scholastics discussed the complexities of transmitting change from the original cause to the things to be effected. Three main sources of intermediating causes were discussed: celestial motion, light, and celestial "influences." Although the accuracy of the Greek and Arabic astronomical tradition of describing celestial motion was slowly improving in the Middle Ages, little was done to reconcile the problems which complex planetary motions posed to a theory of causal transmission. Thus light, rather than celestial movement, appeared much more likely to be the vehicle transmitting change from the Prime Mover. Especially for Robert Grosseteste and his followers, light, by virtue of its ability to pass through and leave unaltered certain objects, such as the transparent celestial spheres, came to be seen as the most significant cause of motion. Also, by virtue of its straight line path the direction of light as cause was deemed understandable according to the rules of geometry. Celestial influences were generally used to explain the effects which seemed to transpire without the presence of light, such as the formation of metals underground or the "spontaneous" generation of worms from dark mud. Influences from the celestial realm, of supreme importance to the medieval science of astrology, were thought to pass, unlike light, through even opaque, dense things to bring about a change. Immaterial celestial intelligences, posited in Arabic Neoplatonism to explain the transmission of being itself, were the ultimate metaphysical derivation in the Middle Ages of the original Greek conception of intermediaries as physical entities.

In Epistemological Positions

The inspirational texts to scholasticism, the works of Aristotle, provided such grist for the medieval epistemological mill that discussions of how human beings come to know extended along numerous tangents. Is the root of all knowledge sense perception or a divinely given capacity to understand? Can human beings understand everything (including God)? What is the proper way to proceed to learn to reason? Is accessible knowledge ordered and if so how? For the medieval scholastics all of these questions pertained to epistemology, the study of the process of human beings' coming to knowledge. Scholastic epistemology offered such an adaptable *modus operandi* for learning that at the thirteenth-century height of scholasticism, virtually everything was deemed accessible to human cognition and classification. Illustration of the results of such a comprehensive approach will be presented in the last chapter of the book, which surveys the principal subject-areas of human thought in the Middle Ages. Here some general theoretical reflections by scholastics on the acquiring of knowledge, or *episteme*, will be addressed.

Human cognition   Two important aspects of human cognition were of particular concern to the scholastics, as they had been to Aristotle and Plato earlier: the object, and the mechanism and agents of apprehension, the human intellect and imagination. On the one hand, the medieval issue of the possible and proper objects of knowledge clearly tied into an ontological question discussed above under the rubric of universals: what truly exists to be known? Do we learn about individuals or about something common to more than one individual thing? As already mentioned above, scholastics generally asserted that the most we can hope to know about things individually or collectively derives from our ability to compare and subsequently to group objects according to their similarities and differences. Many scholastics, following Aristotle, endeavored to obtain conclusions applicable to either the individual or the group through a process of abstraction. The process entailed three steps in abstracting: reasoning from concretre, individualized matter to the commonalities of a group of like material things, reasoning from commonly shared matter and qualities to pure mathematical quantity, and reasoning from the quantity (and any other qualifiers) of an existing thing to "being" itself.

The discussion of the mechanism and agents of human cognition became very detailed in the Middle Ages. Texts which lent themselves to what would today be considered psychology, rather than philosophy, were in abundance. The soul and the intellect were described with great subtlety, as to composition and function, in their relation to human cognition. The discussion had major implications for medieval epistemology. The various opinions on human psychology dictated at least to a degree a scholar's position on the specifically problematic epistemological issue: can certain knowledge be derived from the senses?

Schools of scholastics debated the reliability of sense experience. Each of the two extreme positions, that the senses always deceive and that the senses never deceive, found supporting arguments. Scholastics especially influenced by Augustine maintained that absolutely certain knowledge was accessible only through divine illumination and that, since the senses might well be deceiving, the mechanism for receiving such divinely transmitted knowledge was the intellect. On the other hand, scholastics who held that the senses never deceive, in cases of mistakes did not blame the processes of sense perception, but rather the limitations of human judgement about sense information, as responsible for causing humans to err. Between these extreme positions and explanations fell many stances moderated in one direction or the other.

Hierarchy of knowledge   For the scholastics, regardless of the mechanism and agents involved, not all objects were considered to be equally accessible to cognition. Distinctions stemmed from the ontological status of the objects themselves. Objects were categorized by Aristotle into areas of human knowledge, according to the objects' availability to sense perception. For Aristotle, since the cognitive process was that of abstraction, objects at the level of individualized matter were considered the most accessible to sense perception and to being immediately known. Aristotle classified all objects of knowledge hierarchically thus, according to the level of abstract reasoning required to contemplate them: the sensible objects first; the mathematical next; and metaphysical being, last. His classification-scheme which placed metaphysics (or theology) at its pinnacle was affirmed in its whole by the scholastics' dictum that the act of abstracting is not deception, *abstrahentium non est mendacium*. Within scholastic learning, the notion of cognitive abstraction and the Aristotelian scheme of classification were interpreted to entail, in theory if not in practice, the important idea of specialization or the possible necessity for an individual to devote concentrated study to only one or a few areas of knowledge.

In Theological Positions

The debates over ontological and epistemological issues might evoke with their abstractness and apparent futility the image of the quintessentially scholastic, yet each goes back to a formulation by thinkers who antedated the heyday of scholasticism: the question of universals, back to Boethius in his second commentary on Porphyry's *Isagoge* (the introduction to Aristotle's *Categories*); the roots of the distinction between existence and essence, to Aristotle's *Posterior Analytics* and *On the Soul*, Book III, Boethius' *In What Way Substance* (*Quomodo substantiae*), and the Arabic commentators on Aristotle, Avicenna and Averroes; the analysis of change according to potency and actuality, to Aristotle's *Physics*; discussions of the human intellect and sense perception, to the ideas of Plato's *Meno* and Aristotle's *On the Soul*; and the classification of human knowledge, to Neoplatonist writings and to Aristotle's *Nicomachean Ethics* and *Posterior Analytics*. For some medievals, an issue's being perennial was, however, no sign of its value. John of Salisbury, already exasperated in the mid-twelfth century, noted of the question of universals that it was "a problem over which more time has been lost than the Caesars ever spent in conquering the world, and more money than ever filled the coffers of Croesus."[10] Nevertheless, discussions concerning the ontological and epistemological states of both material and immaterial things were deemed important by most scholastics, and most specifically because beyond philosophy and psychology, they saw implications for theology in the questions of a thing's existence, identity, and knowability.

To isolate the ontological and epistemological issues of scholasticism from the theological is not anachronistic. As the examples themselves already reveal by their origins in Greek and Arabic cultures, each debate had no specific theological relevance nor dictated any particular theological opinion. Christian scholastics such as Albertus Magnus openly asserted clear distinctions between the method and subject-matter of philosophy and theology. Although making a point about the separation of reason and faith, Albertus among others was primarily seeking multiple routes to strengthen Christian belief. As the following will illustrate, in the medieval period philosophical issues were undeniably propelled into prominence for the bearing they were thought to have on Christian theology.

Universals　The question of the existence of universals was connected to theology. Christ and Judas were subjects to demonstrate the potential of the universal "human being" to experience joy and sorrow simultaneously. God was consistently the ultimate entity to which all conclusions were applied. Denial of universals, the tenent of extreme nominalism, had to be rejected by the orthodox Christian, for it seemed to imply that the parts of the Trinity (God, Christ, and the Holy Spirit) had nothing essential in common, shared no divine nature, but were instead three different deities. Some forms of realism were also deemed theologically suspect; for example, the notion of the universal as actually distinct from the individual. Was it not absurd to think of God creating the universal "human being" without creating individual people, or for that matter, individuals without the universal? John Roscelin, Peter Abelard, and William of Ockham were a few who vociferously recognized the important theological implications of the philosophical discussion of universals.

Essence and existence　The discussion of essence and existence was tied to theology through the distinction it permitted between created and creator and as it concerned the existence of the human soul. Only in the unique case of God was the distinction between essence and existence not seen to apply. God's existence was necessary, not merely accidental, and He had only one mode of being. In the case of created things the distinction did apply. Created things received existence from God according to what they were to be, that is, according to their essence. By some, the human soul was considered to be the substantial form of man (a fact which according to Duns Scotus was known by reason, while everything else about the soul is known only by revelation). By others, the soul was identified as the agent of intellection. The Greco-Arabic concept of a separate Agent Intellect, a highest part of the intellect which exists independently of a bodily organ, appealed to certain scholastics. That notion was neatly tied to the Christian belief in a soul immortal after the death of the physical body.

Change Philosophical discussions of change had innumerable implications for medieval theology. Two are of note here: hylomorphism and transubstantiation. Universal hylomorphism, or the concept that all beings (excluding God, but including souls, separate intellects, and angels) were composed of matter and form, was adapted to the context of theological debate. For example, the notion that if souls were composed of matter and form, they would be corruptible like matter, led to conceiving distinctions in kinds of matter, spiritual or material, separated or related to form, etc. Transubstantiation was the theological doctrine adopted in 1215 by the Fourth Lateran Church Council, that the bread and wine of the Eucharistic Mass were, in the celebration, actually changed or transubstantiated into the body and the blood of Christ. Scholastics divided on whether Aristotelian philosophy could support the theological assertion that the attributes of the bread and wine, their color, texture, and taste, remained without the substances of which they were the attributes, and that in their place, instead, Christ existed invisibly with all his attributes. The official Church position in the condemnations of 1277 was to affirm the teaching that God could make an attribute which did not have a substance. Some scholastics, such as Thomas, had proposed that the attributes inhere in the quantity, if not the substance, of the bread and wine. Others discussed the independence of attributes from substance altogether, and how change could occur in them. The succession theory of change, noted above, was developed in numerous texts as the very one to explain changes in the Eucharist where no change of matter was involved.

Human cognition Theories of human cognition were primarily focused theologically on the possibility of human beings to have a relation with their God through perception, reason, or revelation. The degree to which knowledge of the subject-matter of theology (God, the resurrection, the meaning of the sacraments, etc.) was dependent on the medium of revelation was particularly heavily debated during the scholastic period. Schools of scholastics varied dramatically on this question. One extreme form articulated by the Franciscan Bonaventure avowed an inseparable dependence on divine illumination for all knowledge, and especially for enlightenment concerning the divine. Another extreme position espoused by the Dominican Thomas Aquinas saw the same truth fully accessible by reason and faith. Known as the Franciscan and Dominican schools respectively, each had major influence on the evolution of medieval scholastic thought. In effect their extremes represented the tolerated limits of the intellectual field. Both extreme mystics who were thought to reject the use of reason, and Latin Averroists, accused of pushing reason to the point of abandoning Christianity, were criticized for appearing to reject the espoused goal of scholasticism, to understand Christian theology in the context of classical philosophy.

It would be hard to find a medieval thinker who, in theories of cognition regarding theological matters, did not give some role to both belief and the use of reason. Strongly Aristotelian theologians drew heavily upon Platonism and contemporary doctrinal ideas, just as medieval mystics gave Platonic and Aristotelian reason pride of place. Setting limits on extreme conclusions, the episcopal condemnations of 1270 and 1277 rejected, however, both the Platonic teaching of the unity of the intellect in man and the Aristotelian saying that man understands all. While the parallels between Neoplatonism and mysticism on the one hand and Aristotelianism and natural theology on the other were undeniable, for almost all scholastics, Christianity was thought to provide the mind-set which could free its believers from all limitations to human cognition. In their conviction that for Christians God sets no limits to human knowledge, Christians believed that understanding about such subjects as the eternity of the world was considered to be possible for them, as it had not been for earlier pagans.

Hierarchy of knowledge   In the medieval hierarchy of human endeavors, theology was at the top. Either it was a calling and a practice elevated above all others, or it was a "science" served by the conclusions of all other studies. The most crucial issue concerning theology in schemes classifying knowledge was the division of responsibility between philosophy, with its studies of physics and metaphysics, and theology. As a science, theology acknowledged the independent principles and methods of other studies, yet scholastic theologians predominantly thought its role to be that of judging through its own principles the validity of the others' findings. The question of the eternity of the world frequently appeared in medieval discussions of the roles of philosophy and theology. Its treatment by philosophers and theologians gave to both a gracious way of resolving conflict between their different conclusions. It was recognized that the eternity of the world was undemonstrable by the reasoning of the medieval natural philosopher. Without physical proof there is no reason for the natural philosopher not to recognize the premise of metaphysicians and theologians, that the world depends upon God for its existence. The conclusion that God created the world could be in this case harmoniously held by both philosopher and theologian. More frequently, however, the conflict between experience and scripture, on which the classifying of philosophy and theology fundamentally depended, could not be so easily resolved.

Extended Meaning of Medieval Scholasticism

In addition to the particular issues under scholastic inquiry, a fascination with language underlay the whole of the Latin scholastic movement from its origins to its dissolution. John of Salisbury offers a most interesting characterization of one thinker on the question of universals, saying that he

> takes refuge in a new tongue, since he does not have sufficient command of Latin. When he hears the words "genus" and "species," at one time he says they should be understood as universals, and at another that they refer to the *maneries* of things. I do not know in which of the authors he has found this term or this distinction, unless perhaps he has dug it out of lists of abstruse or obsolete words, or it is an item of jargon of present-day doctors.[11]

The lengthy semantic discussions of thirteenth- and fourteenth-century scholasticism seem to have been carrying out Abelard's early scholastic posture, that a controversy can often be solved by demonstrating that a word can have been given different meanings by different authors.

The writings of Aristotle were at the heart of most scholastic issues and their dominance was to provoke a two-fold concern for language. First, Aristotle himself saw semantic clarity as essential to a understanding of the world and therefore devoted a great deal of his texts to distinctions often of a purely linguistic nature. His commentators continued this priority and medieval scholars both inherited and perpetuated it. Avicenna's interpretation of Aristotle's notion of form is one example. Aristotle and Avicenna presented such different understandings that, regardless of whether the later was considered a distortion of the earlier, a confusing choice between consistent and compelling conceptions was offered.

Secondly, the new learning which was to stimulate the scholastic movement was a learning whose meaning was veiled in foreign tongues and novel terminology. Thus the semantic priorities of the Philosopher himself were reinforced in the scholastic preoccupation with "making sense" of the languages in which the new learning was transmitted. The budding scholastic preoccupation with language and logic would acquire even greater urgency when Christians began reflecting on pagan and Muslim commentaries on Aristotle's work, for the Philosopher's paganism also illustrated to them that persuasion could not always be achieved by appeal to revelation. No longer could medieval philosophers begin with Anselmian "faith in search of understanding," even in such discussions of ontology as the question of the existence of God.

One further leading aspect of the scholastic movement was its method of reasoned inquiry. Application of the scholastic method has been found outside the immediate frame of medieval philosophical preoccupations. It has been detected by modern historians in many areas of medieval thought: in law, medicine, architecture, music, etc. Its use in scholastic Latin law ought not to be surprising, it has been argued recently by George Makdisi, for it was already present in Islamic law before scholasticism reached the Latin West. It has also been asserted in the recent scholarly hypothesis of Erwin Panofsky that the *modus operandi* of scholasticism was at work in western medieval Gothic architecture. Panofsky's hypothesis offers detailed argument that the meaning of scholasticism extended well beyond constructions in the mind. Makdisi's and Panofsky's theses illustrating the extensions of Latin scholasticism will be discussed briefly.

Makdisi's Hypothesis: The Influence of Khilaf

The scholastic method made its appearance after a long developmental phase. Dialectic, disputation, and the *"sic et non"* method (Abelard's eleventh-century technique for juxtaposing apparently contradictory extracts from religious works) were three components which took time to coalesce. The scholar George Makdisi has claimed that *khilaf*, or eastern scholasticism, may also have influenced western intellectual practices.[12] Makdisi argues that while no direct influence can yet be established, the scholastic method had already developed in the East before it began to develop in the West. It was, according to Makdisi, through law, not philosophy or theology, that the impetus came for its eastern development, and through law, therefore, that it might have infiltrated into the West.

Most of the criticism of Makdisi's hypothesis has centered upon the inconclusiveness of the evidence to argue for influence or transmission as Makdisi would like. For example, whatever similarities there may have been between the methods in these diverse cultures, there is no evidence that any of the eastern legal scholastic texts was ever translated into Latin. Equally, however scholastic, the Latin texts of law and other subjects make no reference to Arabic law or method of exposition. Nevertheless, it is evident that the Latin scholastic method does show remarkable affinities with the procedure of *khilaf*, and it is possible that Latin scholastic writings reflect the influence of the Arabic tradition.[13] Even if Makdisi's hypothesis as originally stated is unsupportable, it seems that there are excellent reasons for suggesting that Latin scholasticism may well reflect its indebtedness, in addition to the many translations and commentaries in Arabic, to a tradition of thought such as that associated with the *khilaf* of Islamic law.

Panofsky's Hypothesis: Latin Architecture and Scholasticism

Scholars had long regarded the innovations of Gothic architecture as simply another phase in changing aesthetic styles during the medieval period, thus bringing the Middle Ages into line with other periods of cultural change. In a short but important book published in 1957, Erwin Panofsky, however, argued that a very different interpretation was to be placed on the concept of a changing style.[14] According to Panofsky, the Gothic style of architecture ought to be referred back to the Gothic mind-set, deriving from scholasticism (the scholasticism of Thomas Aquinas). Before noting a number of ways in which the ideas of scholasticism appear to have been transmitted into an architectural style, Panofsky announced:

> When asking in what manner the mental habit induced by Early and High Scholasticism may have affected the formation of Early and High Gothic architecture, we shall do well to disregard the notional content of the doctrine and to concentrate, to borrow a term from the schoolmen themselves, upon its *modus operandi*. The changing tenets in such matters as the relation between soul and body or the problem of universals vs. particulars naturally were reflected in the representational arts rather than in architecture. . . . What he who "devised the form of the building while not himself manipulating its matter" could and did apply, directly and qua architect, was rather the particular method of procedure which must have been the first thing to impress itself upon the mind of the layman whenever it came in touch with that of the schoolman.[15]

If Panofsky is right, scholasticism still stands, in the stone of the most strikingly visual of medieval legacies, suggesting that Gothic cathedrals may in fact represent the greatest lasting triumph of an intellectual movement which was well under attack by the end of the Middle Ages.

In the year 1140 Abbot Suger dedicated his newly renovated church at the monastery of St-Denis. Earlier that century, important changes were being introduced into the architectural lexicon, especially those relating to the potential height of a building. Up to that point, builders of large edifices were able to erect structures according to the load-bearing capacities of round arches, barrel vaults, and thick walls. In other words, Romanesque architecture had been perfected, but not yet the techniques of Gothic architecture. With the new features of pointed arch and ribbed vaults, builders would now be able to build, as experience would reveal, to incredible new heights. What brought about this transformation in architectural technique?

A number of scholars have elaborated the thesis of Panofsky, that the method of scholasticism lay behind the adoption and elaboration of Gothic architecture. Important to note, however, is the continuing work of Robert Mark which has been serving in a sense as a kind of test of the hypothesis that there was method behind Gothic architectural achievements.[16] His discoveries have led to detailed conclusions about to what degree specific areas of that medieval phase of construction were undertaken in full awareness of complexity and outcome. His findings have raised a number of questions which remain unanswered about how fundamental a contemporary link was between the Gothic cathedral and scholasticism. Some of them will be considered here.

1   Medieval architects or builders do not seem to have dealt with any written exposition of scholastic procedure. Panofsky's hypothesis, which requires that a builder would have had some notion of scholastic method, is based on the argument of "mentalité." "Small wonder, then that a mentality which deemed it necessary to make faith 'clearer' by an appeal to reason and to make reason 'clearer' by an appeal to imagination, also felt bound to make imagination 'clearer' by an appeal to the senses" in the scholastic fashion.[17] Is it in fact small wonder? If the work of Abbot Suger himself, *On Administration* (*De administratione*) dealing with his efforts to reconstruct and decorate his abbey church, is any testimony, he was not driven by an intellectual desire for clarity in building or in writing about building: as Harning notes,

What holds the narrative of the *De administratione* together is
not an intellectual construct, such as Suger's adaptation of
pseudo-Dionysian light metaphysics or anagogical thought,
but rather an impulse to gather together in one record the
entire spectrum of his interests and accomplishments. This
"collector's impulse" – which Suger manifests as much in his
treatment of objects as in his treatment of words – reminds us,
in so far as it organizes his writings, of the concepts of "collective unity," defined by Saint Bernard of Clairvaus ... as
"when, for example, many stones make one pile".[18]

2 Panofsky referred to Abbot Suger as the instigator of the architectural feature of the west facade rose window, a new round
insertion not yet resolved with the rest of the edifice, poised in
true "*sic et non*" inconclusive style.[19] Since the "*sic et non*," yes
and no style of scholasticism is identifiable with Abelard of the
eleventh century, can one advance with Panofsky a conscious
one-to-one correspondence between components of the twelfth-
century Gothic edifice and Abelard's scholastic rhetorical
approach? Panofsky himself does not pursue the link to a "Senlis
gloss" or a "Notre Dame summa." Further, is there one example
of Gothic architecture which represents the epitome of the scholastic method?

3 Romanesque architecture is specifically identified in mid-twelfth
century documents as a style of design desperately in need of
modification in terms of its size, as well as its small window
openings, suggesting that the Gothic style was predominantly a
sought-out way of remedying those lacks in Romanesque style.

4 From its early phase, 1140–80, Gothic architecture underwent
notable changes to achieve features of the radical flamboyant
style replete in later constructions and the "evolved" style of
Gothic. Historians of art and architecture have posited motivations for these internal stylistic changes. Panofsky presented one
thesis for stylistic and structural alterations: the desire to achieve
the scholastic "final" solution where, for instance, "the window
remained a window and the rose a rose."[20] Robert Mark, whose
work has uncovered in part the level of technological expertise
of the medieval cathedral builders, has been more impressed by
the thesis of Otto von Simpson, that the cathedral builders
strove to realize an architectural ideal, "which aimed for a display of daring structure admitting the maximum amount of
light" for Christian metaphysical reasons.[21] The consensus
among most recent studies seems to be that Panofsky's thesis has
been a valuable stimulus to research on Gothic architecture and

that continued effort should be invested in proposing links
between the contemporary intellectual activity and its very practical, manual counterparts.

Scholasticism as a Social Phenomenon

Some historians have conceived scholasticism to have been a very
different phenomenon sociologically from the breakthrough of
vernacular languages. It has already been seen that the breakthrough
of vernacular language was primarily a secular cultural phenomenon
which achieved wide circulation in the twelfth century in all strata
of European society, though especially in those strata which were
not previously a part of an intellectual environment. As use of
the vernacular languages was, however, also adopted by specific
religious orders,[22] the vernacular breakthrough was clearly an intellectual transformation whose form was received and employed
within a variety of important sociological groups. To assess the
sociological spread of scholasticism as an intellectual movement, it
might therefore be helpful to identify which members of society
were most instrumental in transmitting and developing specific
scholastic ideas.

It has been stated by modern historians of the Reformation, for
example, Alister E. McGrath, that unlike humanism, scholasticism
had virtually no influence outside the sphere of the university.[23]
Even if this were the case, there would be no reason for the further
claim, also made by McGrath, that the appeal of scholasticism was
limited "to those who enjoyed dialectics".[24] In fact, it transformed
the whole of the world of education. Generally speaking, every
member of the university community would have been affected by
scholasticism. Indeed, the main scholastic schools were specifically
linked with individuals or groups of teaching masters at the university. The Dominican teaching masters tended to propagate
Thomism, and the Franciscans, Scotism, although frequently the
same ideas would be shared among the religious orders and certainly
with teaching masters outside the orders. Virtually all university
teaching would have offered instances of the scholastic method.

The impact of scholasticism was in fact most particularly notice-
able on education. The paedagogical background of medieval
intellectuals before the development of scholasticism is of major
importance in appreciating the extent to which it began to influence
all areas of teaching. As the last chapter will illustrate, the transformation of the classification and paedagogy of the seven liberal

arts (whose origins and texts, it has been noted, predate scholasticism), reflects the impact of scholasticism. Along with philosophy, two of the highest branches of university learning, medicine
and law, also show how the scholastic method was enlisted in all
areas of university teaching.[25] Medieval university study began and
ended in the cradle of scholasticism.

   The impact, which emanated from the universities as its intellectual hubs, had, however, an extended appeal outside educational
circles. It was virtually impossible for a literate, not to mention
educated, person to have avoided the influence of scholasticism. Its
force permeated every aspect of intellectual life and expression,
including not only dialectic argumentation, but the whole world of
art and culture. While scholasticism did not independently influence
the different social strata as the vernacular language movement had,
none the less the spread of vernacular language enables one to
understand how scholastic ideas and methods might also have been
adopted with widespread use. Certain literary styles, political
theory, secular and religious administrative techniques, perhaps
even architecture, were all to some extent scholastic in form.

   Furthermore, from the thirteenth century onwards all significant
Church debates were carried out in university scholastic style. The
conciliarists, for example, bent on reforming the life and morals of
the Church of the day, paid attention to scholastic models of presentation and persuasion. Even those who could afford to ridicule
scholasticism had to acknowledge its intellectual presence – and
engage with it directly. Whether in the circles of the educated or
uneducated, in the later Middle Ages the vernacular became the
main channel of expression for ideas of change. The essential difference between scholasticism in Latin and scholastic expression in the
vernacular was that for the former, philosophical Latin had become
virtually the only mode of expression, whereas for the vernacular
tongues, there were many other types of Latin expression which
could serve as models. It seems, in general, that scholastic ideas
were "productively misunderstood" by the vernacular advocates as
embodying a respectable mode of thinking, thus giving scholastic
ideas circulation in circles formerly touched only by folk wisdom
and folk art.

   In sum, the phenomenon of medieval scholasticism had profound
influence on theology and on virtually all areas of medieval thought.
The primary tool of scholasticism, logical reasoning, extended to all
fields of thought a new guide for organization and expression. As
the gilt on the picture of medieval intellectualization, scholasticism
was undeniably responsible for the rich subject–matter and scope of

many intellectualized areas of medieval life, as will be discussed in the last chapter. As a particularly theological movement, scholasticism, however, primarily showed its capability to put the tolerance of the Church for intellectual contemplation *ad absurdum* to the test. In the chapter immediately following, the dictates of the conclusions of scholastic theology and philosophy and their impact on the institution of the late medieval Church will be discussed.

For further reading

To place scholasticism in the context of other philosophical and theological movements, see:

William Wallace, *The Elements of Philosophy: A Compendium for Philosophers and Theologians* (Staten Island, NY, 1977), pp. 288–95.

On philosophical scholasticism, see:

Marilyn McCord Adams, "Universals in the Early Fourteenth Century," in *The Cambridge History of Later Medieval Philosophy: From the Rediscovery of Aristotle to the Disintegration of Scholasticism*, eds Norman Kretzmann et al. (Cambridge, 1982), pp. 411–39.

David Knowles, *The Evolution of Medieval Thought* (London, 2nd ed., 1988).

John Marenbon, *Later Medieval Philosophy (1150–1350): An Introduction* (New York, 1987).

On theological scholasticism, see:

M.-D. Chenu, *Toward Understanding St Thomas*, trs A. M. Londry and D. Hughes (Chicago, 1964).

Gordon Leff, *Medieval Thought: St Augustine to Ockham* (London, 1959), pp. 77–251.

Jaroslav Pelikan, *The Christian Tradition: A History of the Development of Doctrine*, vol. 3: *The Growth of Medieval Theology (600–1300)* (Chicago/London, 1978), pp. 268–307.

For discussion of the wider ramifications of scholasticism, see:

A. Dempf, *Die Hauptform mittelalterlicher Weltanschauung; eine geisteswissenschaftliche Studie über die Summa* (Munich/Berlin, 1925).

Paul Frankl, *Gothic Architecture* (Harmondsworth, England, 1962), pp. 260–70.

Hamilton Gibb, "The Influence of Islamic Culture on Medieval Europe," in *Change in Medieval Society*, ed. Sylvia Thrupp (Toronto, 1964 rpt. 1988), pp. 155–67.

C. S. Lewis, *The Discarded Image: An Introduction to Medieval and Renaissance Literature* (Cambridge, 1964).

Otto G. Von Simpson, "The Gothic Cathedral: Design and Meaning," in *Change in Medieval Society*, ed. Sylvia Thrupp (Toronto, 1964, rpt. 1988), pp. 168–87.

On medieval universities, see:

A. B. Cobban, *The Medieval Universities: Their Development and Organisation* (London, 1975).

Gordon Leff, *Paris and Oxford Universities in the Thirteenth and Fourteenth Centuries: An Institutional and Intellectual History* (New York, 1968).

Anders Piltz, *The World of Medieval Learning* (Totowa, NJ, 1981).

H. Rashdall, *The Universities of Europe in the Middle Ages*, eds F. M. Powicke and A. B. Emden (3 vols: Oxford, 1936, re-ed. 1959).

7

The Dictates of Philosophy and the Late Medieval Church

In many respects, scholastics' views exposed the Achilles' heel of Christian thought. By the thirteenth century, scholastics were faced with two decidedly different comprehensive views of man and his world, Aristotelian and Christian, whose principles and content they could not bring into total harmony. In the case of Aristotelianism, there was no concept of Christ, no church, and no overriding aspiration to a life outside the material world. Knowledge lay within one's rational reach, and no institution (or deity) was responsible for guiding the human soul to knowledge. In the case of Christianity, belief was superior to knowledge, and the Trinity was the supreme object of belief. Christian belief in the Middle Ages was grounded in the institutionalized Church and had acquired thereby a historical continuity and purpose. Most scholastics managed remarkably to carve a middle road between Aristotelianism and Christianity, but some found themselves forced to acknowledge serious inconsistencies and became vulnerable to ecclesiastical censure, as did, for example, the strictest of Aristotelian scholastics. As most thirteenth-century scholastics strove to attempt a reconciliation of pagan philosophy and Christian theology, they could not have been more aware of the tension remaining within the blend. The present discussion considers what proved to be the aspect of the late medieval Church most vulnerable to dispute, its claim to authority.

Dictates of Philosophy

By the end of the thirteenth century, the philosophical system of Aristotle was attracting new attention as a target of criticism from both religious and philosophical factions. While thirteenth-century scholasticism had witnessed at two different intervals the grouping of Aristotle's available works into a distinct corpus, with over 50 works attributed to him in circulation, some scholastics did begin to question the attribution of particular works to Aristotle. Thomas Aquinas, for example, correctly doubted that the work *On Causes* (actually the *Elements of Theology* of the Neoplatonist Proclus) was the work of Aristotle. Most would, however, not see the distinguishing of Platonic, Aristotelian, or even Islamic ideas from one another as easing their task of treating comprehensively the Philosopher's corpus since they continued to undertake the explanation of the connection of others' ideas with those of Aristotle. Why were so many of the scholastic scholars so devoted to the philosophy of Aristotle? To many intellectuals of the fourteenth century, both the anticipation and surprise at the initial receipt of Aristotle's works into the Latin West helped explain why his writings were at first deemed so important. The discussions, however, near the end of the medieval period placed their continued significance in doubt.

For most thirteeth-century medieval writers, intellectual reflection was fostered by studying and teaching at the university. Most scholastics' works derived from the teaching syllabus, and the main purpose of their circulation was to aid the student. Their paedagogical function was fulfilled, in Latin, using the set patterns of the commentary, *questiones*, or *summa* styles. The importance of the written word in guaranteeing both a teaching monopoly and religious orthodoxy was clearly realized in the university environment. Attention was given to controlling works under study and in circulation by enforcing prohibitions on certain books and by regulating the booksellers' trade.

There are several indications, however, that university needs did not and could not fully dictate book production and circulation. Over the course of the thirteenth century, works circulating outside the paedagogical setting, strictly speaking, were becoming an increasingly important medium for spreading current philosophical thought. Unofficial circulation of texts, such as the translations of Aristotle's natural philosophical works during the 1220s, was seen to bring about subsequent curricular changes. The textual commentary became increasingly only one among several writing formats which intellectuals would employ. Outstanding medieval intellectuals such as Dante would even choose to express and circulate their musings or grumblings in a vernacular language.

Although the impact of attempts by the medieval university to dictate the propriety of specific texts and teachings is still highly debated,[1] the successive bannings of Aristotle's writings or ideas in 1210, 1231, and 1270, and the condemning of specific teachings in 1277, probably reoriented the general influence of Aristotle's philosophy. The ensuing approach to his writings was quite different from the one most widely adopted initially. It resulted in the elimination of ideas unacceptable to Christian orthodoxy. In his assessment, the renowned historian Knowles, for example, saw the condemnations of specific teachings as creating "a widespread phobia of Aristotelian philosophy as tending towards determinism and a necessitarian cosmology. Moreover, by setting a stigma upon philosophy, and particularly upon Aristotle, the most 'rational' of philosophers, they did much to shatter the vision of a great synthesis."[2] Not surprisingly, within late medieval scholastic analysis, new premises began to appear.

Two newly popular philosophical premises, the concept of the unlimited *potentia Dei* and the fallibility of the senses, were seemingly a negative response to Aristotelianism, yet their long-term impact on the reworking of Aristotle would be double-edged. As for the premise affirming the limitless power of God (*potentia Dei*), theoretical assumptions circumscribing God's power came to be identified with the exclusive acceptance of Aristotelian ideas on determinism, for example. The rejection of many of Aristotle's ideas as possibilities should, however, also have represented limitations on divine possibilities. As for the premise asserting the fallibility of the senses, questioning the soundness of induction from sense observation meant denying the importance of a crucial part of Aristotle's epistemology. By the same token, it also could have meant acknowledging the psychological possibility that any observer, however, deceived by his senses, might indeed have had reasons for thinking he had observed what he said he had.

Numerous philosophical shifts might be tied to the change in the approach to Aristotle. For one example, a concept of experimentation as something more than an active testimony to authority was emerging.[3] The knowledge that something observed had happened (*cognitio quia*) became as important as knowledge of why something had happened (*cognitio propter quid*). *Experimentum* or observation was seen as the best possible way either to understand the constancy of God's will in His ultimate power, or to combat the possibility that the senses might trick one. John Buridan, for example, maintained that while one might not be able to render the principles and conclusions of natural science absolutely evident, they can be considered sound if they have been confirmed in repeated instances and have not been falsified.[4] The repetition of experiment, rather than authority, was thus increasingly judged to demonstrate the reliability of knowledge.[5]

However multifaceted the implications of both newly adopted premises, the infinite power of God and the deceit of human senses, they were not widely recognized to encompass the reacceptance of Aristotle.[6] Instead, after 1277, one finds serious disagreement over his authority developing within the university scholastic community. As direct successors to the thirteenth-century scholars (such as Albertus Magnus, Thomas Aquinas, and Siger of Brabant), scholars of the fourteenth-century scholastic movement formed schools, most prominently on the one hand, the school of the Latin Averroists, and on the other, that of John Duns Scotus and William of Ockham, distinct in part in their inability to agree on the proper import of Aristotle. Undoubtedly, of the many factors which brought about polarization, different receptions of the condemnations of 1277 and their later annulment in 1325, and the different contexts of intellectual activity in the fourteenth century were certainly significant. After some general observations about the differences between the thirteenth- and fourteenth-century approaches to philosophy, the new intellectual postures will be discussed, with the careers first of William of Ockham and then of Nicholas of Cusa serving to indicate their significance in philosophy, theology, and especially ecclesiology near the end of the Middle Ages.

From the Philosophers' Point of View

Underlying the views of fourteenth-century scholastics are the strains of thirteenth-century scholasticism. The important distinctions between older ideas or the *via antiqua*, and the new ideas or the *via moderna*, in the writings of William of Ockham and Nicholas of Cusa are intricate. It might be thus helpful first to itemize briefly some differences between the older and newer approaches to philosophy to appreciate the impact of their intellectual confrontation.

1   Both thirteenth- and fourteenth-century scholars reflect the evolution of medieval education beyond the early paedagogical scheme limited to the seven liberal arts. After the introduction of the complete works of Aristotle, the Arabic commentaries, etc., the inadequacy of the liberal arts scheme as a net in which to catch the entirety of secular (and religious) learning could hardly be ignored.[7] Whereas Roman culture had specified seven arts worthy of study, all the scholastics insisted that a further level of study, university training in philosophy and theology (or in law or medicine), of which they were the products, ought to be recognized as important and thus to be provided. Thirteenth-century scholars, such as Albertus Magnus and Robert Kil-

wardby, emphasized the formal aspects of education, listing
and prescribing a general route to learning. In the fourteenth
century, John Duns Scotus and William of Ockham, as they
ushered in the wave of epistemological skepticism, stressed
instead the results, rather than the procedure, of university
training. University scholars had now become *philosophi*[8] and
theologi, the intellectuals of society, those who had specialized in
the contemplation of the truth and who, Ockham in particular
thought, ought to by consulted for their ideas.

2 Thirteenth-century scholastics were considerably more traditional in their approach to the authority of the written text than
were fourteenth-century intellectuals. In his comprehensive
treatise, *Summa theologiae*, Thomas Aquinas (d.1274) clearly
reflected his retention of the traditional view of Aristotle as
authority, Authority 2 in reputation and in word. While not
letting his posture be misunderstood as implying acceptance,
Thomas freely included Aristotle's ideas whenever appropriate,
preferably at the outset of a discussion, as those of the main
spokesperson for philosophy.[9] In the fourteenth century
Ockham, however, pushed for the abolition of the concept of
"authority," suggesting anew that the weight formerly given to
the statements of authorities should be reserved for statements of
divine illumination. As a consequence, Aristotle was no longer
to be the center of a natural theology. In addition, while Thomas
had placed great emphasis upon the comprehensive *summa* as the
most thorough form of commentary, Ockham insisted that the
commentary on authoritative texts ought no longer to be the
traditional scholastic focus, but should be replaced by independent discourses.[10]

3 Although all scholastics retained a commitment to language and
the precision of expression, representatives of each century did
so for different reasons. For the thirteenth-century scholastic
realists, words could represent existing things as well as convey
meaning about them, and hence precision of expression was
thought to generate understanding about the real world. For
Ockham and other fourteenth-century nominalists, language
reflected only by convention a connection with the world of
existing things, and hence, for language to function as an effective means of communication,[11] the utmost allegiance to precision, consistency, and efficiency was required.

4 In the thirteenth century scholastics had adopted, as philosophically astute, both Aristotle's assertion concerning (ten) ontological categories and his requirement that the state of a body

in motion be explained. In the fourteenth century, however, Ockham asserted that there are only two categories of being: substance and quality. For Ockham, the other Aristotelian categories – time, relation, place, quantity, activity, passivity, position, and state – are simply names signifying the varying conditions of bodies and their qualities. While for thirteenth-century scholastics, a mover had to be identified to explain a motion, Ockham defended the lack of necessity to "explain" motion in any other way than by defining it as "a body that was in one place, and later will be in another place, in such a way that at no time does it rest in any place."[12] Ockham's thoughts seem to have inspired successors to devise a principle of inertia as an appropriate new way of conceiving motion.

5   Thirteenth-century and fourteenth-century scholastics were not in accord on the nature of the expression *distinctio rationis*, central in the scholastic lexicon. For Thomas, *distinctio rationis* meant a distinction made by the mind between concepts, which was based on the existence outside the mind of the conceived things. For Ockham, such a distinction could have no reality in the things conceived except by analogy. Ultimately, two distinct ways of conceiving God resulted from this disagreement.

6   In both centuries scholastics affirmed a doctrine of transubstantiation. Thomas, relying on scripture and Aristotelian philosophical foundations, articulated strongly the position of the Fourth Lateran Council and the doctrine's basic underlying idea: Christ is really present at the celebration of the Eucharist. Ockham, however, reflected the weakening of the Aristotelian foundation and the plurality of contemporary opinions concerning the doctrine. Contending that diverse opinions can be held, he noted three of the many alternative theories of transubstantiation: the same substances that had been bread and wine were now the flesh and blood of Christ; the substances of bread and wine ceased to exist and the substance of the body and blood of Christ began to exist under the same attributes of the bread and wine (orthodox position); and the substance of the bread and wine remained, together with the body and blood of Christ in the same place.[13]

7   In the thirteenth century, scholars such as Albertus Magnus and Thomas Aquinas understood the realms of philosophy and theology to be distinct but inseparably linked. They thought both could lead to the truths of Christianity. Both were legitimate epistemological avenues to knowledge and understanding. Reason was deemed capable of yielding, and affirming or

demonstrating, the truths of faith. By the fourteenth century, however, for Ockham and others, it was divine illumination alone which permitted faith, and only the receptivity to divine illumination enabled reason to complement faith. For Ockham, conclusions acquired through reason and those obtained directly by divine illumination may indeed not be distinct, except in one crucial respect, their degree of certainty. Only divine illumination is of absolute certainty.

Important differences between thirteenth- and fourteenth-century scholastic thought can be found in their approach to philosophical, ethical, political, and theological issues. In the area of philosophy, changes destabilized the earlier emphasis placed on authority, and on logic as a tool of analysis. Not only did Thomas and Ockham disagree on the authority of Aristotle. They could not even have agreed on an interpretation of phrases such as "I like red bricks" (which Thomas would have interpreted as a reference to species, and Ockham as one to particulars) or "God is wise" (which now, apparently inconsistently, Thomas would have interpreted as pertaining to the particular subject, God, and Ockham as a metaphor by analogy). The linguistic optimism of early scholasticism was sincerely built on precise expression, but however precise, communication, it came to be believed, was not easy to achieve.

As for ethical issues, differences in the posture of scholars in each century ensured a permanent separation into two distinct approaches to ethics, a "perfectibilist"[14] and a "voluntarist." Their differences might again be encapsulated in Thomas' and Ockham's disagreement on a term's meaning, in this case, "good." Thomas understood goodness to be a property of being: a creature was good in so far as it achieved the perfection demanded by its nature. For Ockham the concept of goodness had no ontological connection either to "being" in general or to a creature's "nature" (whose existence he denied). Goodness was a term signifying that something was as it ought to be according to a will exterior to it, and that goodness was pursued according to an interior will. Thomas may have found a moderate path between opposing views on objective and subjective standards of good and evil as advanced by Augustine and Abelard. By the fourteenth century, however, it was increasingly obvious that unless agreement could be reached on the reason for any objectivity in the standard, dissension would again follow.

In a political context, the differences between the two centuries' scholars reinforced the uneasiness of the scholastic union of ecclesiastical and secular interests in the universities. Medieval universities were the training schools of doctors and lawyers and scholars in the arts as well as theologians, and at times divergence in the interests and convictions of the different groups were highly accentuated. Throughout the thirteenth century, it became increasingly clear that if the unity of a university's masters could not be maintained (mendicants and clerical masters, artists and theologians, etc.), the quotidien functioning and the paedagogical purpose of that university would not continue. It had in fact happened that a dissatisfied group at one university had left and moved to a new location to start a new university. For the most part, however, the repute of the university and its self-advocacy as an institution of respected scholars above the rifts of the non-scholarly world increased, and with the reputation grew the prestige of the university masters to offer learned opinions on how to resolve disputes outside the university.

Thus by the time of Ockham and Marsilius of Padua, the opinions of university masters would be sought on issues of political concern, such as the resolution of the Hundred Years' War. When in 1324 Marsilius of Padua wrote his treatise on politics, *Defender of Peace* (*Defensor pacis*), inspired by three distinctive Church–State conflicts of his own experience, he was in principle acting within an accepted role of the university scholar. His choice of delicate subject matter and the position he adopted were, however, not solicited, and Marsilius wisely chose to have the work circulate anonymously. In Padua the city-councils had been virtually powerless in bringing local clergy under the civil code due to long-standing papal interference in the affairs of the city. Further, disputes between Pope Boniface VIII and King Philip IV the Fair of France and between the Emperor-elect Louis of Bavaria and Pope John XXII, were in his mind. There was very little disguising the players in the political situation Marsilius described, and in 1327, Pope John XXII condemned Marsilius, once discovered as the author, for spreading heresy.[15] Suddenly, the traditional teaching of the spiritual hierarchy being espoused right through thirteenth-century scholasticism faced a powerfully articulated intellectual threat in the guise of political thought.

As to their theological impact, intellectual changes from the thirteenth to the fourteenth century raised grave doubts concerning an Augustinian notion, that of the "divine contract with the faithful." The ideas of Thomas and Ockham were in distinct disagreement on the meaning of God's relationship to his believers. Thomas maintained that it was a relationship based on the intelligibility of God and hence on the access that believers have to understanding

Him, whereas for Ockham the relationship was based on the will of God alone to have human beings believe in Him. The enthusiasm for reason, manifest in early scholasticism, was seen to be foundering by the fourteenth century. Scholastics were retreating to faith, as reasoned understanding of the divine seemed far from attainable.

What follows is a detailed examination of the social implications of some of the philosophical convictions of two fourteenth-century thinkers, first, William of Ockham and then, Nicholas of Cusa. The discussion of Ockham's understanding of *potentia Dei* and Cusa's concept of *docta ignorantia* will serve both as a recapitulation and an extension of the points made above.

Ockham's Potentia Dei

In the political treatises William of Ockham wrote during the last two decades of his life, he launched an all-out attack on flaws he perceived in the hierarchical structure of the Roman Christian Church. Drawing on philosophical reasoning, he stated that the traditional use of the Petrine doctrine was not justified by the biblical text. Thus, while the Roman Church recognized a pope, Ockham recognized only at best a believer. According to Ockham, in organized religion only believers, scripture and sacraments, the most essential aspects, exist. Thus, he argued, the traditional hierarchical system of the Church had given a priority totally unfounded in scripture to a single pontiff. Believers, he asserted, were captive to error in three ways:

1 In the practice of conceiving the Church as "the pastoral body" (in other words, comprising only the clergy, and not the laity). There had been a long-standing tradition within Christian theology of seeing the clergy as equivalent to the Church. Rejecting this idea, Ockham argued that the Church comprises the whole of all believers – the community of Christians. The fact that the believer might not have been conscious of being excluded was irrelevant: every believer is a member of the Christian community. Sharing in the celebration of the Eucharist, just as in baptism, ought to be a public demonstration of this membership. According to Ockham, anything else is unjustifiable and a distortion of scripture. Ockham declared that any pretension of the clergy to exclude the laity from the Church (the spiritual institution) was a sin of avarice and pride. This position of Ockham was influential enough to play a role in the ecclesiology of certain fifteenth-century conciliarists.

2   In the doctrines of the hierarchical primacy of the papacy and of the pope's supreme power. These seemed to Ockham to be *non sequiturs*, attempts to rationalize an institution. For Ockham, the issue was that no priest receives his authority except by election or delegation. There is no particular scriptural instance of any other way. If St Peter was himself elected from among the apostles, so was the primacy his, and in that primacy, both the apostles and the received authority are represented. Should not the true historical evidence of scripture be used to establish the roots of the primacy of Peter, instead of permitting the filling-in of missing details, or the extending of the authority of the pastoral role of Peter, according to desire?[16] The succession of the sacred authority of Peter to the Roman popes could not be said to stem from exegesis. What was to be believed, Ockham maintained, was not a doctrine of papal primacy, but rather that Christ quite simply gave the responsibility of "feeding his sheep" to Peter, and that fact cannot be extended to mean that Christ gave Peter the right to designate a head of the Church.

3   In the conception of the Church and State functioning as distinctly different collectives for the individuals which they comprise. For Ockham, this conception was erroneous, for there is only one community of believers, organized spiritually and civilly, such that the common temporal good is safeguarded and the Christian faith defended.[17] Ideally the governing authorities, whether secular or spiritual, are to be concerned with the smooth functioning of a community. In the situations which Ockham experienced, however, secular ruler and pope or bishop were often pitted against one another, aimed at dividing rather than uniting the one community of the faithful.

Interestingly enough, as early as 1324, while waiting his turn to be granted mastership in theology at the University of Oxford, William of Ockham was charged with heresy for his philosophical ideas. He immediately answered a summons from London to the pope in Avignon only to find a trying three-year delay for the hearing of the accusation. There seems to be no evidence that Ockham had any misgivings about his own statements, which, until his trip to the papal court, had focused mainly on Thomistic philosophy.[18] His "ecclesiopolitical breakthroughs," including his questioning of papal primacy, took place during the next 20 years, during which period Ockham, having been excommunicated, sought refuge in the protection of the German emperor and made his noted declarations of the pope's heretical stand on the issues of apostolic poverty and the beatific vision. Those particular issues seem to have played but a small role in his wider assessment of the papal office, which appears indeed to have been foreshadowed in aspects of his earlier critique of scholastic philosophy.

Ockham's hostility to the Thomistic teachings of Lutterell, his contemporary and chancellor of Oxford, was significantly linked with the accusations against him.[19] Already in his *Commentary on the Sentences* (*Super quattuor libros Sententiarum*), the final version of which was finished by 1324, Ockham makes dramatic modifications of numerous thirteenth-century scholastic ideas. Behind Ockham's ecclesiopolitical assertions were many of his essential philosophical principles: (1) his efficiency principle or "Ockham's razor" (more ought not be posited when less will suffice); (2) his rejection of the necessity of nature; (3) his definition of goodness (the state of something being as it ought to be according to a will exterior to it); and (4) his ideas on the category of quality (two qualities can be present in the same person). A fundamental part of the importance of Ockham's antithetical philosophical posture concerns its circumstantial, and, more importantly, substantial connection to his later ecclesiopolitical ideas, particularly to those defining the Church and the papacy. It is this very connection which renders Ockham a product of the fourteenth century, an era in which the worldly implications of medieval philosophical thought were becoming realized.

Ockham rejected outspokenly both "pseudo-exegetical" arguments for papal supremacy and the division of power between pope and king, as well as an interpretation of necessity deriving from traditional practice. He urged scrutiny of the reasons for the acceptance of ideas. To him it was essential that the principle of clarity of thought (which he asserted as fundamental in his programme of logical reform) be applied in the use of *épike* (proper scriptural interpretation). The preeminence of Peter and the popes of the Church over other bishops and over all secular rulers was thought by most theologians through the thirteenth century to have rested on scripture, most specifically on Matt. 16:19 and John 21:17. The interpretation, deemed clarified by the writings of the Church Fathers, especially Augustine, and Pope Gelasius' distinction between *auctoritas* and *potestas*, had yielded an established historical tradition. What came to be the classical Church definition of the proper relationship between ecclesiastical and secular power affirmed that *potestas*, the power of the king (the highest contemporary secular claimant to power) remained limited to the sphere of public order, while *auctoritas*, the sacred authority of the highest priest which is that over divine things, extended over that of the royal power. To interpret scripture thusly, thought Ockham, was to bring about exactly the unrest which had existed and continued to exist between king and pope and against which the biblical texts, Matt. 6:24 and Luke 16:13, had warned "no one can serve two masters." The message was perfectly clear, and seemed to him to admit no other interpretation.

Aside from his own exegetical conclusions, Ockham's positions did not stem from theological dissension. In the case of the division of power, Ockham continued to adhere to the fundamental idea that secular matters belong to one learned in secular institutions, and that spiritual affairs belong to one of faith: "the priestly and secular powers (*potestas*) are distinct jurisdictions."[20] His objections were, however, not to the idea of a distinction in power, but to the *dual way of distributing that power*. A distinction in power did not necessitate distinct administrators. The two powers were merely divided *as* powers, and one person could administer them both. He stated in fact that were he to be shown that the community of Christians could be directed as well by two leaders, a pope and a king/emperor, as by one Christian emperor, then he would be the first to maintain the established order of things.

Giles of Rome, Marsilius of Padua, Hugh of St Victor, and John of Paris among others, who also addressed the question of the two powers, thought the question out differently. To all except Marsilius, it seemed that scripture pointed to the necessity of recognizing a duality. Ockham, disagreeing with each and all, chose, like Marsilius, to dismiss as unfounded the exegetical implications they saw. He did, however, address Marsilius' claim that the papacy was simply a product of Church history and that it ought not simply for historical reasons to be acknowledged as being legitimate. Along with Giles of Rome, Hugh of St Victor, John of Paris, and most medieval theologians, Ockham gave significance to the traditional existence of the papacy. Paradoxically, Ockham's recognition of the traditional institution of the papacy was consistent with his distinction of the two powers.

To Ockham's mind, numerous popes had demonstrated the philosophical principle that two qualities can be found in the same person, such that the responsibility for spiritual leadership could be shared with the responsibility for temporal concerns. Popes had clearly given themselves generously to judicial concerns whenever a secular leadership void presented itself. Thus, for Ockham, spiritual leaders were not merely capable of strengthening the faith; they had occasionally by necessity exercised secular powers of judging and politically organizing the faithful. This papal exercise of secular power he considered a safeguard of the common good of Christians, and a right deriving from one or more of four sources: Christ's wish, natural law, imperial concession, or the supreme law of necessity. In fact, Ockham was to finish by relegating the legitimacy of the papacy to tradition and periodic necessity.

Ockham equally found no problem with a dual role for the king/emperor as it was witnessed in the imperial convocation of Church councils, a king's designation of popes, or his direct interventions in the spiritual realm. The exercise of spiritual authority by a king presupposed only the condition that he be emperor, and hence of the faith. In fact, reminded Ockham, the imperial office was generated by that faith. A king as emperor was confirmed to have spiritual authority, which was necessarily to be exercised regularly. Ockham, in fact, in contrast to some of his reformist contemporaries, like Marsilius of Padua, held that *all* power, spiritual and secular, should reside in the single judge and supreme governor of the Christian emperor. In so doing he was to justify most of the existing practices of the imperial office and certainly to leave room for its expansion.

For Ockham, Church and State represented the same body of people. Being a part of the Church signified not merely being of a spiritual community, but also of a secular community of believers, and viceversa. Ockham felt that for institutional organization, it was simply a matter of choosing one or the other. He chose the State: "the community or congregation of the faithful is best organized (*ordinata*) and in a secular way."[21] In so doing he was also choosing the emperor as the ultimate spiritual and secular authority; but, as he had constantly maintained, not to acknowledge the authority of the emperor in spiritual matters was to demonstrate disloyalty to that office and the Christian community.

Ockham was, none the less, also concerned with a potential difficulty relating to imperial power. The question had been raised of whether imperial authority in spiritual matters could really be justified, especially when the emperors may not have demonstrated their wisdom and will to defend Christianity. Ockham clearly recognized the need to placate any misgivings, and addressed this difficulty in his theory of imperial superiority.[22] Ockham noted that, as recorded in the Bible, kings of the Old Testament punished blasphemy long before there were popes, reflecting their royal responsibility in defending the God of the people of Israel. There were indeed two reasons for the fact that judicial power of the secular authority had been laid down by divine designation to protect divine honor: the efficacy of secular intervention and the instruction of the authoritative laity in the Truth.

Emperors were elected to lead a community to which they belonged. Their protection of Christianity was their role in belonging to that community. The emperors were, according to Ockham, entitled to expel from office even popes who defaulted on their responsibilities due to negligence, misdeeds, or lack of power. Ockham also acknowledged the possibility of the need to judge an emperor, but determined that the "Roman people" would be the only ones justified to do so. As the strength and the religious and political views of the reform papacy at times from as early as the eleventh century posed a major threat to the emperor in Germany or Italy, Ockham's understanding of *Christianitas* as both an ecclesiastical and a civic entity was seen to provide an excellent means of reinforcing the power of the emperor.

Almost all aspects of Ockham's thought were to set his contemporaries reeling. His assertions about the completeness of the imperial office were regarded with awe by intellectuals in Italy, France, and England. To some it seemed that with his nominalist razor of efficiency he was being extremely lucid in making deserved concessions to secular leaders. In Paris he was depicted as the defender of the absolute power of Louis XI the king of France. An astonishing diversity of moves toward a role for secular authorities in spiritual matters became current in royal circles in England under Richard III, in France under Charles VII, and in imperial Germany under Albert II of Austria. None of them can be tied directly to Ockham. His ideas, however, certainly coincided with less sophisticated attempts to exact more spiritual authority for secular leaders.

Nicholas of Cusa's Docta Ignorantia

Like Ockham, Nicholas of Cusa (1401–64) had serious concerns about the contemporary state of the Church. As will be seen, these stemmed, however, from a different philosophical source, Nicholas' concept of "learned ignorance." Early on, Nicholas coined a term, "learned ignorance," which was to have the extended impact of undermining the authority of the Church and of treating the institutional aspects of the Church (a papacy in schism, wealth, etc.) as signs that Christianity had been allowed "to deteriorate into appearance." When Nicholas introduced the expression "learned ignorance" (*docta ignorantia*), his reference was to the state which is attained when individuals have fully realized their own ignorance, and the inadequacy of the human mind and the method of human reasoning.[23] Initially, Nicholas perceived the role of the Christian as one of actively searching, in vain, for knowledge, that is, for the signs of human limitations to acquire knowledge. At that point, Nicholas of Cusa shared with William of Ockham a significant degree of sympathy on the inherent limitations of human knowledge, although as shall be seen directly, the issue of the consequences of these limitations divided them radically.

By May 1437 and the schism within the Council of Basel, evidence that Nicholas of Cusa was to differ from William of Ockham became clear. Nicholas retained the concept of learned ignorance as an enlightened individual state. However, while earlier he had emphasized the effort entailed in acquiring learned ignorance, in perceiving inherent limitations, after 1437 he became more concerned with the consequences of being "learnedly ignorant," attempting reconciliation of all apparent opposites or contradictions. Important to remember is that Nicholas was a pastoral priest before being sent to the Church council at Basel in 1432. Drawing on his experience at the council, Nicholas argued that learned ignorance is primarily a declaration disavowing the principle of noncontradiction. Just as the individual believer learning ignorance accepted the coincidence of opposites in God (in the way of "copulative theology"), so the individual believer practising learned ignorance must work to unite contrasts and differences.[24]

Nicholas used the Latin words *consensus et concordia*, consent and concord, as designations for the essential aspects of any practical union. Consent and concord were the two means used by anyone (of religious or secular station, papal or conciliar affiliation), who either would be, or was already, an authority, to acquire the legitimacy and purpose to act as representative. Consent and concord stemmed from the group as a whole, not from the individual alone. With consent, the believer confirmed his acquiescence to the leadership of the head of the community. In concord, each one affirmed unity amid diversity.

Nicholas initially developed the idea of the papacy as subordinate to the choice of the community of believers. It was their choosing which brought learned ignorance into play: conciliar gatherings and papal elections provided occasions at which the desire for coincidence of differing positions must be publically demonstrated. The choosing by individuals was centrally important, and the councils and the papal office provided the institutional stamp. They confirmed concord.

Further, however, Nicholas developed his understanding of the papacy in its leadership role with a shift in emphasis to its authority, most probably drawing on his experience when representative to the Council of Basel:

> There is nothing in the church which is not first in Peter or his successor, and through the medium of the pope in all others. . . . All power flows from the head of the church, where there is a plenitude of power, and is particularized (*contracta*) in the church. . . . All power which is so unfolded (*explicata*) in the church is contained in the pope as in a causal principle.[25]

The passage, written in the 1440s, reflects the historical context of the schismatic Councils of Basel and Ferrara/Florence. Their existence in May 1437 could be regarded as the beginning of the end for the conciliar movement, for it entailed the division of the representatives to the Council of Basel into two sites for over a decade. The passage above reflects two of Nicholas' main points. First, the pope was the intermediary between Peter and "all others" (incorporated together by their recognition of the pope, of course) as an appearance of God, demonstrating His essential presence in the Church. Similar to Christ, the pope demonstrated the link between God and man initially by reflecting Peter, and further by uniting the followers. The pope was the hierarchical head in fullness of power. Second, the conciliar schism was considered by Nicholas a test of recognition of papal power.

The members of a Church council were in fact for Nicholas manifestations, in a historical context, of the exclusive issuing forth ("unfolding") of them from the pope and of the believer as an effect of papal power. The individuals, whether they followed Pope Eugenius from Basel to Ferrara or remained dissenters in Basel, were testimony to the restriction of the power of each to an active individual membership in the Church. Nicholas' conviction in this nature of the papacy is confirmed by the treatment he had given it in Book II of his treatise *On Learned Ignorance* (*De doeta ignorantia*). The words "being in everything," "plenitude," and "unfolding" were there applied to God signifying, along with "contraction," aspects of the relationship God–man. Nicholas was saying generally, as it were: "I perceive the pope as fulfilling a role analogous (or perhaps more than analogous) to that of God in his relation to human beings, so that when you turn from an orthodox pope who is serving the welfare of the Church at large, you turn by extension from God."

For Nicholas, the Council of Basel significantly had begun in the same spirit as any council legitimately convened by the pope. The dissolution of that same Council by Pope Eugenius in September 1437 and its transfer to Ferrara were important events, but no more or less central to the identity and legitimacy of Church councils than the initial convocation. When the Council at Basel ceased to have the pope as its chief executive, like any other council continuing in session schismatically without the acquiescence of an orthodox pope, it did not reflect the necessary consent and concord to proceed. For Nicholas, a Church council was a true and authoritative representative body only if it possessed the consent of all its members that it was such. Nicholas insisted that the importance of the office of the pope must be respected, eliminating thereby the idea of permanent conciliar supremacy.

The holder of the papal office was thus centrally important to Nicholas, for the pope provided a head to the Church both as the intermediary between God and man and as the source of believers' institutional strength. The members of the Council of Basel, setting off to reconvene in Ferrara, were giving the pope their vote of confidence, particularly in his power to negotiate a settlement with the eastern Church over the centuries-old doctrinal differences with the western Church. The pope, with his plans of schismatic reconciliation, was attempting to carry out labors appropriate to the head of the (western) Church. Interpreting the significance of the papal office would in fact be for all fourteenth- and fifteenth-century theologians the focal point at which totally differing conceptions of the Church itself would collide. Four different conceptions of the papacy found advocates at the time. First, the legacy of the Fourth Lateran Church Council of 1215 was faint but represented the popes themselves. According to that council the pope was deemed to be superior to all other claimants, secular or ecclesiastical, to spiritual authority.

Second, Nicholas of Cusa represented the only view challenging the papacy which still gave it a significant role. He continued to feel justified in affirming that at issue was not the papacy itself, but heretical popes, and obstinate dissension and factionalism within the conciliar body. It was still necessary, Nicholas argued, to give consent to an orthodox pope to lead the Church, for the Church derived power from the papacy. The other two concepts of the office of the papacy posed much greater degrees of challenge to its absolute power. As the conciliar movement continued increasingly to threaten the papacy in the 1430s, popes would come to appreciate the significant support in Nicholas' moderate conciliarism.

The views of William of Ockham and Marsilius of Padua both entailed envisioning the Church as holding within it an institution more powerful even than the papacy, the Church council. As has already been seen, for Ockham to understand the papacy was to return to the historical foundations of its origins, the apostolic church. According to his, the third conception of the papacy, the role of Peter, as caretaker of those who had selected him, had been totally distorted through the assumption of power by the papacy within the Church, but also by its claim to superiority over secular rulers, leading thus to a divorce between the leaders of Church and State. Ockham wished to establish a close alliance of Church and State through the office of the Holy Roman Emperor, thus diminishing the role of the pope to that of spiritual adviser at most. Fourth, Marsilius of Padua also advocated reducing the power and role of the pope, but primarily within the Church structure. He wished to see the pope continue to serve as titular head of the ecclesiastical community in a conception which had inspired the Council of Constance and its conciliar doctrine. Important for their differences, these four conceptions are yet most significant for their similarity. Each emphasizes how closely theology (inspired by philosophical ideas) and Church structure and practices were connected with the politics of the Holy Roman Empire in the fourteenth and fifteenth centurys.

Interpretation by the Late Medieval Church

The interest of intellectuals, such as Ockham and Nicholas, in the institutional Church enhanced the state of the Church under stress. Both intellectual and lay sensitivity to the needs of individual Christians and to the Church's institutional response to those needs was adding great pressure in an already tense period of transition. Rival claimants to the papacy, insecurity in and dislocation from Rome, administrative duplication and disarray distracted the Church leaders from an intellectual contemplation of the Church from within. The survival of the traditional Catholic institution was at stake, and the mere pragmatics of maintaining it were demanding the greatest amount of clerical attention. Reinforcement for political and economic as well as religious actions was drawn *pro forma* from conciliar statements, such as those of the Fourth Lateran Council, and the concept of covenant.

Until the late fourteenth century, the papacy chose as its most obvious course of action to reject objections to its supremacy, but that defensive posture was neither immediately to quiet the challenges, nor to address the events. The late fourteenth-century papal schism which at one point boasted three elected claimants to the papal seat demonstrated critically that a procedural response was needed. The response devised was conciliarism. Intellectuals Jean Gerson and Pierre d'Ailly, and their student, Nicholas of Clémanges, suggested that if contending popes would not resign their claims (*via cessionis*), or take judgement from a board of respected men acceptable to all parties (*via compromissi*), then a Church council would have to be convened. Differences should be resolved by a council "lawfully assembled in the Holy Spirit" with "its authority immediately from Christ."[26]

In the Swiss city of Constance in 1414 a conciliarists' gathering numbering almost 200 clergy brought about the deposition of all three contemporary claimants to the papacy and elected a new pope, Martin V.[27] The Council of Constance was a concrete response to a situation of papal schism, not new but now somehow entrenched. The response incorporated the thirteenth-century ideas of Thomas with the strong fourteenth-century convictions of Marsilius. The conciliarism of Constance denied the belief of Ockham that councils could err in their judgements just as easily as bishops and popes. It did not, however, also follow fully Marsilius' advice that councils are more worthy of the pinnacle of the ecclesiastical hierarchy than are popes, who are merely bishops of Rome, and ought therefore to function constantly. The Council of Constance was a council called to address a particularly critical situation.

The conciliarist ideal of resolution foundered, however, on one in particular among the many points on which intellectuals of the thirteenth and fourteenth centurys, such as Thomas and Marsilius, would never have come to agreement. In their ideas there was no agreement on the supremacy of Church or State. For Thomas, "grace perfects nature" and the pope as guardian of divine grace is supreme over secular authority. Marsilius asserted that the roles of the secular and spiritual leaders are distinct and one is not superior to the other. There was no agreement on the source of a ruler's power. Thomas saw both the secular and spiritual rulers as divinely established, necessary guiding authorities for the realization of man's supernatural end. Marsilius considered the two rulers to exist by virtue of the divinely given authority of two distinct human communities to have chosen them, the citizenry legislating a king into office and the body of the faithful selecting a pope for direction.

Yet one more dividing point was decisive in the conciliar movement. According to the thirteenth-century legacy, Church councils should act only in times of emergency, whereas for Marsilius they should be a constant feature of Church administration. The conciliarists' hope of a united spiritual union, with regular Church councils being called to facilitate communication, was dashed from 1417 onward, as popes immediately from Martin V began to frustrate the operation of regular councils. In 1437, conciliar schism seriously compromised the administrative and spiritual credibility of the Church council vis-à-vis the papacy. By 1460, Pope Pius II had cemented the reassertion of papal authority over councils with his bull *Execrabilis*, a gain helped to no small extent by the political consequences of the continuing strong adherence even among conciliarists to a theory of abiding rights of the pope and the restriction of the councils to emergency instruments.

The efforts of the Church to maintain its strength in the later Middle Ages were undoubtedly challenged by internal administrative discord. Hierarchical disarray left the Church weak before the recommendations of intellectuals for reorganization. Proponents of a conciliar movement made their recommendations, however, without unanimity, and even more independent-minded reformers, such as William of Ockham, could not be ignored. This late medieval intellectual approach to the need of the Church for survival, like its counterpart in the earliest of medieval centuries, was inspired by philosophy. Rather than calculatingly conceiving a Christian theology from classical philosophy, as Augustine and others had done in the fifth and sixth centuries, late medieval intellectuals instead tested the existing theology, especially ecclesiology, expecting it to stand up or yield to the philosophical dictates they had extracted from scholasticism. This was a not wholly propitious intellectual posture for the survival of the Church, but it was a strong reflection of the confidence placed by the late Middle Ages in holding the mirror of reason up to any human activity or institution.

For further reading

For the philosophical views of late medieval philosophers, see:

Marilyn McCord Adams, *William Ockham* (Notre Dame, IN, 1987).
Charles C. Bayley, "Pivotal Concepts in the Political Philosophy of William of Ockham," *Journal of the History of Ideas* 10 (1949), pp. 199–218.
Philotheus Boehner, "A Recent Presentation of Ockham's Philosophy," *Franciscan Studies* 9 (1949), pp. 443–56.
F. C. Copleston, *A History of Medieval Philosophy* (London, 1972).
Alexander Passerin d'Entrèves, *The Medieval Contribution to Medieval Thought: Thomas Aquinas, Marsilius of Padua, Richard Hooker* (Oxford, 1939).

Alan Gewirth, *Marsilius of Padua, The Defender of the Peace* (2 vols: New York, 1951, 1956).

David Knowles, "A Characteristic of the Mental Climate of the Fourteenth Century," in *Mélanges offerts à Etienne Gilson de l'Academie fran baise* (Toronto, 1959).

Gordon Leff, "The Fourteenth Century and the Decline of Scholasticism," *Past and Present* 9 (1956), pp. 30–9.

Paul Vignaux, *History of Medieval Philosophy: An Introduction* (Cleveland, OH, 1962).

For the views of late medieval philosophers on the Church, see:

James E. Beichler, "Nicholas of Cusa and the End of the Conciliar Movement: A Humanist Crisis of Identity," *Church History* 44 (1975), pp. 5–21.

William J. Courtenay, "Nominalism and Late Medieval Religion," in *The Pursuit of Holiness in Late Medieval and Renaissance Religion*, ed. Charles Trinkhaus and Heiko A. Oberman (Leiden, 1974) pp. 26–58.

Gordon Leff, *The Dissolution of the Medieval Outlook: An Essay on Intellectual and Spiritual Change in the Fourteenth Century* (New York, 1976).

Heiko A. Oberman, *Forerunners of the Reformation: The Shape of Late Medieval Thought* (New York, 1966).

——, *The Harvest of Medieval Theology: Gabriel Biel and Late Medieval Nominalism* (Cambridge, MA, 1963).

Steven Ozment, *The Age of Reform 1250–1550: An Intellectual and Religious History of Late Medieval and Reformation Europe* (New Haven/London, 1980).

Brian Tierney, *Ockham, the Conciliar Theory and the Canonists* (Philadelphia, 1971).

8

Domains of Abstract Thought

Distinct intellectual positions on theological and philosophical issues in the Middle Ages have been recounted in previous chapters. They have presented different perspectives on particular questions of concern at the time: from Arian/orthodox interpretations of the Trinity to scholastic/conciliarist opinions on the role of Church and State. The debates reflect that those who discussed Christianity adopted a highly intellectualized posture, no matter whether the issue of concern was the Church as a whole or one small facet of it. The increase throughout the Middle Ages in the intellectualization of Christianity has been traced in the present book. Many further examples of activities or documents of the Church which reflect the facility its members were acquiring to express their religious beliefs on an intellectual plane could be added to those provided: the Petrine Doctrine, to assert the supremacy of the bishop of Rome; the Councils of Carthage, to debate the orthodoxy of beliefs; the Synod of Whitby, to weigh arguments for religious practices; the Donation of Constantine, to recognize the importance of written documents; the Council of Clermont, to bind social circumstances and religious aims; the Concordat of Worms, to assert authority over secular power; the Fourth Lateran Council, to combat heresy and affirm papal strength; the Condemnations of 1277, to censure institutions of learning; and the Council of Constance, to analyze its own institutional weakness. Indeed, it has been maintained throughout that the notion of "medieval thought" entails the recognition of the close connection between the individual and Christian beliefs and institutions in the development and exercise of human intellectuality.

The actual process of thinking as the most important capacity of humans played an important part in medieval Christian thought. "For we are and we know we are, and we love our being and our knowledge of it," wrote Augustine of Hippo.[1] Thinking was part of fulfilling one's place as a human being in the hierarchy of creation. In the Middle Ages the Christian conception of human rationality in the world of God's creation harmonized with the classical valuing of thought by the Greek philosophers and Roman rhetoricians. While the ancients with their views on human intellect did not, however, compromise with theology,[2] the thinkers of the Middle Ages functioned precisely according to such compromises. Indeed, medieval ideas about any number of subjects, such as the role of the secular community and its ruler, reflect theological presuppositions. Historical, political, and social realities awarded the medieval Church a strong intellectual role, which is substantiated by the identifiable activities of known medieval Churchmen and women as preservers, educators, synthesizers, translators, and exegetes of the written word. While medieval thought was not orchestrated monopolistically by the Church, it is, none the less, to that institution the historian must turn in large measure to ascertain its refinement.

Christian thought in the Middle Ages reflected a high degree of abstraction. An exercise in abstraction underlay most medieval religious concepts of absolutes (Truth, Being, Good, etc.). Considerable emphasis was consistently placed on the abstract, immaterial attributes of Being and God. The concern for abstraction which underlay both medieval metaphysics and theology was, however, also to some degree rightly regarded in the same period as fundamental to epistemology and the concept of knowledge in general. The medieval notion of "abstraction" was basically the degree to which concepts in the mind are removed from the individuality and particularity of the instance or item which inspired them. The specific degree or level of abstraction was the essential criterion in medieval schemes of classifying knowledge, with the most abstract concepts and entities associated with the pinnacles of disciplinary study, metaphysics and theology.

As the Middle Ages evinced such a strong interest in classical philosophy, it is understandable that it should have shared not only the Greek epistemological interest in abstraction but also the Greek recognition of the variety of things to be known. As has already been seen, the idea that bodies of thought not specifically Christian, such as the seven liberal arts, could be abstract was indeed entertained during the Middle Ages. The aim of this chapter is to examine in what way abstraction played a role in all areas of medieval thought. Since the notion of abstraction itself was considered primarily by medieval philosophers, and was not consciously a part of most "abstract" medieval endeavors, the role of the historian becomes that of the detective. Not expressed *per se*, the "abstractness" of the subject-matter and procedure of many areas of medieval thought must be sought out in all forms of expression and documentary evidence. Conclusions of this nature are discussed in the present chapter.

Thought

Central to any era which considers thinking and thought interesting, is that era's analysis and delimitation of the process and its product. In other words, its scholars ask themselves "what are we doing when we are thinking?" and "how do we organize our thoughts?" and the answers to their questions can be quite revealing.

About Thinking

The study of the human process of thinking called, since the six-teenth century, "psychology," derives its name from the classical Greek context of the discussion, the study of the *psyche* or soul. The soul was considered to be, among other things, the organ of thought. One of the central *foci* of medieval discussions on the soul was the study of the faculties or powers of the soul. It had come to be thought that separate faculties located in separate places of the body performed the distinct functions necessary for sense perception and intellection, and that those faculties considered all together formed the virtual whole of the soul. One of the important capacities of the soul was "reasoning." It was reasoning, not by virtue of having a soul, but by virtue of having a soul with a higher part, that was thought to be the basis on which human beings show them-selves to be distinct from plants or animals. This observation was made by medieval thinkers as early as Augustine, and throughout the Middle Ages it was to be emphasized to some degree, leading to a sustained interest in "human rationality."

For the medieval psychologist, the brain functioned as that organ of the soul which bestowed the faculty of reasoning on the human body in such a way that both external sensation and internal sen-sation could be understood by the individual. Brain activity, stimu-lated by sense information from outside a person, yielded thought within that person. For a number of later medieval scholars in-fluenced by Aristotle and Averroes, the faculty of reasoning remained predominantly dependent upon the external senses. It was from the five external senses of sight, smell, hearing, taste, and touch that knowledge initially derived. The brain's internal senses, however, functioned to complete or denominate the sensorial perceptions, as if they were part of the sensing individual. The common sense formed a composite image of the sensed object. The imagination apprehended the object separated now from its presence and its matter. The memory either stored it for future reference, or it was sent to the estimation and phantasy, where the "intentions" of the object were apprehended. Some medieval scholars included a last step in which the object was known in terms of a universal concept, abstracted from all the limiting features of its existence as a particular object. In sum, the intellect, reason, mind, or brain effected cognition or knowledge.

The ideas of Aristotle on the soul were developed by Arabic philosophers to yield a medieval doctrine generally known as the knowability of separate substances.[3] In the Middle Ages there was certainly not full agreement on the processes of perception, let alone on the role of the intellect in facilitating rational thought. While Albertus Magnus taught that the intellect may proceed beyond the sense images of the internal senses to contemplation first of itself, then of the celestial intelligences, and finally of God, Thomas Aquinas thought that the soul did not contain such an "intellect" which could understand itself or other intelligences directly. For Albertus, the intellectual soul was fundamentally separable from the body. For Thomas, that soul was the substantial form of the body, inseparable from it. Thomas thus drew a sharp distinction between corporeal modes of cognition (abstractions from sense images, cognition by reflection or analogy) and intellection for a separate substance, designating only the former as accessible to humans and the latter as that of the celestial intelligences and God. For Albertus, both were faculties of the human soul. The act of human thinking (*ratiocinare* and *intelligere*) shares in the activity of separate substances, namely knowledge of self (*se intelligere*). Thomas did actually admit that the human intellect might come to know itself through discourse, but Ockham a little later would state that, if by soul was meant (Albertus' conception of it as) immaterial and incorruptible form, one could not know, "by reason or experience," the soul as the source of knowledge.

The importance here of these developments in psychology is that they denote a definite medieval absorption with understanding the process of human thinking, from sense perception through complete abstract cognition. From as early as Augustine, "rationality" referred to the characteristic of being created both as human and in the image of God. Discussions throughout the Middle Ages reflected on the concept and mechanism of human rationality. It is interesting to note that such discussions encompassed debates concerning the individuality of the soul (and its antithesis, the oneness of the intellect for all men) and the uniqueness of the self.[4]

About Divisions of Thought

The phrase "classification of the sciences" (a post-medieval expression) has come to refer to the medieval way of ordering knowledge. The term "classification" immediately suggests that something – in this case, knowledge – is being organized. Like many other schemes of organizing knowledge developed by philosophers and paedagogues, the medieval mode of classifying is a product of its time. For medieval intellectuals, "science" or "scientia" meant knowledge. It remains, nevertheless, that the English cognate of the Latin designation *scientia* is used in the expression "classification of the sciences."

Medieval classifications of the sciences were linked with Aristotle's hierarchical ranking of divisions of knowledge, according to the "scientific-ness" of their subject matter, mode of investigation, and conclusions. Aristotle's rules concerning "demonstrative" or "scientific" knowledge gained wide medieval support, partly because not all knowledge was considered "scientific" by Aristotle himself.[5] Compilers of classification-schemas generally reflected a certain narrowness concerning the variety of groupings of contemporary thought. Many medievals seem to have believed that the only divisions which could be regarded as belonging to the classification-scheme were those originally included in Aristotle's conception. A comparison of the contents of the classification-scheme of Boethius with that of Robert Kilwardby in the thirteenth century (*De ortu scientiarum*) shows that although both schemes were "Aristotelian," the latter contained a number of divisions which Boethius with his few texts of Aristotle had not included. Aristotle's distinction between the "arts," the "practical sciences," and the "speculative sciences" was, however, already drawn. For Aristotle, the first consisted of gymnastics, grammar, statuary music, logic, rhetoric, and poetry; the second, of moral philosophy or ethics; and the third, of natural philosophy, mathematics, and metaphysics (to which Aristotle devoted whole works, such as his *Physics* and *Metaphysics*).[6]

A fundamental rethinking occurred at the end of the thirteenth century as to the role of Aristotle in European Christian thought. Although by 1255 there was widespread agreement that the works of Aristotle could be used as base texts for teaching university courses, some medievals considered the works of the pagan Aristotle to be dangerous to Christian belief. The Condemnations of 1277 by Etienne Tempier, Bishop of Paris, defining 219 contemporary teachings as "vanities and lying follies," revealed, to some, confusion between interpretations of Aristotle and Aristotle's own ideas. The legacy of this shift, to be felt well into the Renaissance, was first reflected in the attitudes toward Aristotle of different late thirteenth-century groups, the most outspoken being the Averroists.

The ideas of Aristotle were still under as tight scrutiny at the end of the thirteenth century as they had been earlier. For the Averroists, staunch adherence to Aristotle's ideas, as understood by Averroes, was based on the idea that they contained one truth. The implication was that there might be other sources of truth, but that Aristotle's was of no less importance. The opposing view, held by many intellectuals, distinguishable among themselves for other beliefs, was very different. Not only did they attach the status of truth to scripture and divine revelation alone, but they disagreed with the Averroists as to what the proper interpretation of Aristotle was. What was the relevance of this dispute to the classification of the sciences?

One thirteenth-century scholastic practice to which the new dissenters from Aristotle would take particular exception was that of writing strict commentaries on Aristotle's works. To those of the *via moderna*, this practice had rested upon the time-worn phase of the introduction of Aristotle into Europe (the period of translation), and had encouraged both excessive enthusiasm for him, and doctrinal distortion. Some opponents of the *via antiqua* felt they had already surmounted the limitations of the commentary format by incorporating the practice of writing digressions on ideas elicited by the base text. The dissenters from Aristotle, however, having claimed that much of his writing was in error (and hence not authoritative), adopted the posture that, in their view at least, the practice of commentary was no longer appropriate. The obvious riposte from the Aristotelian–Averroist side was that the *via moderna* had abandoned the path of reason, having excluded Aristotle from the canon of knowledge, and had turned from any ideas which appeared to contradict theology.

One outcome of this debate was the writing and circulating of books which were devoted to the discussion of particular questions and issues. The list of *opera omnia* of almost any fourteenth- or fifteenth-century writer reflects the liberation from the corpus of Aristotle, as they include *Questions on . . .* , *Treatise on . . .* , *About . . .* , as opposed to the earlier *Commentary on . . . .* Some even deliberately omitted reference to Aristotle and his works, or else indicated that his ideas were of no relevance in the content under discussion. Of specific importance here is that the classification-scheme of Aristotle was also being severed from the corpus of his works, and the divorce would begin to yield intellectual fruit in the late Middle Ages.

On the Arts

The Middle Ages inherited from Greek antiquity the divisions of *tekne* and *philosophia* – the arts and sciences. The arts underwent further division into "technical" and "liberal." Within this division, actively adopted by paedagogues of the early Middle Ages, gymnastics, arithmetic, geometry, music, astronomy, poetry, grammar, rhetoric, and dialectic (the art of reasoning) were considered the "liberal (or freeman's) arts," and cooking, weaving, tailoring, armament-making, building, commerce, agriculture, hunting, theatrics and medicine, the "technical arts." These two kinds of arts were, though often limited each to seven in number, quite distinct. Underlying this division was a cultural bias of classical Greece against manual labour in the life of the educated freeman.[7] Thus, the technical arts were not related to the study of the liberal arts, although knowledge of reading, writing, and reckoning would certainly prove useful in the study of the former. As Aristotle in the *Nicomachean Ethics* had noted long before the Middle Ages about the technical art of medicine, "Clearly you do not become a physician by books. Nevertheless the writers of books try to describe not only the remedies but the general and special methods of therapeutic too, with respect to the individual case. That would be useful for the skilled man, but the untrained ones gain no use from it."[8]

The division of the arts according to manual and cerebral skills had meant pragmatically that the technical arts were seen purely as ends in themselves. Artisans, whether officially trained or not, would not be equipped with any further knowledge to move beyond their trade. As was seen earlier, such isolation was one of the barriers to progression through the intellectual ranks which the use of vernacular language began to demolish. Convinced in the twelfth century that the technical arts ought not to be ignored, Hugh of St Victor gave them a significant place in his classification-scheme, as "adulterate" arts. He wrote in the *Didascalicon*, his treatise on education:

> These sciences are called mechanical, that is adulterate, because their concern is with the artificer's product, which borrows its

form from nature. Similarly, the other seven are called liberal either because they require minds which are liberal, that is, liberated and practical (for these sciences pursue subtle inquiries into the causes of things), or because in antiquity only free and noble men were accustomed to study them, while the populace and the sons of men not free sought operative skill in things mechanical.[9]

Hugh had virtually abolished the stigmatic division between the manual and the cerebral arts within classification-schemes. He fully recognized the traditional distinctions between the divisions of the arts, insisting, however, that these differences were not based on an inherent relative value of the studies (or the student). Assuming that all the arts were included in his lists of seven technical and seven liberal, he asserted that the technical arts, by virtue of their undertaking, belong paired one to one with the other more often honored studies. For Hugh, the mechanical arts had their own value, the redemption of the fallen nature of humankind through active labor. Since, however, medieval classification-schemes were effected through both philosophical convictions and the practical divisions at work in the contemporary environment, it is worth asking whether after Hugh there was any continued push for the recognition of the technical arts. In the intellectual realm, Robert Kilwardby in the late thirteenth century established a classification-scheme based on the distinction between the "practical" (including the technical arts and ethics) and the "speculative" studies.[10] Also among the later, more mystical intellectuals such as Bonaventure, the mechanical arts have a prominence.[11]

In the workaday world, Hugh of St Victor did not have to remind others that Jesus was a carpenter, Paul a tent-maker, or Peter a fisherman. Religious movements in the later Middle Ages were peopled with believers who consciously chose to practise a trade, to pursue a technical art in imitation of the first Christians. Those pursuing the technical arts needed no guidance either from the classifying philosopher as to how their profession should evolve. Artisans were increasingly applying intellectual categories to their own efforts, and acting according to them. Just as long-told stories in the vernacular were being put into writing, so the artisan was recording long-practised (as well as new) techniques of the trade.

Hugh's elevation of the technical arts into higher profile in classification-schemes may well have been the intellectual reflection of the increasingly higher profile the pursuit of technical skills was acquiring in the contemporary medieval society at large. Just as Hugh of St Victor, artisans themselves began to emphasize the different but equal value of their technical skills to the skills of pure intellectual endeavor. "Producing" was placed on an equal footing with "imagining." While the medieval student was beginning to rely more heavily on the written word to provide instruction in medicine, law, and philosophy, the artisan through books and diagrams was also slowly becoming freer from the physical presence and guidance of the master.[12] Such intellectualizing would call former standards of dividing the manual from the cerebral into question, far more so than had the fact that all individuals in medieval society had "liberated" access to knowledge.[13]

Rendering technical expertise a component of medieval thought was effected through many sources: through classifiers of knowledge like Hugh of St Victor, through patrons of technical production, and through the artisans themselves, as well as through technical change and the written word. When spiritual bishops and temporal kings desired artifacts of improved or novel technique thereby to possess graphic, concrete symbols of their power, they were playing an important part in medieval technological thought. In the sphere of authority concerning the well-being of their realm, they could effect practical changes. They might themselves be the artisans of those changes, but more often, since medieval temporal authorities were involved primarily in leading an life of ease, their own needs entailed enlisting the work of others. Whether the kings or nobles realized it or not, they were performing a role in intellectualizing the technical arts. Frederick II himself wrote his falconry book, *On the Art of Hunting with Birds* (*Dearte venandi cumavibus*). Abbot Suger wrote an account of the reconstruction of St-Denis whose renovation was made possible by the royal patronage of Louis VII of France.

Patronage ordained that intellectual conception would be imposed upon production, for the purposes of ensuring the expression of intent and novelty. There were three types of patrons within medieval society: the immediate or local sponsor of an endeavor, who would perhaps be part of the operation him/herself (reflecting the power of wealth and expertise combined); the nobility, who exercised political and social as much as economic authority, and were fundamentally interested in the tangible results of the activities they patronized; and the clergy, who exercised both economic and spiritual authority, with an eye as well, however, to tangible results. Patronage from each of these depended on more than a single word promising something in return for support. The institution of patronage required both that sufficient knowledge about the procedure be communicated from, and that an adequate fulfillment of the desired final product be reflected by, the recipient of patronage back to the non-artisan sponsor.

For Hugh of St Victor, reason (or thought yielding invention) and the production of things coexisted within the practice of the technical arts. Hugh established his classification of the sciences in part on the affirmation that there were some "things which human beings do not possess naturally, things which have to be invented by reasoning" and then produced.[14] "Invention" and "production" could be *distinguished*, but it was recognized that they could not be *isolated*. Knowledge for production might be transmitted through apprentices by imitation, but the reasoning for invention must be ruled by abstract thought: "Indeed, man's reasoning shines forth much more brilliantly in inventing these very things than ever it would have had man naturally possessed them."[15] Hugh was insisting that the populace at work in the kitchens, workshops, construction sites, markets, fields, forests, and village squares might well be contributing to the body of medieval thought. He seemed also to have recognized that it would be utterly unrealistic to assume that human society could exist without the artifacts it has invented and produced. Hugh might have found it appropriate if somehow everyone were involved in the technical arts; at the very least he believed that expressions of technical and intellectual thought must coexist in human society.

Hugh of St Victor's classification-scheme appears to indicate that two different types of intellectualization were occurring in tandem within the technical arts: "experimentation" and personalized rules-of-thumb, and the use of the written word. The first type of intellectualization reflected the need for adaptation to innovation and change, and challenged earlier theoretical preconceptions of how materials can be used. "Experimentation" and personalized rules-of-thumb were rooted in the economic reality of competition, in which the artisan creatively/intellectually responded to the market and the availability of raw materials. The use of the written word, based upon the preexisting, relatively static level of literacy in the world of the artisan, was to fix accounts of technical processes for their later reproduction. The use of the written word was also based upon the rapidity of technical change and upon a new enthusiasm for the products of invention. The literate and technically astute committed their ideas and techniques to writing for an audience beyond the atelier.

Medieval cathedral-building is a splendid example of both strains of intellectualization. Throughout the Middle Ages the practical, hands-on imitative approach to technical knowledge continued to dominate the *teckne*, in the manner in which it had in Greek and Roman antiquity. Thus, the two noted characteristics of technical intellectualization, experimentation and written accounts, exemplified in cathedral-building by Abbot Suger's *On Consideration* (*De consideratione*) and *On Administration* or the sketch book of Villard de Honnecourt, are not representative of the general sophistication of technical thought in the Middle Ages. Hugh and his enlightened successors omit from their classificationlists such technical arts as milling, ale and wine making, musical-instrument making, pottery, and ceramics. These trades were, however, also actively undertaken at the time (and equally important parts of medieval culture). Quite probably their omission reflects that their professions were in a less visible state of transition and therefore not incorporating as obviously as cathedral-building, perhaps, the attributes of intellectualization, either in experimentation or in written documentation.

Abstract thought about artisan endeavors began to play a role of intermediary between patron and artisan, and master and apprentice. New professionals, the *ingeniator* ("engineer") and architect, used both ingenuity and creativity, as well as years in service, to assert themselves, not because such service was inherently any less obligatory, but because the novelty and demand for their particular expertise was great. It could be noted that had the Middle Ages experienced no technical changes, no general intellectualization of its technical arts would have been necessary. Every apprentice would have continued to recognize the wisdom of the master, and accordingly to imitate his experienced skills. The feudal, economic and political system of medieval Europe established, however, an era of sufficient prosperity to foster human technical expression and creativity, resulting in change and the remarkable intellectual expansion of the most practical dimension of medieval thought.

On the Practical Sciences

The place of ethics in the classification of the sciences has already been alluded to in previous sections as a three-part component of the practical-science division. Even since the beginning of classification-schemes with Aristotle, classifiers appear to have designated ethics as composed of ethics of the individual (called ethics), ethics of "domestic society" or the family (called monastics or economics), and ethics of "civil society" or the state (called politics). While there continued to be active discussion of ethics throughout the Middle Ages, it focused very little on the reformulation of these divisions as such. Aristotle considered his ethical theories both practical and scientific. Recognizing, as did Plato, the contemporary political realities of his time and the apparent reliance of human societies on hierarchical structures, Aristotle reinforced his concept of human societal groupings by grounding it in his notion of human perfectibility. The law of nature governed all material things (including the individual) in the gradual process of their potential capabilities becoming actual. Each rational human being was a product of nature, and in realizing their potential to be fully human, individuals banded together for their common good.

The authority of Aristotle in the study of ethics was all-pervasive, though not restrictive, after the translation of his two works, *Ethics* and *Nicomachean Ethics*. Medieval ethics concerned itself exclusively with the Christian believer and primarily with his soul, though by extension with his goods, in economics, and his person, in politics. The study of ethics in the Middle Ages, highly intellectualized from the start, appears, given the texts of Aristotle, to have been able to step outside the strictures of Christian scriptural ethics to appreciate that the existence of a particular ethical standard was not presupposed by the study itself and that God's part in establishing human ethics could come under discussion. No medieval scholar of ethics would go so far as to posit two separate ethical arenas, one with a standard and one without, but the scope of the study certainly would have permitted the discussion. The role of factors determining ethical behavior – sense, will, and intellect or reason as well as attributes of personality – was encompassed by the medieval study of ethics.

The subjects of medieval ethics seemed to shift between an emphasis on the choice of the individual and the importance of God's grace. Human notions of right and wrong, standards of conduct, and the forums of ethical activity were all under discussion. These were especially significant in the areas of economics and politics. Unlike reflections on individual ethics, and even the contemplation of political systems, the study of economics in the Middle Ages really only began with the reception of Aristotle's ideas, thereby commencing, none the less, at a sophisticated level of discourse. There is no virtual delineation of an economic system to be found among the medieval scholars of economic ideas. The scope of their discussion was oriented instead toward the ethical values which should be at work in any economic system.

In commentaries on Aristotle's ethical works as well as in more wide-ranging theological treatises, medieval scholars attempted to determine the standards of "equity" which ought to rule economic and social relations. These were based on several generally held premises. (1) The immediate distribution of wealth, in God's hand, was unequal. (2) The eventual distribution of wealth, within man's capability, was legitimately achieved only by specific kinds of transactions among individuals. (3) The value of goods and services was determined by their capacity to satisfy a need (utility or *indigentia*). There was no place in ethical economics for a discussion of the belief that God distributed wealth, in His design, according to birth, merit, individual capacities, occupation, and need. The legitimacy of certain kinds of transactions was, however, of much concern, as it lay within the sphere of just (and unjust) human acts. Economic exchange was seen as a contract in which fair wages must be the return for fair prices, with the cost of production deemed the minimum measure of the rate of return. Since the value of goods was considered determined by their utility, supply and demand were deemed the appropriate market forces in a exchange forum of free trade and competition. Activities such as price regulation by monopolies or tariffs and taxation through authoritative intervention were debated for the ethical as well as purely economic anomalies they would bring into a free-trade context. The role of intermediaries, commercial or financial, also came under discussion in the later medieval period, which could no longer deny the important role of merchants, despite their price mark-ups, and bankers, despite their profiteering from currency exchanges and money-lending.

Politics was the broadest in scale of the ethical studies. The practical science of politics in the Middle Ages undertook to consider the form of protection of a territory or people and the recognition of authority responsible for that protection. Just as the scope of economics was not seen to be limited to any particular economic system, so too was the discussion of political ethics not intended to support any particular political system. With, however, a hierarchical system presupposed either as a necessity or as a natural aspect of social groupings, under debate were the form of governing body, the kind of political offices, their responsibilities and exercise of control, and the role of the individual in the social structure. Late medieval notions of consent and active involvement of individuals in the civil (and Church) government, which have already been discussed, would reform politics in content, but not really in scope. For late medieval writers, rather than ethical studies of distinct kinds, individual ethics, economics, and politics reflected simply different levels of individual ethical activity.[16] In this context as well, political ethics of civil government was not seen to differ from the political ethics of Church government, in that the responsible behavior of the individual in each context ought be the same. Both the believer and the citizen were under obligation to God, in that they had both been entrusted with acting as Christians within their community, Church or State.

Aristotle's ideas, once available in the later Middle Ages, determined the widest scope of medieval political theory. Inspired by his *Nicomachean Ethics*, the topics under discussion included society and state as natural institutions, the common good, legitimate authority and its limits, and the rights of those subject to authority. "There are three forms of constitution, kingship, aristocracy, and that of communities (*communitatum*). And of these, kingship is the best," Aristotle had written,[17] and his opinion was until the late Middle Ages respected as most authoritative. In fact, well before the impact of Aristotle's theory, the medieval abstract ideal of civil political organization was the monarchy, and the king was considered the ideal ruler. Medieval thinkers identified the Holy Roman Empire as a theocracy, and increasingly kings of other realms maintained that their power was divinely given. Rulers were obliged to carry out their work as Christian monarchs. Until the time of William of Ockham and the conciliarist movement discussed above, the monarch, emperor, and pope alike were deemed all to be charged with leading the Christian community. Even with the later textual and interpretative alterations to Aristotle which were to thrust the community or commune into political prominence, the sphere of politics as a domain of abstract thought underwent very little change.

Law and medicine were two further practical studies which clearly reached a high level of intellectual sophistication in the Middle Ages. They share the feature of finding themselves somewhat misrepresented as studies by the classification-schemes. Medicine, when it was classified by philosophers, appeared as a (technical) art, though, as was frequently noted by physicians such as Peter of Abano, for many of its characteristics it deserved consideration among the (practical) sciences, no less than law. Law, in fact, was not usually classified among the known studies at all, yet there were whole schools devoted exclusively to its study from the twelfth century on. There are further parallels between the studies of law and medicine which can be identified.

1 In some respects the most practical aspects of both medieval law and medicine were based on an ethical foundation and thus entailed a definition of "good": the "good" or healthy functioning of the body, the "good" and legal, or not-good and illegal act, etc. Both also attributed proper legal conduct or good health

to sense, will, and intellect, as the instruments of ethical behavior. As Abelard wrote concerning law, conscience must be aware of the law; the will must put it into practice.

2 Both considered the community as a whole in need of the learning of law and medicine to be Christian. While the focus of canon law was of course exclusively Christian, even medieval codes of civil law and medicine were clearly tailored to a Christian audience. Both law and medicine were invoked when the individual was "erring" either in body or soul. As law encompassed the erring of the soul, and medicine the "erring" of the body, it was considered legitimate for practitioners to treat the conditions as infractions against the good Christian life.

3 Only those who were professionals were permitted to exercise the authority of doctors of law or medicine. Among the truly intellectualized disciplines, degrees in law and medicine were the first to function as required signs of sufficient "vocational" training.

4 Both law and medicine were deemed important areas of expertise in the medieval community. Training in the law often led to the holding of political positions, thus influencing the community at large. Charlemagne was well aware that without training in rhetoric, the ruler himself stood weak against an articulate lawyer. As for medicine, even before the medical schools of the eleventh century, an experienced practitioner was sought out as one more likely to effect good health quickly and appropriately than the inexperienced, and was to be consulted by reason of experience. The change that the further intellectualization and institutionalization of legal and medical training brought was that where previously experience had been the qualification for the vocation, now practitioners had degrees (and schooling) to "prove" their expertise.

5 The professions of law and medicine both exemplify the growing medieval awareness of a distinction in lay vocations between the private individual and the public persona. The ethical dictates of both professions (for example, not to condemn the ill-doer oneself but to leave that to the court of law, and to administer care even to one's personal enemies) were to become applied to the public professional. Infractions of ethical codes were considered sanctionable against the individual as public persona, if not against him/her as private person. Boccaccio points out scathingly that doctors fled Florence and did not stay to care for the masses dying of the plague in the fourteenth century.

6 Law and medicine each recognized the different sources of its

knowledge. They distinguished those of custom from the information in learned texts. Medieval law-codes were developed both from customary legal traditions concerned with the preservation of time-honored institutions arising as the response of the group to wars, migrations, wealth, or penury, and from the written codes of various cultures testifying to specific circumstances which had been deemed by them to require legal formulation. Originally, as a source to medieval law, customary law served as a font reflecting practice, while written codes told of the authoritarian desire that certain practices should be entertained. When both were united and imposed, law would have the power to change human behavior.

In medicine there was also a distinction to be made between customary practice and written accounts. Customary practice reflected the local practical folk wisdom of disease detection, care, and prevention. Written medical documents circulating in the Middle Ages suggested practical techniques both of local origin and from farther afield. They captured as well the synthesis of theory and practice yielding divisions of the discipline worthy of the titles therapeutics (using diatetics and pharmaceutics, notions of habit and teleology), traumatology (mental and linguistic), preventative medicine (mostly diatetics), surgery and anatomy, symtomatology, and aetiology. The phase of intellectualization of law and medicine which took place over the second half of the Middle Ages was to unite the periodically opposed sources into a more cohesive body of knowledge accessible to students of the professions.

On the Speculative Sciences

Natural Science

For Aristotle, natural science, because of its manifestations in the world, is the first body of knowledge accessible to human experience and understanding. This conception was of both theoretical and practical importance. Robert Grosseteste, the first medieval scholar to have attempted to understand Aristotle's concept of the science of nature, between 1220 and 1240, effectively ensured that the Philosopher would be recognized as having authority to dictate the agenda for its study. While Grosseteste certainly considered the study of nature to be an investigation for the sake of a greater understanding of God, natural science seems to have attained by the end of the Middle Ages a position in which it was really an investigation of Aristotelian inspiration undertaken for the sake of a greater understanding of nature itself. Even before the translations of Aristotle reached the Latin West, another aspect of medieval culture which was to have an impact on its studies of natural science was already flourishing. "Whoever understands the natural world has dominion over it" was espoused by intellectuals and practised by craftsmen from the ninth century onwards, as already alluded to above. This led to the flourishing of the conviction from Marius to Theodoric of Freiburg (d. c.1310) that matters which belong to natural science can be dealt with by observation and "experimentation" and "test." Their persuasion often carried the accompanying reminder that the real aim was to understand not the descriptive aspects of phenomena, but the causal reasons for their occurrence.

But what was the medieval science of nature? Aristotle draws distinctions to yield many divisions: biology, botany, the study of motion (natural or self-motivated and forced motions), the study of growth and decay, mineralogy, meteorology, geology, cosmology, and physics. In the Middle Ages, separate sciences, of weights (*mechanica*) and of optics (*perspectiva*), joined the collection denoted by Aristotle. In the discussion of the grouping of these sciences, medieval writers display an epistemological and ontological understanding which seems to owe virtually nothing to any specifically Christian insight. In many ways, the discussions of classification, method, and content reflect those of a highly philosophical era, with its emphasis upon cumulative analytical analysis rather than inspirational conviction.

To Aristotle and thinkers of the Middle Ages, the divisions of the natural sciences were hardly arbitrary; their scope and relationship were determined on the basis of (their perception of) nature itself. Nature was composed of simple or compound material compositions, and the inanimate and animate. The animate fell into two distinct groups: plants and animals. The animating organ of living bodies, the soul, functioned in distinct ways for distinct classes of living things: vegetative or nutritive in plants, animals, and humans; sensitive in animals and humans; and intellective or rational in humans alone. Natural change was seen to take place distinguishably by motion or by change in size, kind, or characteristic. Aristotle had pointed out that there should be no shortcomings in the systematic investigation of nature, since "scientific knowledge is judgement about things that are universal and necessary, and the conclusions of demonstration, and all scientific knowledge, follow from first principles (for scientific knowledge involves apprehension of a rational ground)."[18]

Investigations into the natural sciences according to the inherited Aristotelian divisions were sustained by even those late medieval thinkers who could find God to be the only universal and necessary being. The divisions would not, in fact, be fundamentally reorganized until the distinction between the sublunary and the supralunary world was no longer considered valid by Kepler and Galileo. Well before this reorganization happened in the seventeenth century, the principles that nature dictates the results of its own investigation, and that a cumulation of information means greater knowledge for human beings of their natural world, had become adopted premises. For all it has been maligned, medieval science in its many branches possessed the strong influence of Aristotelian methodology and with it the sense of accountability on the part of its investigators, recognizing and attempting to avoid reliance on both the shortcomings of opinion and the revelations of faith. Using Aristotelian logic, natural science was the *model* intellectual endeavor.

There are sharp contrasts in the role attributed to logic in the Middle Ages. Aristotle's ideas on logic which entered the Latin West in the first and dominant texts of his works comprised for some an independent field worthy of investigation and expansion. For others logic remained, in Aristotle's perspective, a tool of investigation. The varying attitudes to logic permit the historian also to appreciate the differing importance placed upon various of the speculative sciences. For some, demonstrative knowledge could not be ascertained about anything. Although writers of the late Middle Ages occasionally admitted that "laws" could be stated, their works are replete with passages which clearly imply that affirmations of certainly were impossible.[19]

Earlier scholastics and strict followers of Aristotle were more persuaded that necessity and constancy underlay many aspects of the world, and that the rigors of a logical method could definitely reveal them. Aristotle was careful to lay down the conditions under which a conclusion could be considered certain. Misunderstanding the premises for scientific knowledge, for defining a subject, or for specifying a universal could lead to errors; semantic and logical precision must be adhered to wherever possible. Since a strain of thought which favored a logical (or, at least, a systematic) mode of thinking survived throughout the Middle Ages, various approaches to logic were pointed to as the means by which specific issues might be addressed; for example, Platonic dialectic for the resolution of opposing positions; Aristotelian syllogism for demonstrative affirmation; or the speculative logic of the fourteenth century for the study of "the conceptual order that parallels the synthetic structure internal to the things."[20] The scope and purpose of logic as a domain of abstract thought was thus somewhat changeable. One advantage of a formalized system of medieval education was that the student encountered knowledge ordered, making the organization of thought, however subtly, a "subtext" accessible for being learned. Logic, as such, was also periodically advocated as a subject of direct study, deposing grammar as the premier study and thus further fostering systematic endeavors.

Mathematics

Mathematics in the Middle Ages, like natural science, was both practical and theoretical. Recognizing, along with Plato, number and quantity as fundamental to human abstraction, and, along with Aristotle, a reliance upon the numerical and quantifiable to understand nature, medieval intellectuals periodically reinforced the actual study of mathematics, as medieval artisans sporadically wedded it to their expertise. An oft-reaffirmed medieval conviction was that mathematics permitted knowledge of the real world ("reality" meant either Platonic "Ideas" or Aristotelian "Individuals") through its abstraction from all material aspects of things to the purely quantitative or formal. As material things have quantity and form, the most thorough study of them would inevitably lead to a higher study of quantity and form, that is, to the branches of pure mathematics.

What, however, it might reasonably be asked, comprised the study of mathematics in the Middle Ages? Did the culture, dominated by Christian learning, perceive a use for such study, and its applications? As has already been seen, in the early Middle Ages, although the pure mathematical arts of arithmetic and geometry appeared as part of the quadrivium, their actual role in the curriculum was modest and unsophisticated. Thus clearly many paedagogues thought there was little to be gained from mathematics, and this remained the case until the twelfth century, when philosophy, rather than religion, began to dominate medieval teaching and when the newly translated texts began to offer ideas in mathematics for study. As Al-Khwārizmī's *Introductory Book* (*Liber Ysagogarum*), *Algebra* (*Ludus algebrae et almucgrabalaeque*), and *Astronomical Tables* (*Zīj*), Euclid's *Elements*, Fibonacci's *Book of the Abacus* (*Liber Abaci*), and Archimedes' corpus loomed on the horizon, it seems that the deficiencies of Boethius' textbooks, the encyclopedists' summaries, the Roman *agrimensores'* treatises on surveying, and the compilation on geometry known as *Geometry of Gerbert* (*Geometria Gerberti*), were becoming obvious. The new texts brought both new abstract mathematical ideas and new techniques. The logic of Euclidian and Archimedian justifications and proofs, algorisms, Arabic numerals and a decimal place-value system, and the sexigesimal system of degrees all were newly inherited infusions into medieval mathematics.

Artisans as well as students began to integrate the new mathematical learning into their discourse. Thus, again in the twelfth century, Hugh of St Victor in his *Applied Geometry* (*Practica geometriae*) made a distinction between theoretical and practical geometry: "The theoretical is that which investigates spaces and distances of rational dimensions only by speculative reasoning; the practical is that which is done by means of certain instruments, and which makes judgments by proportionally joining together one thing with another."[21] Hugh also developed a tripartite division of practical geometry: altimetry (the investigation of heights and depths), planimetry (for seeking the extent of a plane), and cosimetry (measurement of the world). Algebra became the tool of such practical investigations with the translation of several texts in the Arabic tradition of measurement. Mathematics was undeniably considered a practical tool in the *scientiae mediae* of the later Middle Ages, optics, mechanics, music, and astronomy, and by medieval master masons in their version of "constructive geometry."[22] None the less, the predominating evidence concerning its investigation and transmission as an independent study reveals that it served the primarily didactic and philosophical abstract role depicted in the classification-schemes of both Platonic and Aristotelian inspiration.

Metaphysics/Theology

As has already been stated, metaphysics and theology were the pinnacle studies in medieval classification-schemes. They were, however, never one and the same. Metaphysics, the classical study of non-corporeal being ("above physics") predated Christianity, and figured in the classification-scheme of Aristotle. Theology did not. However, just as the works of Aristotle were being rendered "Christian" upon their integration into Latin learning, so too was the Aristotelian classification-scheme. Scholastic theology either extended the classification–pyramid higher than metaphysics, or supplanted it entirely.

Metaphysics continued to exist with an independence of subject, although it had its scope determined by Christian doctrine. The theological limits of metaphysics were drawn at the discussion of the number of divine beings and at the explanations provided by other fields of investigation, such as natural science or ethics. The question, for example, "did God create us or we God?" could not find articulation, nor were mysteries (defined as such by other fields) embraced. Medieval metaphysics encompassed vigorous discussions, however, about its "proper" subjects: being (essence and existence), universals, forms, the incorporeal and its nature and relation to the corporeal, *telos* (the end or purpose), time, change, motion, and free will. The content and method of medieval metaphysics were adopted from the extremely influential model of Aristotle's *Metaphysics*.

Medieval theology was far less unified than metaphysics. Before the eleventh century, the Bible and the *ad hoc* conciliar or papal formulation of doctrine had been its only sources of organization. Its foundation was the study of scripture, and exegetical methods rigorized its procedure. Four persons' works were, however, to dramatically alter theological absorption with exegesis and the establishing of doctrine. The *Sentences* (*Quatuor libri sententiarum*) of Peter Lombard and the *Yes and No* of Peter Abelard were to render theology systematic, that is, able to extract, address, and confront Church doctrines and scriptural texts thematically. The *Concordance of Discordant Canons*, or the *Decretum*, of Gratian brought greater organization still to Church theology with its systematic ordering of Church "law." The translations of Aristotle pushed medieval theology yet one step beyond system into speculation.

Medieval theology continued to struggle with contradictions in authoritative statements, within the Bible and within the writings of the Church Fathers and later Christian thinkers, but it also addressed issues whose significance stemmed from their treatment by (Aristotelian) philosophy or other religions. The principal subject-matter of medieval theology remained throughout the Middle Ages the relationship of God and human beings; God's gift of saving grace, and the effect of that gift on his creatures, body and soul. Both eschatology and ecclesiology were thus included in medieval theology. It was particularly these two areas of theology which most touched Christian believers and interested theologians of every stripe, academic or lay, orthodox or heretical. In them theology had its most obvious visage as *praxis* as well as *logos*.

Theologizing the institution of the Church was, as noted in chapters 1 and 2, among the very first preoccupations of intellectual Christians. It was the omnipresent focus on the concept of *ecclesia* that actually transformed the late Middle Ages into the Reformation. Christian ideas on death, judgement, and the future state of the soul also led to abstract theological concepts and to theological change. For a study at the pinnacle of abstract thought, medieval theology was as caught in the practical world as any other human endeavor. Victims of their own highly successful attempts at intellectualizing Christ's teachings, medieval theologians were, however, to be exposed as far less conscious of their remove from the "real world" than any medieval writer on agriculture, economics, or astronomy.[23]

Abstract interpretation by the laity of penitential acts as varied as pilgrimage, confession, indulgences, and flagellation, repeatedly had the disrupting effect of heretically severing practices from the institution. Yet "one cannot find in the literature on confession and penitential practice even a notion that religiously earnest laity may require a distinctive piety of their own, or that a moderated clerical regimen may not be the most satisfying spirituality for laity."[24] In an even more dramatic fashion, abstract lay notions of the true *ecclesia* led some Christians to severe themselves, as an institution, from the Roman Catholic Church. Calvin's true church was "to be found where the gospel is rightly preached, and the sacraments rightly administered – and understood to be included within this definition is a specific form of ecclesiastical institution and administration."[25] Western medieval theology finally reached a point where its abstraction rendered it no longer viably represented by a single institution, the Roman Catholic Church. Yet from longer ago than Boethius, the intellectualizing agenda had been well established. In medieval theology, "purely intellectual concepts were to control the inquiry: 'in divine matters it is necessary to be engaged intellectually.'"[26]

For further reading

David L. Jeffrey, ed., *By Things Seen: Reference and Recognition in Medieval Thought* (Ottawa, 1979).

Norman Kretzmann et al., eds, *The Cambridge History of Later Medieval Philosophy: From the Rediscovery of Aristotle to the Disintegration of Scholasticism 1100–1600* (Cambridge, 1982).

Alain de Libera, *La philosophie médiévale* (Paris, 1989).

David Lindberg, ed., *Science in the Middle Ages* (Chicago History of Science and Medicine: Chicago/London, 1978).

William A. Wallace, *The Elements of Philosophy: A Compendium for Philosophers and Theologians* (Staten Island, NY, 1977).

Lynn White, Jr., *Medieval Religion and Technology* (Berkeley, 1978).

Conclusion

It is suitable that the present book should end with the most practical results of western Christian medieval thought, the disunity
of the institutional construct it had created, the Roman Catholic
Church. The first efforts of Christian intellectuality had been, given
doctrinal diversity, to unite and strengthen the fledgling group of
believers into a cohesive Church. Christian thought had also
struggled to deal with ideas other than those of its own making,
those of the classical liberal arts and philosophy. It had adopted
reason, logic, and a systematic approach before the challenge of
the Aristotelian corpus. With intellectual rigor, Christianity had
developed its own counterpart of Islamic determinism and Greek
rationality, scholasticism. Both reason and contemplation had been
used to maintain and extend, to safeguard and defend, the beliefs,
the ideas, and the edifice of the western medieval Church.

Disintegration of western Christian institutional unity provides a
convenient place to end, for with its schism came the end of the
dominant influence of the Roman Catholic Church on intellectual
activity. What might one say in conclusion about that influence?
First, there were two strains of intellectualization of Christianity: the
internally and the externally motivated. Tests of unity by self-
proclaiming Christians in the form of practical changes or more
intellectual formulations recurred throughout the medieval period.
The response from within, already established among believers of
the first centuries, was to "clarify" the intellectual roots of Christianity and to seek consensus on ideas and rituals as the expression of
the ideas. There were, however, also external catalysts to the intellectualization of Christianity. Greek philosophy was written into the
Gospel of John; Plato's *Timaeus* was a "likely story" of creation;
Aristotle's system of knowledge set metaphysics, or rather theology,
at the top. These all represent periodic jolts to unified Christian
thought during the Middle Ages, to which the Church, its teachers,
theologians, and lay believers responded intellectually.

The Christianization of medieval thought was both progressive and encompassing. Historians have echoed this observation in any number of ways. "The witness of records makes it evident that medieval thought is, summarily, Christian thought."[1] "Medieval thought was governed by its Christian framework."[2] "The intellectual history of the Middle Ages . . . involves a continuing attempt to fit increasing natural knowledge into the unquestioned doctrinal and institutional framework of Christianity . . . The medieval mind continually sought a *summa*, a comprehension of all knowledge as it became available within the framework of basic Christian dogma. The struggle to achieve this *summa*, the contradictions to be resolved and the adjustments and re-definitions to be made, are reflected in the literature and art as well as in the philosophy of the Middle Ages."[3]

By the fourteenth and fifteenth centuries, however, the results of the extremes of theological and philosophical abstraction were revealing their weakness. "The universalism of the Church's authority was the source of the unity of a Christian outlook; on the other hand, it could be maintained only by Christianizing human experience."[4] When the Church lost interest in the human experience, it could be argued, it lost control. Christian intellectualizing had brought about a "divorce between thought and life, and between dialectic and the muses. Life and physical universe no longer continued to supply the philosopher with impetus for thought."[5]

The least abstract of the arts and sciences were to have the most appeal to the immediate successors to medieval intellectuals, Renaissance scholars. History, literature, painting, and the classical technical arts of architecture, military engineering, and sculpture were all continued with great verve beyond the Middle Ages. Although their level of abstraction had increased somewhat in the medieval period, it is more probable that their lack of rarified abstraction,[6] their connection to both life and thought, rendered them both accessible and desirable for study in the new era. Medieval thought had undeniably soared on the wings of Christianity, but with medieval Christianity's attraction to further and further heights of abstraction, it, like Daedalus, only barely escaped being swallowed by the "seas," of the Renaissance and Reformation.

Appendix 1

A Glossary of Philosophical, Theological, and Historical Terms

In English, the standard reference work to consult for the discussion of philosophical terminology is *The Encyclopedia of Philosophy*, ed. P. Edwards (New York, 1967). Useful information can also be provided by the earlier reference works, *Dictionary of Philosophy and Psychology*, ed. J. M. Baldwin (New York, 1928–) and *The Dictionary of Philosophy*, ed. D. D. Runes (New York, 1942). A specialized glossary relating to scholastic philosophy is provided by the *Dictionary of Scholastic Philosophy*, ed. B. Wuellner (Milwaukee, WI, 1956). For a general discussion of theological terminology in English, a reference work to consult is *Dictionary of Theology*, ed. L. Bouyer, tr. C. U. Quinn (New York, 1965).

There are also many terms useful in discussions of medieval thought which are not connected to medieval philosophy or theology. In English, the standard general reference work on the Middle Ages organized according to important terminology or key words is *Dictionary of the Middle Ages*, ed. J. R. Strayer (12 vols: New York, 1982–9). Useful information can also be provided by the shorter reference work, *Dictionary of Medieval Civilization*, ed. J. Dahmus (New York, 1984). Glossaries and analyses of vocabulary relating to specific fields of medieval study also exist. Some of these are mentioned here.

Agriculture
J. L. Fisher, *A Medieval Farming Glossary of Latin and English Words* (London, 1968).

Architecture
J. Harris and J. Lever, *Illustrated Glossary of Architecture: 850–1830* (London, 1966).

Violet-le-Duc, *Dictionnaire raisonné de l'architecture francaise du XIe au XVIe siècle* (10 vols: Paris, 1854–68).

R. Willis, *Architectural Nomenclature of the Middle Ages* (Cambridge, 1844).

Botany

W. T. Stern, *Botanical Latin, History, Grammar, Syntax, Terminology and Vocabulary* (Newton Abbot, England, 1973).

Hunting

D. Dalby, *Lexicon of the Medieval German Hunt* (Berlin, 1965).

Law

A. Berger, *Encyclopedic Dictionary of Roman Law* (Philadelphia, 1953).

R. Naz, *Dictionnaire de droit canonique* (Paris, 1935–).

Music

In his bibliography, *Medieval Music: The Sixth Liberal Art* (Toronto, 1974), A. Hughes lists numerous studies of medieval music terminology. Of them G. Reaney, "Terminology and Medieval Music," in *Festschrift für Heinrich Besseler* (Leipzig, 1961), pp. 149–53 is one of the few in English.

Religion

J. G. Davies, *A Dictionary of Liturgy and Worship* (London, 1972).

J. M. Harden, *Dictionary of the Vulgate New Testament* (London, 1921).

G. W. H. Lampe, *A Patristic Greek Lexicon* (Oxford, 1961).

J. L. McKenzie, *Dictionary of the Bible* (Milwaukee, WI, 1965).

P. K. Meagher, T. C. O'Brian, and C. M. Aherne, *Encyclopedic Dictionary of Religion* (Philadelphia, 1979).

Most interesting recent work in the area of medieval vocabulary is being fostered by the group Comité International du Vocabulaire des Institutions et de la Communication Intellectuelles au Moyen Age (CIVICIMA) founded in 1985. It is publishing a series of studies, *Etudes sur le vocabulaire intellectuel du moyen âge*, pertinent to medieval vocabulary. Thus far:

Terminologie de la vie intellectuelle au moyen âge, ed. O. Weijers (Turnhout, 1988).

Vocabulaire du livre et de l'écriture au moyen âge, ed. O. Weijers (Turnhout, 1989).

The glossary provided here is designed more to enable the reader to pursue further reading in the area of medieval thought than to assist specifically in the understanding of this volume, whose vocabulary, it is hoped, is explained within the body of the text itself.

A silentio
Latin, literally, "from silence." An argument which is not (or cannot be) solidly reinforced with evidence is said to be advanced *a silentio*. For example, historical conclusions about the Middle Ages may have been drawn *a silentio* when evidence concerning certain episodes or ideas is scarce. It is important to recognize *a silentio* conclusions as such to avoid adopting and building upon them with unmerited enthusiasm.

Allegory
Greek, literally, "a speaking otherwise." In ancient times, the term referred to a trope or figure of diction in which one thing is stated in terms of another. It was treated by classical rhetoricians as closely akin to metaphor, by which a particular meaning of a word would be transferred to another thing. Even before the Middle Ages allegory assumed a more general significance which it would retain, classified as a figure of thought whose significations are made explicit and in which any analogy is developed in a relatively regular and sustained way. (See *Exemplum*.)

Ancilla
Latin for "maid" or "servant," found in the scholastic metaphor of philosophy as the handmaiden of theology, "*philosophia ancilla theologiae*." Also used to mean "nun."

Apostolicus
A revered title used at first to denote only the immediate followers of Jesus of Nazareth, then in the Middle Ages applied to any bishop, to be later restricted only to popes.

Auctor or **Auctoritas**
A honorific title of a writer who is deemed to have *augmented* the knowledge and wisdom of humanity. Those classical and Christian writers considered to be *auctores* during the Middle Ages were thought to have already said almost everything worth saying (see pp. 70–3 for the two ways in which writers were honored as *auctoritates*).

Babylonian Captivity
A historical term used to refer to the "captivity" of the papacy in Frankish territory, 1308–78, during which period the popes held court at Avignon (see p. 154). The term alludes to the earlier challenge to the faith of dislocation in the deporting of the Jews to Babylon in the first millennium BC.

Barbarian
A term used by the Romans to designate populations which did not speak either Latin or Greek. With the invasion of such peoples into the heart of the Roman empire, the name became applied pejoratively to describe them, the Huns, Goths, Vandals, etc. collectively, as rude, savage, or uncivilized.

Category
A term of logic dealing with systems of organization according to which everything that exists and/or everything that is conceived is classified. The system of nine categories devised by Aristotle according to both conceivable *and* existing objects was fundamental to all medieval logic.

Christology
The part of Christian theology which is particularly concerned with Jesus Christ. Medieval Christological debates centered around the predominant importance of Jesus' divine or human nature. The Christological positions of Nestorianism and Monophysitism in the fourth century played a significant role in the formulating of Roman Christian orthodox Christology.

Chronicle
A type of medieval written work having something in common with medieval histories in that it recorded the past. Whether universal or particular in character, a chronicle, was often written with picturesque details and anecdotes, to be a pleasing rather than an instructive historical account of the past.

Clerk
From Latin *clericus*. A term used in two major senses. First, it referred to those men who were planning to become priests and had therefore already taken first tonsure (or ritual haircutting) and vows in the form of one or more of the minor orders. Second, it was used to refer to "regulars," those living under a rule (Latin *regula*) in monasteries, friaries, priories, and nunneries, or as priests in a secular setting.

Codex
The term refers to the form of bound book known to the Middle Ages. A codex, usually made of sheets of parchment (or animal hide) of relatively uniform size, on both of whose sides a text had been handwritten, might contain any variety of works between its leather or wooden covers. The study of medieval codices is revealing not only of the state of book technology but also of the kinds of texts which were collected and bound together.

Copyist
One who copies a written text to reproduce it. The degree to which a medieval copyist would reproduce a text without altera-

tion varied greatly. Many types of additions ("scribal inter-polations," as they are known to manuscript editors) and changes to texts can be attributed to copyists (see **Exemplar**). Also known as scribes (Latin *scriptores*), copyists were, in the era before printing, responsible for the availability of almost all written works, some of which were actually dictated to them by the "author."

Courtoisie, Courtly love

A medieval form of amorous relationship in which the love expressed is illicit and potentially adulterous; its immortalization in literature is owed predominantly to the lyric poetry of the medieval French vernaculars.

Deacon

Title denoting a medieval clergyman of rank just below a priest; the second of the three major orders: subdeacon, deacon, priest.

Doctor

From Latin *doctus* meaning "learned." In the Middle Ages "doctor" was not strictly speaking a professional title (as "master" was), but rather it identified one who was acknowledged as learned.

Dominus

A medieval title usually translated as "lord," given to prelates, the lesser nobility, knights, and Benedictine monks.

Double Truth

A term used to refer to a theory or assertion in the later Middle Ages that the studies of philosophy and theology impart two separate truths. This assertion derived from Averroes and was advanced by the Latin Averroists, attributed most notably to Boethius of Dacia. See pp. 88–9.

Ecclesiology

The part of Christian theology which is particularly concerned with understanding what is meant by the Christian "Church" (Latin *ecclesia*). See pp. 19–21. Periodically throughout the Middle Ages, but especially in its later centuries, attention turned to ecclesiology as discussion arose about what group of Christians was considered to comprise the "true Church": the saints, or the saints and clergy alone, or all who affirmed belief. See pp. 152 and 187.

Elements

According to ancient Greek cosmology which was adopted by the Romans and later the medievals, all material things in the universe were made of one or more of the four "elements": Fire, Air, Water, and Earth.

Exegesis
The study of interpreting a written text, usually used with reference to the Bible. Following the hermeneutic (or interpretational) approach of Origen (184–254), medieval exegetes customarily distinguished four possible different levels of interpretation: the *literal or historical sense* (often significantly conveying a statement of fact), the *allegorical sense* (in which facts or events are treated as metaphors), *the tropological or moral sense*, and the *anagogical sense* (in which the meaning alludes to and is thereby seen to uplift toward the eternal mysteries of Christianity). See p. 60.

Exemplar
The model copy of a work which a copyist was to follow. Within medieval university circles the original writer of the work would often approve an exemplar for its reproduction by booksellers and students or their copyists.

Exemplum
A situation, perhaps allegorical, serving as illustration for a moral example or lesson, which was provided or repeated for the benefit of medieval listeners or readers. *Exemplum* could also refer to the specific genre of narrative which employs such illustrative situations to attract the attention of the audience.

Explicit
The closing words or sentences of a written work which in a medieval manuscript may provide the only indication of the author or title of the work (See *Incipit*.)

Hexaemeron
Greek, literally, "of the six days." The term can refer to either the six days of the Creation or to the Biblical text of Genesis (and commentaries) dealing with the Creation.

Illumination
The decoration of a medieval written work by means of gold and silver and colorful inks. The purpose, as well as the origin, of a copy of a medieval written work is often divulged, in part, by the presence of illumination. Works destined to serious textual analysis, as in university circles, were infrequently illustrated, while those prepared for religious display or for the private libraries of the noble or wealthy who were quite possibly illiterate were often embellished with the most elaborately illuminated letters and pictures.

Incipit
The beginning words or sentence of a written work which in a medieval manuscript may provide the only indication of the author or title of the work. (See *Explicit*.)

Library
In the case of medieval monasteries, the term can legitimately rafer to a physical premise given over to books. In the case of medieval academic or royal culture, the term must refer simply to the collection of books owned by an individual, whether housed together or in disparate locations.

Literature
The contemporary working notion of literature comprises only works of fiction: poetry, prose fiction, and plays. To acquire an appreciation of literate activity during the Middle Ages, the notion must be extended to include also nonfiction works: treatises, histories, chronicles, letters, sermons, travel books, and auto-biographies, for at least two reasons. First, in many respects the distinction between fictive and non-fictive works did not play an important part in the medieval typology of texts. Second, in some vernacular languages virtually the only traces of literate activity are non-fictive works.

Liturgy
The verbal and usually scripted portion of a religious service. Although aspects of the Christian liturgy predated the theologiz-ing of Christianity, as Christian belief became a product of theo-logy, the official Christian liturgy would be transformed to reflect changes in orthodox theology. See pp. 17–19.

Middle Ages
An expression (Latin, *medium aevum*) coined by Renaissance humanists to denote the whole period which lay between the fall of classical civilization and the establishment of their own culture. They characterized the period as an intervening or middle age of barbarism between two periods of high cultural achievement.

Opus (pl. ***Opera***)
Latin term for "work," found in expressions such as *magnum opus*, an author's or artist's great or "greatest" work, and *opera omnia*, literally "all the works" of a writer or artist, usually used in reference to the "collected works" of the individual.

Organon
Term used specifically to descibe the corpus of logical works by Aristotle (384/3–322/1BC). Returning to the Greek etymology of the term ("fundamental"), Roger Bacon (thirteenth century) in-cluded also mathematics, optics, and the "experimental sciences" as well as logic within the corpus of his organon.

Orthodoxy
Greek, literally "right opinion." A term which became current in the second century to identify approved religious beliefs as

distinct from beliefs which were not deemed to be "right." Acknowledging an early Christian teaching as orthodox entailed recognizing an individual or institution as the authority to define it as orthodox. The papacy and the Roman Catholic Church would slowly acquire that authority. See pp. 46–9.

Pentateuch
Greek, literally, "five books." The first five books of the Old Testament, Genesis, Exodus, Leviticus, Numbers, Deuteronomy, were called collectively the Pentateuch.

Prime Mover
Aristotle's concept of the ultimate Being, a First Cause of all change or motion. With Christian reception of Aristotelian ideas the Prime Mover was transformed into God.

Quadrivium
A late Roman division of knowledge into arithmetic, geometry, music, and astronomy. Together the trivium and quadrivium formed the medieval corpus of the liberal arts. Throughout the early Middle Ages the quadrivium was thought to encompass the scientific part of learning. When the works of Aristotle began to influence medieval categories and paedagogy, however, the quadrivium was recognized to have allotted no place to natural philosophy or physics and to quasi-mathematical sciences other than music and astronomy, such as mechanics and optics. The "new learning" caused the dissolution of the quadrivium.

Question
A technical term of the scholastic method, meaning the discussion of a stated issue which is considered polemical.

Renaissance
Literally, "rebirth." It might be most broadly defined as a rebirth or reawakening to Greek and Roman cultures with their intellectual artifacts after a period in which such cultures figured little. The term was orignally, and continues to be, used normatively, setting the "renaissance" in question as a positive change out of a "dark age" or setback in the general knowledge of a culture. See further Warren Treadgold, *Renaissances before the Renaissance: Cultural Revivals of Late Antiquity and the Middle Ages* (Stanford, 1984).

Rumination
The audible "chewing over" of the words of a text as it is being read. For most of the Middle Ages the reader was dependent upon hearing as well as seeing the text. Due to its oral component most reading was thus, even within the monasteries, an act of performance.

Sacrament
A Christian religious ritual commemorating events significant to the life of Jesus and in the lives of believers thereafter, as it is believed to impart the truth and grace of Christian mystery. Baptism and the Eucharist, or commemoration of the Last Supper of Jesus and his apostles, were the earliest sacraments practised by Christians. See p. 10. By the thirteenth century, the Roman Church had recognized in theology and ritual five more sacraments: confirmation, penance, marriage, ordination, and extreme unction.

Schism
A dramatic break in the formal unity within the Church. It might stem from doctrinal disagreements, as in the case of early Church ruptures, or from deliberate organizational fracture, as was the case when more than one pope had come to be elected. One period in medieval religious history has come to be denoted as the period of the "Great Schism," 1378–1417, during which time the Church found itself in the difficult situation of comprising factions who recognized as legitimate the reign of two different popes, one in Rome and one in Avignon.

Septuagint
Translation of the Old Testament of the Bible into Greek, dated to the third century BC.

Translatio studii
A medieval Latin *topos* wich encapsulated a general notion about the historical transmission (*translatio*), or evolution, of western learning (*studii*) or culture according to which knowledge originated in ancient Greece, was carried to Rome, and then brought in the Middle Ages to specific locations in Europe (Aachen, Paris, Germania).

Transmontane (or **Cismontane**)
Adjective or noun referring to the culture or the people of north of the Alps; hence in the Middle Ages it refers to the Frankish and Germanic cultures and peoples as distinct from the medieval Roman (religious) culture and people. (See **Ultramontane**.)

Transubstantiation
A doctrine stated formally by the Roman Christian Church in 1215 that in the celebration of the Eucharist the bread and wine, though they appear unchanged, actually become the body and blood of Christ. See p. 150.

Trivium
A division of knowledge into grammar, rhetoric, and dialectic or logic. Together the trivium and quadrivium formed the medieval

corpus of the liberal arts. Throughout the Middle Ages, the trivium was thought to assure the teaching of the use of language in the correct way through grammar, in the ornate way through rhetoric, and in the truthful way through logic. Grammar was the study of the use of words and rules for their interconnection. Rhetoric taught of the ways to organize, deliver, express, and evoke words to convey a desired meaning. Logic was the study of the quality of reasoning behind language constructions.

Ultramontane
Adjective or noun referring to the culture or the people of the culture south of the Alps. It has come to refer most specifically to the Italian religious and political culture of the Middle Ages or its legacy fostered by the papacy or those sympathetic it. (See **Transmontane**.)

Vulgate
A term of two related uses. Vulgate refers to the Latin translation of the Bible which was predominantely executed by Jerome (d. 420). Jerome's Old and New Testament combined with earlier translations of the missing Psalms, from the Gallican Psalter, and the apocryphal books of Wisdom, Ecclesiastics, I and II Maccabees, and Baruch, from the Old Latin Version of the Bible, to form the most popular version of the Bible in circulation throughout the whole of the Middle Ages. Vulgate can also mean the type of Latin in use during Jerome's day and thereafter. Less sophisticated than classical Ciceronian Latin, it was known as Vulgar Latin or Vulgate.

Writer
The term may evoke the contemporary meaning of one who makes a living by writing books; however, as applied to the Middle Ages, it can only mean "one who writes or has written his/her own works." While an appropriate title for the many medievals who either added clarification to another's text by way of commentary or wrote primarily on their own, the term ought not to suggest their profession. Very few medieval writers were able to make a living from their writing (see **Copyist**).

Appendix 2

Major Primary Sources and English Translations

The ultimate source of almost all medieval works is the parchment manuscript, housed today in library archives or private collections. These were written in Greek, and in the varieties of medieval Latin, Arabic, Hebrew, and vernacular languages; often the handwriting was difficult to read originally, not to mention now with the wear and tear of time on the pages. Fortunately the subject of medieval intellectual history is increasingly well served with printed editions of the extant works of the period. These editions are extremely useful, whether they take the form of a clean transcription of a single manuscript's text or a critical reconstruction of the author's original work from all extant manuscripts. Due to the abundance of editions, only the most recent comprehensive ones of single author works, still in progress, will be identified here. It is to be noted that many others can be found in the series of text editions listed under Primary Source Abbreviations in appendix 3, and that the edition of any individual works would appear in a library's catalogue under the medieval author's name.

Albertus Magnus, *Opera omnia*, ed. B. Geyer (Munster i. W., 1951–).
This new critical edition is undertaken by the Albertus Magnus Institute in Cologne and is often referred to as the Cologne edition.
Thomas Aquinas, *Opera omnia*, Leonine edition (Rome, 1882–).
Aristotle, *Aristoteles Latinus*, eds L. Minio-Paluello et al. (Bruges/ Paris, 1961–).
Augustine, *Opera omnia* (Turnholt, 1956–).
This is a new critical edition of Augustine in the *Corpus Christianorum* series.

Averroes, *Corpus Commentariorum Averrois in Aristotelem*, eds H. A. Wolfson, D. Baneth, and F. H. Fobes (Cambridge, MA, 1958–).

Avicenna, *Avicenna Latinus*, ed. S. Van Riet (Louvain/Leiden, 1968–).

John Duns Scotus, *Opera omnia*, ed. C. Balic (Vatican City, 1950–).

In addition to editions, translations of medieval works are also often very useful. There exist publishers' collections which specialize in or include the publication of ancient and medieval works in translation. The following collections provide translations into English:

Everyman's Library (London/New York: J. M. Dent and Co./E. P. Dutton and Co.).

Fathers of the Church, a new Translation (Washington, DC: Catholic University Press of America).

The Garland Library of Medieval Literature (New York: Garland).

Great Books of the Western World (Chicago: Encyclopedia Britannica).

The Library of Christian Classics (Philadelphia/London: Westminster Press/SCM Press).

The Library of Liberal Arts (Indianapolis: The Bobbs-Merrill Co., Inc.).

The Loeb Classical Library (Boston, MA/London: Harvard University Press/William Heinemann Ltd).

Medieval Sources in Translation (Toronto: Pontifical Institute of Medieval Studies).

The Modern Library (New York: The Modern Library.).

The Norton Anthology of . . . (New York: W. W. Norton and Co., Inc.).

Pengiun Classics (Harmondsworth, England/New York: Penguin Books).

Two kinds of compilations of translations are also very useful: bibliographies of works in translation and anthologies of text selections in translation. Suggested bibliographies are the following:

C. P. Farrar and A. P. Evans, *Bibliography of English Translations from Medieval Sources* (New York, 1946).

M. A. Ferguson, *Bibliography of English Translations from Medieval Sources 1943–1967* (New York, 1974).

See also the serials *Speculum* (1973–) and *Repertorium Fontium Historiae Medii Aevi* (Rome, 1962–) for listings.

Collections of medieval "readings" translated into English are quite numerous. The following collections might be interesting:

H. Adelson, ed., *Medieval Commerce* (Princeton, NJ, 1962).

M. Alexander and F. Riddy, eds, *The Middle Ages 700–1550* (Macmillan Anthologies of English Literature, Vol. 1: Houndsmills, England, 1989).

M. W. Baldwin, ed., *Christianity Through the Thirteenth Century* (Documentary History of Western Civilization: New York/London, 1970)

H. Bettenson, ed., *Documents of the Christian Church* (The World's Classics, 495: London, 1959).

N. Cantor, ed., *The Medieval World 300–1300* (New York/London, 1963).

L. Clendening, ed., *Source Book of Medical History* (New York, 1960).

J. Collins, ed., *Readings in Ancient and Medieval Philosophy* (Westminster, MD, 1960).

A. S. Cook and C. B. Tinker, eds, *Select Translations from Old English Prose* (Boston, MA, 1935).

E. R. Fairweather, ed., *A Scholastic Miscellany: Anselm to Ockham* (The Library of Christian Classics, 10: Philadelphia, 1956).

R. K. Gordon, tr., *Anglo-Saxon Poetry* (Everyman's Library, New York, 1954).

E. Grant, ed., *A Source Book in Medieval Science* (Cambridge, MA, 1974).

D. Herlihy, ed., *Medieval Culture and Society* (New York, 1968).

C. W. Hollister et al., eds, *Medieval Europe: A Short Source-book* (New York, 1982).

A. Hyman and J. J. Walsh, eds, *Philosophy in the Middle Ages: The Christian, Islamic and Jewish Traditions* (Indianapolis, IN, 1973).

C. W. Kennedy, tr., *An Anthology of Old English Poetry* (New York, 1960).

R. Lerner and M. Mahdi, eds and trs, *Medieval Political Philosophy: A Sourcebook* (Ithaca, NY, 1963).

B. Lewis, ed. and tr., *Islam from the Prophet Muhammad to the Capture of Constantinople* (2 vols: New York/Oxford, 1987).

R. McKeon, ed. and tr., *Selections from Medieval Philosophers* (2 vols: New York, 1929/30).

W. H. McNeill and S. Houser, eds, *Medieval Europe* (London, 1971).

A. S. Preminger, O. B. Hardison, and K. Kerrane, eds, *Classical and Medieval Literary Criticism: Translations and Interpretations* (New York, 1974).

H. Shapiro, ed., *Medieval Philosophy* (New York, 1964).

D. Sherman, ed., *Western Civilization*, vol. 1: *Images and Interpretations* (New York, 1983).

B. Tierney, *The Crisis of Church and State 1050–1300* (Englewood Cliffs, NJ, 1964).

B. Tierney, ed., *The Middle Ages*, vol. 1: *Sources of Medieval History* (1970, New York: 4th ed., 1983).

C. Vollert, L. Kendzierski, and P. Byrne, eds, *On the Eternity of the World* (Milwaukee, WI, 1964).

K. M. Wilson, ed, *Medieval Women Writers* (Athens, GA, 1984).

J. F. Wippel and A. B. Wolter, eds, *Medieval Philosophy from St Augustine to Nicholas of Cusa* (New York, 1969).

Appendix 3

Standard Abbreviations of Major Sources and Journals

Works of frequent use by modern scholars of the Middle Ages are often denoted by abbreviations. Although it is important to be aware of these abbreviations, in the context of an introductory look at medieval thought it is even more useful to know of the existence of the works in question. This appendix with its list of abbreviations offers thus some of the more significant and fundamental journals and source series available for the study of medieval intellectual history. This list should prove especially helpful if consulted in conjunction with appendices 2 and 4.

A listing of many abbreviations designating works of secondary literature can also be found in J. S. Wellington, *Dictionary of Bibliographic Abbrevations Found in the Scholarship of Classical Studies and Related Disciplines* (Westport, CT, 1983) and S. Schwertner, *Internationales Abkürzungsverzeichnis für Theologie und Grenzgebiete* (Berlin/New York: de Gruyter, 1974), itself abbreviated frequently as *IATG*.

Primary Sources

ANTS   The Anglo-Norman Text Society (Oxford).

Archives   *Archives d'histoire doctrinale et littéraire du moyen âge* (Paris, 1926–).

AS   *Acta Sanctorum ex latinis et graecis aliarumque gentium antiquis monumentis* (Paris, 1863–75).

ASPR   *The Anglo-Saxon Poetic Records* (6 vols: London and New York, 1931–42).

Beiträge, BGPM   *Beiträge zur Geschichte der Philosophie des Mittelalters* (43 vols: Munster i. W., 1891–1980; new series: 1970–).

CCCM   *Corpus Christianorum Continuatio Mediaevalis* (Turnholt, 1971–).

CCSL   *Corpus Christianorum, Series Latina* (Turnholt, 1954–).
CFMA   *Les classiques français du Moyen Age* (Paris, 1910–).
CIC   *Corpus Iuris Canonici* (2 vols: Graz, 1959).
CICiv   *Corpus Iuris Civilis* (3 vols: Berlin, 1872–1908).
CIMAGL   *Cahiers l'institut du moyen-âge grec et latin* (Copenhagen).
CPD   *Corpus Philosophorum Danicorum Medii Aevi* (Copenhagen, 1955–).
CPMA   *Corpus Platonicum Medii Aevii* (London, 1943–).
CPR   Calendar of Patent Rolls (Public Record Office, London).
CSEL   *Corpus Scriptorum Ecclesiasticorum Latinorum* (Vienna, 1866–).
EETS   Early English Text Society, Original, Extra and Supplementary Series (London).
MGH   *Monumenta Germaniae Historica* (Stuttgart, 1938–).
Migne, *MPL, Pat. Lat., Patrologia Latina, PL*   J. P. Migne, *Patrologiae, cursus completus, Patres Ecclesiae, Series Latina* (221 vols: Paris, 1844–64); *Supplementum*, ed. A. Hamman (Paris, 1958).
Migne, *PG*   J. P. Migne, *Patrologiae, cursus completus, Patres Ecclesiae, Series Graeca* (162 vols: Paris, 1857–66).
Nelson's   Nelson's Medieval Classics, eds V. H. Galbraith and R. A. B. Mynors (London).
PBel   *Les philosophes belges. Textes et études* (Louvain).
PIMS   *Pontifical Institute of Medieval Studies, Toronto. Studies and texts* (Toronto).
PM   *Philosophes médiévaux* (Louvain).
REED   Records of Early English Drama (Toronto, 1979–).
Rolls Series, RS   *Rerum Britannicarum Medii Aevii Scriptores*, or *Chronicles and Memorials of Great Britain and Ireland* (published under the direction of the Master of the Rolls: London, 1858–).
SATF   Société des anciens texts français (Paris, 1875–).
SBon   *Spicilegium bonaventurianum* (Grottaferrata).
SC   *Sources Chrétiennes*, eds H. de Lubac and J. Daniélou (Paris, 1941–).
SRG   *Scriptores Rerum Germanicarum* (Hanover).
SSL   *Spicilegium sacrum lovaniense. Etudes et documents* (Louvain, 1922).
YMT   York Medieval Texts (London).

Secondary Sources and Journals

AHDLMA   *Archives d'histoire doctrinale et littéraire du moyen âge* (Paris, 1926/27–).
DNB   *Dictionary of National Biography*, eds L. Stephen and S. Lee

(vols 1–63, suppl. vols: London, 1885–1901, 1949–).

DSB Dictionary of Scientific Biography, ed. C. Gillisby (New York, 1970–8).

DTC Dictionnaire de théologie catholique (Paris, 1923–50).

FcS Franciscan Studies (St Bonaventure, NY, 1924; new series: 1941–).

FS Franziskanische Studien (Munster i. W.).

MM Miscellanea Mediaevalia (Berlin, 1962; New York, 1971–).

MRS Medieval and Renaissance Studies (Champaign, IL, 1971–).

MS Medieval Studies (New York, 1939–40; Toronto, 1941–).

RSPT Revue des sciences philosophiques et théologiques (Paris).

RTAM Recherches de théologie ancienne et médiévale (Louvain, 1929–).

SBAW Sitzungsberichte der bayerischen Akademie der Wissenschaften, Philosophisch-theologische und historische Klasse (Munich).

SM Studi medievali 3a Serie (Spoleto, 1960–).

Appendix 4
Tools for Using Manuscripts

Many studies of the Middle Ages assume their readers are familiar with the languages and sources of medieval texts. Interpreting references to primary documents or understanding the original languages is often considered an essential part of reading those studies. Material presented under this assumption can appear quite foreboding. The purpose of this appendix is to equip the reader with references to some works which might be of use should he or she to choose to pursue paleography (the art or science of deciphering manuscripts) and the study of medieval Latin or vernacular languages.

Paleography

B. Bischoff, *Latin Paleography, Antiquity and the Middle Ages*, trs D. O. Croinin and D. Ganz (Cambridge, 1990).
L. E. Boyle, *Medieval Latin Paleography: A Bibliographical Introduction* (Toronto, 1984).
A. Cappelli, *Dizionario di abbreviature latine ed italiane* (Milan, 1961).

A few works have appeared within the last decade acknowledging the wonderful assistance computer technology is beginning to offer manuscript scholars. Among them are:

R. F. Allen, ed., *Data Bases in the Humanities and Social Sciences* (Proceedings of the annual International Conference on Data Bases in the Humanities and Social Science: Osprey, FL, 1983–).
A. Glimour-Bryson, ed., *Computer Applications to Medieval Studies* (Kalamazoo, MI, 1984).
N. L. Hahn and J. B. Smith, *The Benjamin Data Bank and BAG/2. A Case History and User Manual for Encoding, Storing and Retrieving Information on Medieval Manuscripts* (Francis S. Benjamin Data

Bank of Medieval Scientific Manuscripts in Latin: Dunellen, NJ, 1983).

R. C. Van Caenegem and F. L. Ganshof, *Guide to the Sources of Medieval History*, Part V, Ch. 8 (Amsterdam, 1978).

Medieval Latin

M. R. P. McGuire, *Introduction to Medieval Latin Studies, a Syllabus and Bibliographical Guide* (Washington, DC, 1965).

K. Strecker, *Introduction to Medieval Latin*, tr. and rev. by R. B. Palmer (Berlin, 1957).

There are several useful dictionaries of medieval Latin. The most comprehensive to date is:

C. du Fresne du Cange, *Glossarium Mediae et Infimae Latinitatis (Lexicon of Mediaeval Latin)*, rev. by L. Favre (10 vols: Graz, 1954).

There are many others, either in process, more specialized, or simply less ambitious:

R. E. Latham, *Revised Medieval Latin Word-List* (London, 1965).
A Latin–English Dictionary of St Thomas Aquinas based on the Summa Theologica *and selected passages of his other works* (Boston, MA, 1960).
Mediae Latinitatis Lexicon Minus (Leyden, 1954). Definitions are given in English and French.
Mittellateinisches Wörterbuch bis zum ausgehenden 13. Jahrhundert (Munich, 1960–).
Novum Glossarium Mediae latinitatis, ab anno DCCC usque ad annum MCC, eds Fr. Arnaldi et al. (Copenhagen, 1957–) Definitions in French.
A. Souter, *Glossary of Later Latin* (Oxford, 1949). Especially valuable for the study of the early Church Fathers.

For study of the language itself the following works could be useful:

K. P. Harrington, *Mediaeval Latin* (Chicago, 1962) and the companion guidebook, J. Heironimus, *Latin 563, Medieval Latin* (Madison, WI, 1971).
E. Lofstedt, *Late Latin* (Oslo, 1959).

Vernacular Languages

English

Dictionary of Old English (Toronto, 1986–).
A Manual of the Writings in Middle English, 1050–1500; vols 1–2, ed.
J. B. Severs; vols 3–, ed. A. E. Hartung (New Haven, CT, 1969–).
A. H. Marckwardt and J. L. Rosier, *Old English: Language and Literature* (New York, 1972).
H. Sweet, *The Student's Dictionary of Anglo-Saxon* (New York, 1911).
J. R. R. Tolkien, *A Middle English Vocabulary* (Oxford, 1925).

Also:

M. W. Bloomfield and L. Newmark, *A Linguistic Introduction to the History of English* (New York, 1963).
G. L. Brook, *A History of the English Language* (London, 1960).

French

J. Anglade, *Grammaire élémentaire de l'ancien français* (Paris, 1965).
Ch. Bruneau, *Petite histoire de la langue française: Des origines à la Révolution* (Paris, 1969).
E. Einhorn, *Old French: a concise handbook* (Cambridge, 1974).
F. E. Godefroy, *Dictionnaire de l'ancienne langue française* (Paris, 1881–1902).
M. K. Pope, *From Latin to Modern French with Especial Consideration of Anglo-Norman* (Manchester, 1956).

German

L. Armitage, *An Introduction to the Study of Old High German* (Oxford, 1911).
C. C. Barber, *An Old High German Reader* (Oxford, 1951).
W. Braune, *Althochdeutsche Grammatik* (Halle, 1925).
—— , *Althochdeutsches Lesebuch* (Halle, 1928).
F. Jelinek, *Mittelhochdeutsches Wörterbuch* (Heidelberg, 1911).
A. Lubben, *Mittelniederdeutsche Grammatik* (Osnabruck, 1970).
R. Schutzeichel, *Althochdeutsches Wörterbuch* (Tubingen, 1969).
K. Weinhold, *Kleine Mittlhochdeutsche Grammatik*, re-ed. G. Ehrismann (Vienna, 1947).

Appendix 5

Bibliographies of Medieval Thought

The present volume contains its own bibliography of selected works concerning medieval thought. Awareness of much more comprehensive and/or specialized bibliographies is, however, also essential, particularly in the field of medieval intellectual history which has so many dimensions. There are two types of bibliographies important in the study of medieval thought: bibliographies of primary source documents and bibliographies of secondary works. In the case of the study of the Middle Ages, bibliographies of primary source documents are simply catalogues of medieval manuscripts, organized variously according to their present archival location, attributed authorship, subject matter or period, etc. Manuscript listings pertinent to a particular investigation might therefore be located by surveying either the catalogues of the holdings of major and minor manuscript archives (often connected to the world's most prominent museums), the introductions to modern editions of a particular medieval author's work, or works dedicated to listing manuscripts related according to their subject matter or general date of execution. For the names of medieval writers after 1100, the following is useful: A. Franklin, *Dictionnaire des noms, surnoms et pseudonymes latins de l'histoire littéraire du moyen âge* (Paris, 1875). Some further information for locating primary sources is provided in appendices 2 and 3.

The abundant bibliographies of secondary literature are also very important to the study of medieval intellectual history. They are of two kinds: works published at one point in time containing bibliographic information on, in their authors' opinion, the most useful works published to date; and bibliographies which incorporate only the most recently appeared work and are themselves published serially. Both kinds of bibliographies can prove to be extremely useful: the former, for the preselection and overview an author's choice might provide and the latter, for its notice of most recent publications. The following are suggestions for both kinds of bibliographies.

Bibliographic Monographs

These are general bibliographies. While many fine specialized bibliographies exist, none specific to a single author or narrow subject has been included here.

G. C. Boyce, *Literature of Medieval History, 1930–1975: A Supplement to Louis J. Paetow's "A Guide to the Study of Medieval History"* (5 vols: New York, 1981).

R. C. van Caenegem and F. L. Ganshof, *Guide to the Sources of Medieval History* (Amsterdam, 1978).

S. J. Case et al., *A Bibliographical Guide to the History of Christianity* (New York, 1951).

O. Chadwick, *The History of the Church: A Select Bibliography* (Historical Association, London, 1962).

J. H. Fisher, ed., *The Medieval Literature of Western Europe: A Review of Research, Mainly 1930–1960* (New York, 1966).

K. Koerner, "Medieval Linguistic Thought: A Comprehensive Bibliography," in *Studies in Medieval Linguistic Thought Dedicated to Geoffrey L. Bursill-Hall*, ed. E. F. K. Koerner (Amsterdam, 1980), pp. 265–99.

J. de Menasce, *Arabische Philosophie* (Bibliographische Einführungen in das Studium der Philosophie, vol. 6: Bern, 1948).

L. J. Paetow, *A Guide to the Study of Medieval History*, rev. by G. C. Boyce and an addendum by L. Thorndike (New York, 1980).

F. van Steenberghen, *Philosophie des Mittelalters* (Bibliographische Einführungen in das Studium der Philosophie, vol. 17: Bern, 1950).

E. A. Synan, "Latin Philosophies of the Middle Ages," in *Medieval Studies: An Introduction*, ed. J. M. Powell (Syracuse, NY, 1976), pp. 277–311.

G. Vajda, *Jüdische Philosophie* (Bibliographische Einführungen in das Studium der Philosophie, vol. 19: Bern, 1950).

D. A. Zesmer and S. B. Greenfield, *Guide to English Literature from Beowulf through Chaucer and Medieval Drama* (College Outline Series: New York, 1961).

Bibliographic Series and Review Journals

R. H. Rouse, *A Guide to Serial Bibliographies for Medieval Studies* (Berkeley, 1969).
This bibliography covers about 283 journals in various languages.

Generally each issue in these series lists articles, notes etc. in journals (up to 759 in number), Festschriften, colloquium papers, and collected essays, for a specific period.

Bibliographische Einführungen in das Studium de Philosophie (Bern).

Bibliography of the History of Medicine (US Department of Health, Education, and Welfare: Bethesda, MD, 1965–).

This bibliography, covering all chronological periods and geographical areas, is divided into three parts: biographies, subjects, and authors.

Cahiers de civilisation médiévale Xe–XIIe siècles (Poitiers, 1958–).

The journal includes an annual bibliographic supplement, with a list of authors, places, and subjects.

S. Forde, present ed., *International Medieval Bibliography* (Leeds, 1967–).

A list of the publications included is presented at the opening. The Bibliography is organized thematically within the chronological limits of AD 450–1500.

Garland Medieval Bibliographies, Garland Reference Library of the Humanities (New York).

Isis Cumulative Bibliography (Philadelphia, 1966–75; 1976–85).

Mediaeval and Renaissance Studies (London, 1941–).

Medieval Studies (New York, 1939–40; Toronto, 1941–).

Medium Aevum (London, 1932–59; Oxford, 1960–).

Moyen Age (Brussels, 1888–).

Rassegna di Letteratura Tomistica (Rome/Naples, 1966–).

Rassegna continues the work of the no-longer-published *Bulletin thomiste* (Le Saulchoir, Etiolles, Seine et Oise).

Recherches de théologie ancienne et médiévale (Louvain, 1929–).

Répertoire bibliographique de la philosophie (Louvain, 1949–).

Revue d'histoire ecclésiastique (Louvain, 1900–).

Three times a year the journal carries a comprehensive bibliography of books and articles related to church history.

Scriptorium (Antwerp-Brussels 1946/47–68; Ghent, 1969–).

Since vol. 13 (1959), annotated bibliographies are a part of each issue.

Speculum (Cambridge, MA, 1926–).

Studi Medievali (Torino, 1904–13; Nuova Serie: 1928–52; 3a Serie: Spoleto, 1960–).

Technology and Culture (Chicago, 1959/60–).

Traditio (New York, 1943–).

Vivarium (Assen, 1963–73; Leiden, 1974–).

Reference Volumes (Dictionaries, Encyclopedias)

Most reference volumes, while important for their own articles, also frequently include bibliographic information as part of their entries.

Dictionary of the Middle Ages, ed. J. R. Strayer (New York, 1982–).
Dictionnaire de spiritualité ascetique et mystique (Paris, 1932–).
Dictionnaire de théologie Catholique (Paris, 1951–70).
Encyclopedia Britannica (New York, 1989).
Encyclopedia of Islam (Leiden/Paris, 1989).
Encyclopedia of Religion, ed. M. Eliade (New York, 1987–).
The New Catholic Encyclopaedia (15 vols: San Francisco, 1967).
F. Van Der Meer and C. Mohrmann, *Atlas of the Early Christian World* (London, 1958).

Appendix 6

Chronology of Political and Intellectual History

For further chronological information, the following could be consulted:

C. Capelli, *Cronologia, cronografia e calandario perpetuo* (Milan, 1930).
C. R. Cheney, *Handbook of Dates for Students of English History* (London, 1970).
F. Lebrun et al., *Les grandes dates du christianisme* (Paris, 1989).
R. D. Ware, "Medieval Chronology: Theory and Practice," in *Medieval Studies: An Introduction*, ed. J. M. Powell (Syracuse, NY, 1976), pp. 213–37.

Many surveys of medieval history include chronological lists of the popes, emperors, and medieval ruling houses. Useful chronological information can be found as well in the following reference works:

Encyclopedia of the Papacy, ed. H. Kuhner, tr. K. J. Northcott (New York, 1958).

C. McEvedy, *The Penguin Atlas of Medieval History* (Harmondsworth, England, 1983).

c.0–c.33	Life of Jesus of Nazareth.
48	Council of Jerusalem, first Christian church council.
48–62	Christian apostle Paul's missionary journeys.
189–c.199	Pontificate of Victor, first Latin-speaking pope.
c.270	Saint Anthony establishes himself in the desert.
303–6	Great persecution of Christians begins under Diocletian.
306–37	Reign of Constantine, first emperor to recognize Christianity.

311	Donatist schism begins.
325	Council of Nicaea. Nicaean Creed formulated.
330	Dedication of Constantinople, capital of eastern Roman empire.
339–97	Saint Ambrose of Milan, Christian theologian.
354–430	Saint Augustine of Hippo, Christian theologian.
383	Saint Jerome begins his translation of the Bible.
395	Final Division of the eastern and western Roman empires.
410	Visigoths under Alaric sack Rome, a mortal blow to Roman power.
440–61	Pontificate of Leo I the Great. He deters Huns from attacking the city of Rome.
451	Council of Chalcedon. Chalcedonian definition formulated.
475	Last western Roman emperor deposed by barbarian Odovacar.
c.480–523	Boethius, late Roman intellectual.
481–511	Clovis rules Franks, converts to Christianity.
493–526	Theodoric the Ostrogoth rules Italy for eastern emperor.
501	Law of the Burgundians, *Loi Gombette*, in writing.
506	Law of the Visigoths, *Breviary* of Alaric, in writing.
508	*Salic Law* of the Franks in writing.
514–84	fl. Cassiodorus, late Roman statesman and educator.
527–65	Reign of Justinian, eastern emperor.
529	Completion of the first part of the Justinian code of law (*codex*).
533	Completion of the Justinian code of law, *Digest* and *Institutes*.
c.534	Composition of the Benedictine *Rule* of Benedict of Nursia.
c.571–632	Muhammad, founder of the Muslim faith.
c.590	Founding of the monastery of Luxeuil by monk Colomban.
596	Augustine of Canturbury's conversionary mission to England.
622	The hegira to Medina, beginning date of the Muslim calendar.
661–750	Umayyad Dynasty at Damascus, conquers North Africa and Spain.
664	Synod of Whitby. Roman liturgy dominates Celtic in England.

687	Carolingian Dynasty asserts power through Pepin of Heristal.
732	Arabs defeated at Tours by Carolingians under Charles Martel.
750–1258	Abbasid Dynasty at Baghdad.
768–814	Reign of Charlemagne, King of the Franks.
800	Charlemagne crowned Holy Roman Emperor in Rome by Pope Leo III.
842	Oaths of Strasbourg, vernacular document in Frankish languages.
865	Great army of Danes lands in Anglo-Saxon England.
871–99	Reign of Alfred, uniting of Anglo-Saxon kingdoms.
909–10	Founding of the monastery of Cluny and the Cluniac Order.
936–73	Reign of Otto the Great. Ottonian cultural revival.
c.980–1037	Ibn Sīnā (Avicenna), Muslim intellectual.
987–1328	Rule of Capetian Dynasty, replaces Carolingian Dynasty.
999–1003	Pontificate of Gerbert of Aurillac, Pope Sylvester II.
1033–1109	Anselm of Canterbury, theologian.
1060–91	Sicily conquered by Normans.
c.1065	Composition of *Chanson de Roland*.
1066	Norman Conquest of England; Norman *langue d'öil* in England.
1066–87	Reign of William the Conqueror as King of England.
1073–85	Pontificate of Gregory VII, rival of Holy Roman Emperors.
1076	Council of Worms over episcopal investiture privileges.
1079–1142	Peter Abelard, intellectual.
1085	Capture of Toledo from Arabs by Christians in *Reconquista*.
1085	Compilation of the *Doomsday Book*, Norman "census" in England.
1090–1153	Bernard of Clairvaux, prominant Cistercian theologian.
1093–1109	Romanesque Durham Cathedral (England) built.
1095	Calling of the First Crusade at the Council of Clermont.

1098/9	Monastery of Citeaux founded. Beginnings of Cistercian Order.
1099	First Crusaders take Jerusalem.
c.1115–1180	John of Salisbury, intellectual.
1122	Concordat of Worms, resolution of investiture struggle.
1126–98/99	Ibn Rushd (Averroes), Muslim intellectual.
c.1132–c.1140	Gothic reconstruction begins at the monastery of St-Denis.
1135–1204	Moses Maimonides, Jewish philosopher.
1140	Gratian complies *The Concordance of Discordant Canons (Decretum)* of canon law.
1147	Second Crusade. City of Lisbon (Portugal) captured.
c.1150	Peter Lombard produces his book of *Sentences*.
1158	Emperor Frederick I Barbarossa issues *Authenticum Habita*.
1170–1221	Domingo de Guzman (Saint Dominic), founder of Dominican Order.
1182–1226	Saint Francis of Assisi, founder of Franciscan Order.
1187	Jerusalem taken from the Crusaders by Saladdin.
1189	Third Crusade launched to recapture Jerusalem.
1198–1216	Pontificate of Innocent III.
1199–1216	Reign of King John of England.
c.1200–1280	Albertus Magnus (Albert the Great), intellectual.
1200	Parisian *universitas* chartered by French King Philip II.
1203–4	Loss of Normandy by the English to the French Crown.
1204	Fourth Crusade. Crusaders take Constantinople.
1208/9–29	Pope Innocent III's crusade against heretic Albigensians.
1214–92	Roger Bacon, intellectual.
1215	Fourth Lateran Council.
1215	Magna Carta, English monarchy rendered subject to law of land.
1217–74	Saint Bonaventure, theologian.
1224	Emperor Frederick II founds the University of Naples.
c.1225–1274	Thomas Aquinas, theologian.
1252	Papal decretal *Ad extirpanda* permits torture in inquisitions.

c.1254–1324	Marco Polo, explorer to China from Italy.
1265–1308	John Duns Scotus, intellectual.
1265–1321	Dante Alighieri, Italian writer.
1274	Second Council of Lyons, ideas of Thomas Aquinas defended.
1275–1324	Marsiglio of Padua, political writer.
1277	Condemnations of 219 propositions at the University of Paris.
1282–1302	War of the Sicilian Vespers.
1285/99–1349	William of Ockham, intellectual.
c.1290–c.1360	John Buridan, intellectual.
1291	Crusaders driven from the Holy Land.
1294–1303	Pontificate of Boniface VIII.
1305–14	Pontificate of Clement V. Papacy moves to Avignon.
1313–75	Giovanni Boccaccio, writer.
1324–84	John Wycliff, religious reformer.
1358–1589	Rule of Valois Dynasty, replaces Capetian Dynasty in France.
1337–1453	Hundred Years' War between France and England.
1348–50	Black Death (Bubonic Plague) sweeps Europe.
1358	Peasants' Jacquerie Rebellion in French Kingdom.
1378–1417	The Great Schism. Rival popes are seated in Avignon and Rome.
1381	Peasants' Revolt in England.
1414–18	Council of Constance. The Great Papal Schism resolved.
1422–31	Reign of French King Charles VII.
1429–31	Career of Joan of Arc.
1453	Fall of Constantinople to Ottoman Turks.
1455–85	Wars of the Roses, English dynastic struggle.

Appendix 7
Medieval Paedagogical Syllabus

Embedded in a number of medieval works is information about the paedagogical syllabus at the time. The following, ordered chronologically, are examples of such works:

Augustine of Hippo (354–430):
De doctrina Christiana, tr. D. W. Robertson, On Christian Doctrine (Indianapolis, 1958).
Martianus Capella (early fifth century):
De nuptiis Philologiae et Mercurii, trans. in W. H. Stahl, R. Johnson, and E. L. Burge, Martianus Capella and the Seven Liberal Arts (New York, 1977).
Cassiodorus (fl. 525–60):
Institutiones (c.562), tr. L. W. Jones, An Introduction to Divine and Human Readings by Cassiodorus Senator (New York, 1946).
Isidore of Seville (d. 636):
Etymologiae, ed. W. M. Lindsay (Oxford, 1911). For selections in translation see E. Brehaut, An Encyclopedist of the Dark Ages (New York, 1912).
Al-Fārābī (d. 950/51):
De scientiis, tr. Gerard of Cremona (before 1187), modern ed. A. Palencia in Catalogo de las ciencias (Madrid, 1953).
Hugh of St Victor (d. 1141):
Didascalion, De studio legendi, tr. J. Taylor, The Didascalion of Hugh of St. Victor (New York/London, 1961).
Domingo Gundisalvo (fl. 1140):
De divisione philosophiae, ed. L. Bauer in Beiträge zur Geschichte der Philosophie des Mittelalters, Texte und Untersuchungen, Band IV, Heft 2–3 (Munster i. W., 1903). For selections in translation see E. Grant, A Source Book in Medieval Science (Cambridge, MA, 1974), pp. 59–76.

Thierry of Chartres (d. after 1151):
Heptateuchon (c.1140). (Cf. A. Clerval, *Les Ecoles de Chartres au Moyen Age* (Paris, 1895), esp. pp. 222–3.)
Alexander Neckam (1157–1217):
Sacerdos ad altare (c.1200). (Cf. C. H. Haskins, *Studies in the History of Medieval Science* (New York, 1960), pp. 357–71.)
Robert Kilwardby (c.1215–79):
De ortu scientiarum (c.1250), edited by A. G. Judy, *Robert Kilwardby, O. P., De ortu scientarum* (London, 1976).

Documents from the medieval University of Paris (chartered 1215), including those which stipulate curriculum, were edited by H. Denifle and A. Chatelain, *Chartularium universitatis Parisiensis* (4 vols: Paris, 1889–97). Some of these documents are translated in L. Thorndike, ed., *University Records and Life in the Middle Ages* (New York, 1971).

Two curricula are provided here to permit observation of the most dramatic shift in the teaching corpus which occurred with the wave of new translations of Greek and Arabic works in the thirteenth century. The first curriculum is that of Thierry of Chartres (see above), dating from just before the new translations became integrated. The second is, in fact, a composite curriculum for European universities in use from the beginning of the thirteenth until the end of the fourteenth century. It incorporates both the highly idealized version of the Parisian curriculum of about 1200 by the English author Alexander Neckam (see above) and the additions made to that curriculum starting less than ten years later. Neckham's list probably includes more literature than was actually being read at the time, but it does give an idea of the variety of works available for teaching and reading at the beginning of the thirteenth century, some of which (those identified with an asterisk) continued to be prominent for more than a century. Works which were not mentioned by Neckham, but which figured prominently in the university curriculum, are set furthest to the right in the list, followed by their earliest date of inclusion (See R. Dales, *The Intellectual Life of Western Europe in the Middle Ages* (Washington, DC, 1980), pp. 221–6.)

The university arts curriculum was not, in fact, arranged by subjects but by books; textbooks determined the curriculum. To facilitate comparison, however, the canon of the seven liberal arts will be used in each list, and the authors and works ordered alphabetically.

Curriculum of Thierry of Chartres (c.1140)

Trivium

Grammar

Donatus, *Ars minor* [*The Lesser Art*, 3 books]
Donatus, *Barbarismus* [*Barbarisms* or Book III of *Ars minor*]
Priscian, *Institutiones grammaticae* [*On grammar*, Books I–XVI *Priscianus major* and Books XVII–XVIII *Priscianus minor*]

Rhetoric

Cicero, *De inventione* or *De rhetorica* [*Rhetoric*]
Cicero, *De oratore* [*On Oration and Orators*]
Martianus Capella, *De rhetorica* (Book V of *De nuptiis Mercurii et Philologiae*) [*On the Marriage of Mercury and Philology*]
J. Severianus, *Syntomata ac precepta artis rhetoricae* [*Rules and Exceptions of the Art of Rhetoric*]

Dialectic/Logic

Anonymous, *De logica* [*On Logic*]
Aristotle, *Analytica priora* [*Prior Analytics*]
Aristotle, *Categoriae* [*Categories*]
Aristotle, *De interpretatione* [*On Interpretation*]
Aristotle, *De sophisticis elenchis* [*On Sophistical Refutations*]
Aristotle, *Topica* [*Topics*]
Boethius, *De definitionis* [*On Definition*]
Boethius, *De divisione* [*On Division*]
Boethius, *De hypotheticis syllogismis* [*Hypothetical Syllogisms*]
Boethius, *De syllogismo categorico* [*Categorical Syllogisms*]
Boethius, *De topicis differentiis* [*On Different Topics*]
Boethius, *In Ciceronis topica* [*Topics of Cicero*]
Boethius, *Introductio ad syllogismos categoricos* [*Introduction to the Categorical Syllogisms*]
Porphyry, *Isagoge* [*Introduction*]

Quadrivium

Arithmetic

Anonymous, *De arithmetica* [*On Arithmetic*]
Boethius, *De arithmetica* [*On Arithmetic*]
Martianus Capella, *De arithmetica* [*On Arithmetic*]

Geometry

Adelard, *De corporibus regularibus fragmentum* [*A Fragment on Regular Shapes*]
Anonymous, *De geometria* [*On Geometry*]
Anonymous, *De mensuris* [*On Measurements*]
Boethius, *De geometria* [*On Geometry*]
Columelle, *De re rustica*, V [*On Things Rural*]
Frontin, *De mensuris* [*On Measurements*]
Gerbert, *De mensuris* [*On Measurements*]
Gerland, *Liber abaci* [*Book of the Abacus*]
Isidore of Seville, *Etymologiae*, VX, 15 [*Etymologies*]

Music

Boethius, *De musica* [*On Music*]

Astronomy

Hygenius, *Astronomicon* [*On Astronomy*]
Ptolemy, *Tabulae astronomicae* [*Astronomical Tables*]
Ptolemy, *Canon Ptolomei* [*On the Use of Astronomical Tables*]

Composite Curriculum (Neckham c.1200; University, 1210–)

Trivium

Grammar

Donatus
Priscian, *Institutiones grammaticae* [*On Grammar* Books I–XVI *Priscianus major*]
Alexander of Villa-Dei, *Doctrinale puerorum* (1199) [*The Teaching of Boys*]
Eberhard of Béthune, *Graecismus* [*On "Greekisms"* (1214)]

Rhetoric

Cicero, *De inventione* or *De rhetorica* [*Rhetoric*]*
Cicero, *De oratore* [*On Oration and Orators*]
pseudo-Cicero, *Rhetorica ad Herrennium* [*Rhetoric for Herrennius*]
Quintillian, *De institutione oratoris* [*On the Education of the Orator*]
Aristotle, *De rhetoricae* [*Rhetoric*]
Boethius, *De topicis differentiis* [*On Different Topics*]

Logic

Apulieus, *De interpretatione* [*On Interpretation*]
Aristotle, *Analytica posteriora* [*Posterior Analytics*]*
Aristotle, *Analytica priora* [*Prior Analytics*]*
Aristotle, *De anima* [*On the Soul*]
Aristotle, *De categoriae* [*Categories*]*
Aristotle, *De generatione et corruptione* [*On Generation and Corruption*]*
Aristotle, *De interpretatione* [*On Interpretation*]*
Aristotle, *De sophisticis elenchis* [*On Sophistical Refutations*]*
Aristotle, *Metaphysica* [*Metaphysics*]*
Boethius, *De syllogismo categorico* [*Categorical Syllogisms*]
Boethius, *De topicis differentiis* [*On Different Topics*]
Cicero, *Topica* [*Topics*]
Porphyry, *Isagoge* [*Introduction*]*
   Aristotle, *Topica* [*Topics*]
   pseudo-Gilbert de la Porrée, *De sex principiis* [*On the Six Principles*]

Quadrivium

Arithmetic

Boethius, *De arithmetica* [*On Arithmetic*]
Euclid, *Elementa* [*Elements* (Books VII–X)]
   Boethius, *De arithmetica* [*On Arithmetic* (in an abbreviated version by Thomas Bradwardine, late XIIIth)]
   John of Holywood (Sacrobosco), *Algorismus vulgaris* [*Common Functions of Arithmetic*]

Geometry

Euclid, *Elementa* [*Elements*]
   Euclid, *Elementa geometricae* [*Elements*] (translation by Adelard of Bath, often abridged)

Optics

Euclid, *Catoptrica* [*Mirrors*]
Euclid, *Optica* [*Optics*]
Pecham, *Perspectiva* [*Optics*]
Ptolemy, *Optica* [*Optics*]

Music

Boethius, *De musica* [*On Music*]

Astronomy

Alfraganus Al-Farghānī, *Rudimenta astronomica* [*Introduction to Astronomy*]
Ptolemy, *Canon Ptolomei* [*On the Use of Astronomical Tables*]
Al-Bitrūjī (Alpetragius), *De motibus caelorum* [*On the Motions of the Heavens*]
Anonymous, *Computus* (various texts)
Anonymous, *Theorica planetarum* [*Theory of the Planets*]
Aristotle, *De caelo et mundo* [*On the Heavens*]
Aristotle, *Metaphysica* [*Metaphysics*]
John of Holywood (Sacrobosco), *Sphaera* [*The Sphere*]
Ptolemy, *Libri almagesti* [*Almagest*]

Natural Philosophy

Aristotle, *Physica* [*Physics*]
    Aristotle, *De anima* [*On the Soul*]
    Aristotle, *De caelo* [*On the Heavens*]
    Aristotle, *De generatione animalium* [*On the Generation of Animals (1220)*]
    Aristotle, *De generatione et corruptione* [*On Generation and Corruption*]
    Aristotle, *De historia animalium* [*The History of Animals (1220)*]
    Aristotle, *De meteorologica* [*Meteorology*]
    Aristotle, *De partibus animalium* [*On the Parts of Animals (1220)*]
    Aristotle, *Parva naturalia* [*Small* [*works on*] *Natural Philosophy*]
    pseudo-Aristotle, *De causis et proprietatibus elementorum* [*On the Causes and the Properties of the Elements*]

Moral Philosophy

Aristotle, *Ethica Nicomachae* [*Nicomachean Ethics*]
Aristotle, *Politica* [*Politics*]
    Aristotle, *Economica* [*Economics*]

Metaphysics

Aristotle, *Metaphysica* [*Metaphysics*]

Notes

Introduction

1 "Whole governmental systems were exclusively based on an abstract idea, on programmatic blue-prints, on an abstract principle from which the last ounce of argument was squeezed out and doctrinally deduced." Walter Ullmann, *Medieval Political Thought* (Harmondsworth, England, 1965, rpt. 1979), p. 230.

Chapter 1 The Christian Impress

1 The word *called* (*appellabat*) that appears here is not from the ordinary verb for giving a name (*nominare* or *vocare*), but a term that indicates a person with respect to a business or special interest. Tacitus, *Annals* XV, 44, 4.

2 On Jerome's translation of the Bible, called the Vulgate, see R. Loewe, "The Medieval History of the Latin Vulgate," in *Cambridge History of the Bible*, vol. 2: *The West from the Fathers to the Reformation*, ed. G. W. H. Lampe (Cambridge, 1969), pp. 102–54.

3 Chrétien de Troyes, *Erec et Enide*, ed. Mario Roques (Paris, 1959), 11. 23–5. Cited and tr. by R. W. Hanning, "'Ut enim faber . . . sic creator': Divine Creation as the Context for Human Creativity in the Twelfth Century," in *Word, Picture and Spectacle*, ed. Clifford Davidson (Early Drama, Art, and Music Monograph Series, 5: Kalamazoo, MI, 1984), p. 130.

4 Fernand Auberjonois, "Gislebertus hoc fecit," in *The Light of the Past* (New York, 1965), p. 112.

5 "Opus Dei, opus naturae, opus artificis imitantis naturam" ("God's work, nature's work, work of the maker imitating nature"). Thierry of Chartres, *De septem diebus*, ed. Nikolaus Haring, in "The Creation and Creator of the World According to Thierry of Chartres and Clarenbaldus of Arras," *Archives d'histoire doctrinale et littéraire du moyen âge*, 30 (1955), p. 148, sections 6–12.

6 Hanning, "'Ut enim faber . . . sic creator,'" in *Word, Picture and Spectacle*, ed. Davidson, p. 110.

7 Tertullian of Carthage, *De corona*, 3 (Ante-Nicene Fathers, New York, 1907), vol. 3, p. 94.

8 Justin Martyr, describing the liturgy of the second-century Christian community for his pagan Gentile readers, said that at the end of the prayers, "all the people present express their assent by saying 'Amen.'" *First Apology*, 65.4 (Fathers of the Church: Washington, DC, 1965).

9 See Humbert of Romans, *De eruditione praedicatorum (On the Teaching of Preachers)*, (Maxima Bibliotheca Veterum Patrum, xxv: Lyons, 1677), II, Tract I, ch. 86, p. 499A, ch. 76, pp. 493G and 494AB, ch. 83, p. 497C, and ch. 98, p. 505C.

10 Jerome (d. 420) speaks of women and a few men who live in "prolonged and rigorous fasting, the wearing of coarse, even squalid clothing, the neglect of personal appearance, and the avoidance of personal comforts like baths, above all, in chastity . . . Their devotion was profoundly Jesus-centered." Cited by J. N. D. Kelly, *Jerome: His Life, Writings, and Controversies* (London, 1975), pp. 93–4.

11 Benedict, *Rule*, I. See John Chamberlin, ed., *The Rule of St Benedict: The Abingdon Copy* (Toronto, 1982), pp. 20–1.

12 Benedict, *Rule*, Prologue. See Chamberlin, ed., *Rule of St Benedict*, p. 20.

13 See Beryl Smalley, *The Study of the Bible in the Middle Ages* (Oxford, 1983), pp. 1–2.

Chapter 2 Early Medieval Religious Thought

1 See, for example, Warren Treadgold, ed., *Renaissances before the Renaissance: Cultural Revivals of Late Antiquity and the Middle Ages* (Standford, 1984), chs 1–5.

2 W. H. C. Frend, *The Rise of Christianity* (Philadelphia, 1984).

3 See W. H. C. Frend, "Popular Religion and Christological Controversy in the Fifth Century," in *Popular Practice and Belief*, eds G. J. Cuming and D. Baker (Cambridge, 1972), pp. 19–29.

4 Irenaeus, *Against Heresies* IV.26.2 (written c.180) (Ante-Nicene Christian Library: Edinburgh, 1868).

5 "It is as if church organization suddenly spoke out against free and independent charismatic practices in the name of the survival of the experiment as a whole." Eduardo Hoornaert, *The Memory of the Christian People* (Maryknoll, NY, 1988), p. 193. See also R. P. C. Hanson, *Christian Priesthood Examined* (London, 1978); R. Gryson, "L'autorite des docteurs dans l'Eglise ancienne et médiévale," *Revue Théologique de Louvain* 13 (1982), pp. 63–73.

6 For further discussion of these two passages ("*Et tibi dabo claves regni caelorum . . .*" Matt. 16:19; "*. . . Pasce oves meas*" John 21:17), see chapter 7.

7 See Paul Johnson, *A History of Christianity* (London, 1976), pp. 166–70.

8 Declaration of the Church Council of Sardica, 341. Cited by Johnson, *History of Christianity*, p. 77.

9 Jaroslav Pelikan, *The Christian Tradition: A History of the Development of*

Doctrine, vol. 1: *The Emergence of the Catholic Tradition (100–600)* (Chicago/London, 1971), p. 315.

10 Pelikan, *Christian Tradition*, vol. 1, p. 315.

11 "*Pelagianae pravitatis reliquiae*," Prosper of Aquitaine, *Epistle to Augustine*, in J. P. Migne, *Patrologia Latina*, vol. 51, p. 72.

12 Johnson's conclusion that Augustine was quite "optimistic" about the effect of the decision, for which he cites Augustine's "Rome has spoken; the debate is over," leads him to draw conclusions decidedly different from those advanced here in the next paragraph (pp. 38–9). See Johnson, *History of Christianity*, p. 156.

13 "An injustice may have been done, here as in other dogmatic debates, but it was an injustice that made history." Pelikan, *Christian Tradition*, vol. 1, p. 313. "In circumstances other than those of the first decade of the fifth century his [Pelagius'] teaching might have provided a basis for a Christian ethic which would have put the seal on the conversion of the Empire. Medieval Europe might possibly have been built on different and more optimistic foundations." Frend, *Rise of Christianity*, p. 675.

14 Theodoret of Cyrrhus, *Ecclesiastical History*, I, 27 (Die grieschichen christlichen Schriftsteller der ersten drei Jahrhunderten: Leipzig, 1954).

15 This excerpt from the acts of the Council of Chalcedon can be found in a number of collections of translated documents of Christianity. See, for example, Henry Bettenson, ed., *Documents of the Christian Church* (London, 1959), p. 73.

16 By the fifth and sixth centuries these were recognized criteria for the orthodox status of a teaching.

17 Johnson, *History of Christianity*, pp. 90–1.

18 See R. W. Southern, *Western Society and the Church in the Middle Ages* (London, 1970), pp. 72–90.

Chapter 3   Christianity and the Liberal Arts

1 There is still a residual of this idea in its English language uses today: The *Oxford English Dictionary*, ed. 1971, makes the distinction between education as "systematic instruction, schooling or training . . . Often with limiting words . . . as *classical, legal, medical*" and education as "Culture or development of powers, formation of character . . . Often with limiting words, as *intellectual, moral, physical*." *Educare* (to rear, bring up) is offered as the strict etymological source in both meanings, with the latter influenced further "by the quasi-etymological notion" from *educe*.

2 Pierre Riché, *Les écoles et l'enseignement dans l'occident chrétien de la fin du Ve siècle* (Paris, 1979), p. 218. See also the invaluable earlier study of E. Lesne, *Historie de la propriété ecclésiastique en France*, Vol. 5, *Les écoles de la fin du VIIIe siècle à la fin du XIIe siècle* (Lille, 1940).

3 On schools, see J. Fried, ed., *Schülen und Studium im Socialen Wandel des Hohen und Späten Mittelalters* (Vorträge und Forschungen, 30, ed. by

Konstanzer Arbeitskreis fur mittelalterliche Geschichte: Sigmaringen, 1986); on patronage, see Georges Duby, "The Culture of the Knightly Class: Audience and Patronage," in *Renaissance and Renewal in the Twelfth Century*, eds Robert L. Benson et al. (Cambridge, MA, 1982), pp. 248–62.

4 See, for example, William Harris Stahl and Richard Johnson, with E. L. Burge, *Martianus Capella and the Seven Liberal Arts* (New York, 1971).

5 See David Wagner, "The Seven Liberal Arts and Classical Scholarship," in *The Seven Liberal Arts in the Middle Ages*, ed. David L. Wagner (Bloomington, IN, 1986), pp. 1–31.

6 Jean Leclerq, *The Love of Learning and the Desire for God* (New York, 1961), pp. 144–5.

7 See, for example, the cleric who wrote that "the aim in going to the schools of the grammarians is to leave them behind, once one has become perfect in their art" (J. P. Migne, ed., *Patrologia Latina*, vol. 144, p. 393) or Peter Damien's comment, "It is a great shame that a member of the Church should keep quiet out of ignorance while those who are outside [the Church] throw false accusations and that a Christian not knowing how to make sense of Christ withdraws conquered and confused beneath the insults of his enemies" (*Patrologia Latina*, vol. 145, p. 41). Riché quotes an apparently common medieval proverb: *Claustrum sine armario quasi castrum sine armamentario* ("A monastery without a library is like a fortress without arms"). Riché, *Écoles et l'enseignement*, p. 215.

8 See Richard McKeon, "Rhetoric in the Middle Ages," in *Critics and Criticism, Ancient and Modern*, ed. R. S. Crane (Chicago, 1952), pp. 260–96; James J. Murphy, *Rhetoric in the Middle Ages* (Berkeley, 1974).

9 Eleonore Stump, "Dialectic," in *Seven Liberal Arts*, pp. 125–46.

10 These excesses were in fact reported as a warning to others who might be tempted to follow. Raoul Glaber wrote of Vilgard, "corrupted by this diabolical mystification [of the poets Virgil, Horace and Juvenal], he began to teach with emphasis many things contrary to sacred belief: he declared that the words of the poets ought to be believed on all points" (Raoul Glaber, *Five Books of Histories* (*Historiarum libri quinque*) Book II, ch. 12, in M. Prou, ed., *Raoul Glaber: Les cinq livres de ses histories* (Paris, 1886)).

11 For a general survey of the serious place of magic in the learning of the Middle Ages, see Lynn Thorndike, *A History of Magic and Experimental Science*, vols 1–4 (New York, 1923–58); and Bert Hansen, "Science and Magic," in *Science in the Middle Ages*, ed. David C. Lindberg (Chicago History of Science and Medicine: Chicago, 1978) pp. 483–506.

12 Richard Dales, *The Intellectual Life of Western Europe in the Middle Ages* (Washington, DC, 1980), p. 38, and Paul Johnson, *A History of Christianity* (New York, 1976), pp. 153 and 183–4.

13 "The monk, who wishes to anticipate knowledge of scripture, ought

never waste his efforts on books of commentary, but rather to extend all the activity of his mind and all the intention of his heart to purification from carnal vices. If it is true not that the grace of the Holy Spirit has not taught the mysteries of the scripture, in order that they might be unknown or obscure, but that these mysteries have become such by our fault, since the veil of sin darkens the eyes of the heart, as soon as these vices are driven away, the eyes of the heart, with the veil of the passions lifted, will contemplate the mysteries naturally." John Cassian, *Institutes* V, 34, in E. C. S. Gibson, tr., John Cassian, *Institutes* (Nicene and Post-Nicene Library of the Fathers: Oxford, 1894).

14 "In the winter, from the autumnal equinox, which is 24 September, until Easter, given that it is cold and the brothers are not able to do manual labour in the morning, from Prime to Terce diverse groups of ten will separate themselves in location each from the others, in order to avoid the assembling of the whole community and the mutual disturbing of groups of ten by the sound of [others'] voices. In other words, the groups devote themselves to reading. One of the ten, in each spot, will read and the others in his group will listen." *Rule of the Master* L, 9–15. See A. de Vogüe, ed., *Règle du maître* (Sources chrétiennes: Paris, 1965).

15 "Idleness is the enemy of the soul and therefore the brothers ought to be busy at certain seasons in manual labour, and at certain times in lectio divina. We think that we should adjust these arrangements to the seasons. Thus from Easter to the Calends of October, the brothers will leave the monastery in the morning. They will work manually at whatever is necessary from Prime until around 4 o'clock. From 4 until 6 o'clock they will attend to reading. After 6 o'clock, when they rise from the dinner table, they will rest on their beds in complete silence. If anyone would wish to read, let him read to himself, without disturbing anyone. . . . At Lent, all the brothers will individually receive books from the library which they ought to read from start to finish. These books are to be given out on the first day of Lent. Above all, it is a good idea to designate one or two among the oldest brothers to walk around the monastery during the hours when the brothers are attending to reading to see if they find by chance any negligent brother who abandons himself to idleness or to vain stories and who is not plunged into his reading. This idleness is without fruit for him and diverts the others." Benedict, *Rule*, XLVIII. See Chamberlin, ed., *Rule of St Benedict*, pp. 54–5.

16 Latin and English quoted from Robert M. Grant, *A Short History of the Interpretation of the Bible* (New York, 1963), p. 85. By the twelfth century the student of biblical exegesis could turn to the *Glossa Ordinaria*, in *Walfridi Strabi Fuldensis Monachi Opera Omnia, Patrologia Latina*, ed. J. P. Migne, CXIII, CXIV (1879). It became the standard medieval corpus of biblical glosses, providing commentaries on a high proportion of verses in the Vulgate Bible. The authors of the glosses are identified as Origen, Augustine, John Chrysostom, Jerome,

Ambrose, Gregory the Great, Rhabanus Maurus, Bede, Alcuin, etc., the works of Augustine being the most frequently cited. Most of the commentaries dwell on only one of the four levels of figurative meaning of a word, phrase, or verse.

17 For two short intellectual biographical essays, see John Matthews, "Anicius Manlius Severinus Boethius," in *Boethius: His Life, Thought and Influence* (Oxford, 1981), pp. 15–43, and Helen Kirkby, "The Scholar and his Public," ibid., pp. 44–69.

18 The word *"philosophia"* literally means "love of wisdom," and came to have many meanings. The definition of Cicero was considered authoritative: "If you would like to explain it, philosophy is nothing other than the study of wisdom; the wisdom is of things divine and human and of the causes by which these things are encompassed by knowledge." (*"Nec quicquam alius est philosophia, si interpretari velis, praeter studium sapientiae; sapientia autem est rerum divinarum et humanarum causarumque quibus eae res continentur scientia"*) *On Offices* (*De officis*), II, ii, 45. For Boethius, in addition to the "study of wisdom" at least two further understandings are involved: knowledge obtained by reason (as opposed to by revelation) and the mental attitude or habit of contemplating knowledge, which brings serenity in disturbing circumstances.

19 See, for example, G. Boissier, "Le christianisme de Boèce," *Journal des Savants* (1889), pp. 449–62; J. D. de Vogel, "The Problem of Philosophy and Christian Faith in Boethius' Consolatio," in *Romanitas et Christianitas: Studia J. H. Waszink* W. den Boer, ed. (Amsterdam, 1973), pp. 357–70.

20 See, for example, David Pingree, "Boethius' Geometry and Astronomy," in Gibson, ed., *Boethius*, pp. 155–61, where Boethius' access to Euclid's *Elements* in Greek is highly questioned.

21 On Boethius and the medieval teaching curriculum, see John Caldwell, "The *De Institutione Arithmetica* and the *De Institutione Musica*," and Alison White, "Boethius in the Medieval Quadrivium," in Gibson, ed., *Boethius*, pp. 133–54 and 162–205.

22 For further details, see Rosamond McKitterick, *The Frankish Kingdoms under the Carolingians, 751–987* (London, 1983), pp. 140–68.

23 John J. Contreni, "The Carolingian Renaissance," in *Renaissances before the Renaissance: Cultural Revivals of Late Antiquity and the Middle Ages*, ed. Warren Treadgold (Stanford, 1984), p. 59.

Chapter 4   The Return to Plato and Aristotle

1 No one study can capture the monumental impact of Plato and Aristotle on western culture, but the following have attempted to do it justice. For their general impact, see F. Brunner, *Platonisme et Aristotélisme* (Louvain, 1963). For their impact in specific areas see, for example, on philosophy, Frederick Copleston, *A History of Philosophy* (London, 1972); on logic, Anton Dumitriu, *History of Logic* (4 vols: Tunbridge

Wells, England, 1977); on political theory, George H. Sabine, *A History of Political Philosophy* (Hinsdale, IL, 4th ed., 1973) or L. Strauss and J. Cropsy, eds, *A History of Political Philosophy* (Chicago, 3rd ed., 1987).

2 Two major studies of this theme and a companion one: "if it is not in Plato and Aristotle, it was not written in antiquity and it is up to us, of the Middle Ages, to complete the gaps," should be noted: Michael Haren, *Medieval Thought: The Western Intellectual Tradition from Antiquity to the Thirteenth Century* (London, 1985), and David Knowles, *The Evolution of Medieval Thought* (London, 1962; 2nd ed., 1988). Scholars have also drawn attention to the lesser influence of Stoic philosophy. See, for example, Michael Lapidge, "The Stoic Inheritance," in *A History of Twelfth-Century Western Philosophy*, ed. Peter Dronke (Cambridge, 1988), pp. 81–112.

3 The presence of the concept of "Authority 1" can be seen in the discussion of Platonism by R. A. Markus, "Marius Victorinus and Augustine," in *The Cambridge History of Later Greek and Early Medieval Philosophy*, ed. A. H. Armstrong, (Cambridge, 1967), pp. 348ff., and of "Authority 2" in the analysis of Aristotelianism by C. H. Lohr, "The Medieval Interpretation of Aristotle," in *The Cambridge History of Later Medieval Philosophy: From the Rediscovery of Aristotle to the Disintegration of Scholasticism 1100–1600*, eds Norman Kretzmann et al. (Cambridge, 1982), p. 91.

4 Augustine offers the analogy of the Egyptians and the Israelites to illustrate a biblical precedent for the appropriation of pagan riches. St Augustine, *On Christian Doctrine* II. 40, tr. D. W. Robertson, Jr. (The Library of Liberal Arts Press, Indianapolis, 1958), p. 75.

5 At this point in the research of classical texts, "pseudo-Platonic," strictly speaking, designates any work attributed to Plato which has not been edited as Plato's in, for example, the Loeb Classical Library Series (3 vols: London, 1966–7). "Pseudo-Aristotelian" could refer for English readers to any work attributed to Aristotle which has not been translated by J. A. Smith and W. D. Ross, *The Works of Aristotle Translated into English* (Oxford, 1910–52).

6 See Bernard G. Dod, "Aristoteles latinus," in *Cambridge History of Later Medieval Philosophy*, pp. 45–79.

7 The *Aristoteles Latinus* editions are presently coordinated by an editorial board at the Catholic University of Leuven. See examples of the series in L. Minio-Paluello, ed., *Aristoteles Latinus*, vols I-III, V, VI (Leiden, 1961–75). *Plato Latinus* is published out of London/Leiden as the *Corpus Platonicum Medii Aevi*. See also, for Aristotle, L. Minio-Paluello, *Opuscula: the Latin Aristotle* (Amsterdam, 1972).

8 See M. T. d'Alverny, "Translations and Translators," in *Renaissance and Renewal in the Twelfth Century*, eds Robert L. Benson et al. (Cambridge, MA, 1982), pp. 421–62.

9 Dod, "Aristoteles," in *Cambridge History of Later Medieval Philosophy*, p. 77.

10 Thomas Aquinas, _Summa theologiae_, I, 84, 5. For the twentieth-century echo of Thomas, see Knowles, _The Evolution of Medieval Thought_, p. 32: ". . . where Scripture gave no lead, Augustine accepted from the _Timaeus_ and _Meno_ of Plato and the _Enneads_ of Plotinus the explanations they gave of the intellectual problems that engaged his attention, and if a reader of Augustine is in doubt as to the origin [Augustine's source] of a particular philosophical idea, he will usually find the answer in Plotinus."

11 See Tullio Gregory, "The Platonic Inheritance," in _A History of Twelfth-Century Western Philosophy_, ed. Peter Dronke (Cambridge, 1988), pp. 54–80.

12 See D. E. Luscombe, "Peter Abelard," in _History of Twelfth-Century Western Philosophy_, pp. 288–92.

13 See Dod, "Aristoteles," in _Cambridge History of Later Medieval Philosophy_, p. 50.

14 This list stems from "a late thirteenth-century manuscript in the Stiftsbibliothek at Admont (no. 126)," Dod, "Aristoteles," p. 50.

15 Dod, "Aristoteles," p. 51.

16 _Alfarabi's Philosophy of Plato and Aristotle_, ed. and tr. Muhsin Mahdi (Glencoe, IL, 1962), pp. 49–50.

17 See Pierre Duhem, _Le système du monde: histoire des doctrines cosmologiques de Platon à Copernic_ (7 vols: Paris, 1913–56).

18 Henry Chadwick, _Boethius: The Consolations of Music, Logic, Theology, and Philosophy_ (Oxford, 1981), p. 125.

19 Albertus Magnus, _Opera_, ed. Augustus Borgnet, (Paris, 1890–9), vol. 35, pp. 16, 34.

20 Knowles, _Evolution of Medieval Thought_, p. 240.

21 Thomas Aquinas, _Summa theologiae_ I, q.32, a.1. For a most recent translation of the _Summa theologiae_, see _Summa theologiae: a concise translation_, ed. and tr. Timothy McDermott (London, 1989). See also Aquinas' commentary on Aristotle's _On the Heavens_, II, lec. 17. (_Sancti Thomae Aquinatis Opera Omnia_ (Paris, 1882), vol. 3).

22 Articles 87 and 90 from the Condemnations of 1277, quoted from E. L. Fortrin and P. O. O'Neill, trs, in _Medieval Political Philosophy: A Sourcebook_, eds R. Lerner and M. Mahdi (Ithaca, NY, 1963), pp. 337–54.

23 Rosamond McKitterick, _The Carolingians and the Written Word_ (Cambridge, 1989), p. 4.

24 Jordanus of Saxony, _Opera_, ed. J. J. Bertheir (Friburghi Helvetiorum 1891), 4.

25 Bonaventure, "Collation XIX. 12" in _Collationes in Hexameron et Bonventuriana Quaedam Selecta_, ed. F. Delormé (Quaracchi, 1934), p. 290.

26 See, for example, the masters' prescribed lecture texts in the Faculty of Arts at Paris, 1254, which included no religious works. Lynn Thorndike, tr. and ed., _University Records and Life in the Middle Ages_ (New York, 1944), pp. 64–6.

Chapter 5   The Vernacular Breakthrough

1 For introductions to Latin in the Middle Ages, see L. R. Palmer, *The Latin Language* (London, 1954) and J. W. Thompson, *The Literacy of the Laity in the Middle Ages* (New York, 1965).

2 See *The Carolingians and the Written Word* (Cambridge, 1989), in which Rosamond McKitterick has most recently contributed to the discussion of the role of Latin in the early Middle Ages with her evidence to support the ideas that Latin may have been the Carolingians' "native tongue in its regularized and conventionalized written representation" and "the study of Latin was used to improve the use of a known language, not to learn it as a new one" (pp. 13, 20).

3 For background on the barbarian invasions, see Lucien Musset, *The Germanic Invasions* (State College, PA, 1975).

4 J. Cremona, "The Romance Languages," in *The Mediaeval World*, eds David Daiches and Anthony Thorlby (Literature and Western Civilization, vol. 2: London, 1973), p. 37.

5 Jacques Paul, *Historie intellectuelle de l'occident médiéval* (Paris, 1973), p. 93.

6 Even the panegyrics of Ennodius and Cassiodorus for Theodoric, king of the Ostrogoths, the poetry of Fortunatus at the Merovingian court of Sigibert, the biography of Charlemagne by Einhard, the poetry of Theodulf and Ermoldus Nigellus for the Carolingian kings, the tales of Apollonius, King of Tyre, or the Seven Sages of Rome were not enough to preserve classical Latinity.

7 See George Hardin Brown, "The Anglo-Saxon Monastic Revival," in *Renaissances before the Renaissance: Cultural Revivals of Late Antiquity and the Middle Ages*, ed. Warren Treadgold (Stanford, 1984), pp. 99–113.

8 See Ralph McInerny, "Beyond the Liberal Arts," in *The Seven Liberal Arts in the Middle Ages*, ed. David L. Wagner (Bloomington, IN, 1986), pp. 258–60, for the positive twist he gives to Chenu's assessment of the Scholastics' "inward and outward style" of "austerity," "special rhetoric," and "procedures in which reason cruelly exploits imagination." Cited is M.-D. Chenu, *Introduction à l'étude de Saint Thomas d'Aquin* (Paris, 1954), p. 52, which has also appeared in translation as Chenu, *Toward Understanding St Thomas*, trs A. M. Landry and D. Hughes (Chicago, 1964). See also Jean Jolivet, "The Arabic Influence," in *A History of Twelfth-Century Western Philosophy*, ed. Peter Dronke (Cambridge, 1988), pp. 118–23.

9 Orosius, *The Seven Books of History against the Pagans (Historia adversus paganos)* VII, 43, tr. Roy J. Deferrari (Fathers of the Church: Washington, DC, 1964).

10 See Cremona, "The Romance Languages," and M. B. Parkes, "The Literacy of the Laity," in *Mediaeval World*, eds Daiches and Thorlby, pp. 51–4, and 558–62, for examples and analysis of the pragmatic use of the vernacular.

11 For details of vernacular texts in the original and in English translation, see appendices 2 and 5. For clarity and brevity's sake, only a exemplary selection of the texts can be noted in the present work.

12 The reasons for the early sophisticated use of prose in English lie undoubtedly in its successful role as both a *substrate* and *superstrate* language. For a sketch of the debate over *substratum/superstratum* theories in the context of the Romance languages, see Cremona, "Romance Languages," in *Mediaeval World*, pp. 49–50. A useful essay worth consulting on the English language is R. M. Wilson, "On the Continuity of English Prose," *Mélanges de linguistique et de philologie: F. Mossé in Memoriam* (Paris, 1959), pp. 489–94.

13 For further details on each language, see the appropriate chapters in Daiches and Thorlby, eds, *Mediaeval World*.

14 For further details, see Cremona, "Romance Languages," in *Mediaeval World*, pp. 57–62, especially n. 12.

15 See Richard C. Dales, *The Intellectual Life of Western Europe in the Middle Ages* (Washington, DC, 1980), p. 290.

16 It would also have marked the passing of an era which a prominent analyst of the *fabliaux* described as one which "no longer possesses the power of collective creation and does not yet have the idea of art." J. Bédier, *Les fabliaux* (Paris, 5th ed., 1925), p. 432.

17 Serge Lusignan, *Parler vulgairement, Les intellectuels et la langue française aux XIIIe et XIVe siècles* (Paris/Montreal, 1987), p. 86.

18 Cited by Dales, *Intellectual Life*, p. 147.

19 See Marie-Dominique Chenu, *Nature, Man and Society in the Twelfth Century: Essays on New Theological Perspectives in the West* (Chicago, 1968).

20 See Jean-Jacques Ampère, *Historie littéraire de France avant le douzième siècle* (3 vols: Paris, 1839–40), vol. 3, p. 457, and Louis J. Paetow, *Guide to the Study of Medieval History* (New York, 1917, re-ed., 1931), p. 411.

21 See Christopher Brooke, *The Twelfth-Century Renaissance* (London, 1969); Richard W. Southern, "Medieval Humanism," in his *Medieval Humanism and Other Essays* (New York, 1970); and Colin Morris, *The Discovery of the Individual, 1050–1200* (New York/London, 1972).

22 See Stephen C. Ferruolo, "The Twelfth Century Renaissance," in *Renaissances*, ed. Treadgold, pp. 114–43.

23 Urban T. Holmes, "The Idea of a Twelfth-Century Renaissance," *Speculum* 26 (1951), p. 651.

24 See Charles Homer Haskins, *The Renaissance of the Twelfth Century* (Cambridge, MA, 1927), and Ferruolo, "Twelfth-Century Renaissance," p. 136.

25 It is also to ignore, which these same historians do not, religious orders which used the vernacular. See Haskins, *Renaissance*, pp. 13 and 159, and Ferruolo, "Twelfth-Century Renaissance," p. 130.

26 Ferruolo, "Twelfth-Century Renaissance," p. 143.

27 John C. Moore, *Love in Twelfth-Century France* (Philadelphia, 1972).

28 Colin Morris, *The Discovery of the Individual 1050–1200* (New York, 1972). On the vernacular "self," see especially pp. 33–6 and 109–19.
29 Ferruolo, "Twelfth-Century Renaissance," p. 143.
30 Peter Dronke, "Profane Elements in Literature," in *Renaissance and Renewal in the Twelfth Century*, eds Robert Benson et al. (Cambridge, MA, 1982) pp. 577, 579.
31 Per Nykrog, "The Rise of Literary Fiction," in *Renaissance and Renewal*, pp. 593–612.
32 Walter Ullmann, *Medieval Political Thought* (Harmondsworth, England, 1965, rpt. 1979) pp. 155, 159–67, 174–85; John B. Morrall, *Political Thought in Medieval Times* (New York, 1962), pp. 61–2, 70–86.
33 In one of the Novels of the Justinian Code, Latin was called "the ancient and national language" (*Novel* XXII. 2).
34 Cited in Morrall, *Political Thought*, p. 61.

Chapter 6   Scholasticism

1 See, for example, Sten Ebbesen, "Ancient Scholastic Logic as the Source of Medieval Scholastic Logic," and John A. Trentman, "Scholasticism in the Seventeenth Century," in *The Cambridge History of Later Medieval Philosophy: From the Rediscovery of Aristotle to the Disintegration of Scholasticism 1100–1600*, eds Norman Kretzmann et al. (Cambridge, 1982), pp. 101–27 and 818–37.
2 See, for example, Ebbesen, "Scholastic Logic," in *Cambridge History of Later Medieval Philosophy*, pp. 101–2; and Paul Oskar Kristeller, *Medieval Aspects of Renaissance Learning* (Durham, NC, 1974), pp. 2–25, esp. 5–10.
3 See David Knowles, *The Evolution of Medieval Thought* (London, 2nd ed., 1988), pp. 139–261; Jaroslav Pelikan, *The Christian Tradition: A History of the Development of Doctrine*, vol. 3: *The Growth of Medieval Theology (600–1300)* (Chicago/London, 1978), pp. 255–93.
4 For example, on the use of the arguments in Aristotle's *Physics* by Thomas Aquinas in his proofs for the existence of God, see Armand A. Maurer, *Medieval Philosophy* (The Etienne Gilson Series 4: Toronto, 1962, 2nd ed., 1982), pp. 166–8.
5 See F. van Steenberghen, *Aristotle in the West: The Origins of Latin Aristotelianism* (Louvain, 2nd ed., 1970); Lynn Thorndike, tr. and ed., *University Records and Life in the Middle Ages* (New York, 1944), pp. 26–7, 64–5, 85–6. A particularly helpful essay on the critical ecclesiastical response to Aristotle is J. F. Wippel, "The Condemnations of 1270 and 1277 at Paris," *Journal of Medieval and Renaissance Studies* 7 (1977), pp. 169–210.
6 On the problem of universals, see John Hospers, *An Introduction to Philosophical Analysis* (Englewood Cliffs, NJ, 2nd revised ed., 1976), pp. 354–67. On realism and nominalism in the Middle Ages, see Etienne Gilson, *History of Christian Philosophy in the Middle Ages* (New

York/London, 1955, rpt. 1978), pp. 489–98; M. H. Carré, *Realists and Nominalists* (Oxford, 1946).

7   John of Salisbury, *Metalogicon* II, ch. 17, in *The Metalogicon of John of Salisbury. A Twelfth-Century Defense of the Verbal and Logical Arts of the Trivium*, tr. Daniel D. McGarry (Gloucester, MA, 1971), pp. 111–16.

8   On the distinction between essence and existence, see John F. Wippel, "Essence and Existence," in *Cambridge History of Later Medieval Philosophy* , pp. 385–410. On Avicenna and reactions to his philosophy, see A. M. Goichon, *La philosophie d'Avicenne et son influence en Europe médiévale* (Paris, 1944, re-ed., 1951).

9   For a survey of medieval scientific activity, and the issues involved, see David C. Lindberg, *Science in the Middle Ages* (Chicago History of Science and Medicine: Chicago/London, 1978). On Parisian and Oxonian natural philosophers, see James A. Weisheipl, *The Development of Physical Theory in the Middle Ages* (Ann Arbor, MI, 1959, re-ed. 1971).

10   Cited by Herman Shapiro, ed. and tr., *Medieval Philosophy, Selected Readings from Augustine to Buridan* (New York, 1964), p. 177.

11   John of Salisbury, *Metalogicon* II, ch. 17, tr. McGarry, p. 116.

12   George Makdisi, "The Scholastic Method in Medieval Education: An Inquiry into its Origins in Law and Theology," *Speculum* 49 (1974), pp. 640–61.

13   For other aspects of East–West transmission, see F. E. Peters, *Aristotle and the Arabs: The Aristotelian Tradition in Islam* (New York/London, 1968), pp. 221–37.

14   Erwin Panofsky, *Gothic Architecture and Scholasticism* (New York, 1957).

15   Panofsky, *Gothic Architecture*, pp. 27–8.

16   See Robert Mark, *Experiments in Gothic Structure* (Cambridge, MA/London, 1982).

17   Panofsky, *Gothic Architecture*, p. 38.

18   Robert W. Hanning, "Suger's Literary Style and Vision," in *Abbot Suger and Saint-Denis: A Symposium*, ed. Paula Lieber Gerson (New York, 1986), p. 145.

19   Panofsky, *Gothic Architecture*, pp. 70–1.

20   Panofsky, *Gothic Architecture*, p. 73.

21   Mark, *Experiments*, p. 4, and Otto von Simpson, *The Gothic Cathedral* (New York, 1962), pp. 50–8.

22   See David Jeffrey, "Franciscan Spirituality and the Growth of Vernacular Culture," in *By Things Seen: Reference and Recognition in Medieval Thought*, ed. David L. Jeffrey (Ottawa, 1979), pp. 143–60.

23   Alister E. McGrath, *Reformation Thought: An Introduction* (Oxford, 1988), p. 52.

24   McGrath, *Reformation Thought*, p. 52.

25   "The practice of writing *consilia* was part of the general movement toward strictness in presenting evidence in theology as well as in the profane sciences, and sometimes it led to an emphasis on logical form to the detriment of observation, as when *consilia* were prepared and

medical advice given from reports on ᵐⁿˢᵉᵉn patients." A. C. Crombie, *Medieval and Early Modern Science*, vol. 1: *Science in the Middle Ages: V–XIII Centuries* (Garden City, NY, 1959), p. 226.

Chapter 7   The Dictates of Philosophy and the Late Medieval Church

1   The cautious assessment in 1980 of Richard Dales in *The Intellectual Life of Western Europe in the Middle Ages* (Washington, DC, 1980), p. 254, that "The effects of the 1277 condemnation are not yet fully understood, so any cause–effect relationship . . . must be considered as tentative" seems to have given way to the more confident assessments of historians such as Armand Maurer [*Medieval Philosophy* (The Etienne Gilson Series 4: Toronto, 1962, 2nd ed., 1982), pp. 204–7], Edward Grant ["The Effect of the Condemnation of 1277," in *The Cambridge History of Later Medieval Philosophy: From the Rediscovery of Aristotle to the Disintegration of Scholasticism 1100–1600*, eds Norman Kretzmann et al. (Cambridge, 1982), pp. 537–9], and David Knowles [*The Evolution of Medieval Thought* (London, 2nd ed., 1988), pp. 272–3], who see that the impact of the condemnation was revealed in a "progressive separation of faith and reason" (Maurer, p. 207); in "appeals to God's absolute power" (Grant), and in strengthening "unduly the conservative theologians," among other things (Knowles, p. 273).

2   Knowles, *Evolution of Medieval Thought*, p. 273.

3   Compare Charles Burnett, "Scientific Speculations," in *A History of Twelfth-Century Western Philosophy*, ed. Peter Dronke (Cambridge, 1988) pp. 152–5 with C. H. Lohr, "The Medieval Interpretation of Aristotle," in *Cambridge History of Later Medieval Philosophy*, pp. 95–8.

4   John Buridan, *Questions on the Metaphysics of Aristotle*, Book II, q. I, f. 9rb.

5   The appearance of the genre of "recipe book" is testimony that confidence in the practical effectiveness of repetition was also present in non-academic popular culture. See Bruno Roy, "The Household Encyclopedia as Magic Kit: Medieval Popular Interest in Pranks and Illusions," in *Popular Culture in the Middle Ages*, ed. Josie P. Cambell (Bowling Green, OH, 1986), pp. 29–38.

6   For the piecemeal use of Aristotle after the thirteenth century, see Lohr, "Medieval Interpretation," pp. 96–8.

7   Ralph McInerny, "Beyond the Liberal Arts," in *The Seven Liberal Arts in the Middle Ages*, ed. David L. Wagner (Bloomington, IN, 1986), pp. 257–8.

8   See Lohr, "Medieval Interpretation," p. 88.

9   See James A. Weisheipl, *Friar Thomas D'Aquino: His Life, Thought, and Work* (Garden City, NY, 1974), passim.

10   See Lohr, "Medieval Interpretation," pp. 95–6.

11   See Paul Vincent Spade, "The Semantics of Terms," in *Cambridge History of Later Medieval Philosophy*, pp. 189–90.

12 Tractatus de successivis attributed to William [of] Ockham; ed. P. Boehner
    (St Bonaventure, NY, 1944), p. 45.
13 Jaroslav Pelikan, The Christian Tradition: A History of the Development
    of Doctrine, vol. 4: Reformation of Church and Dogma (1300–1700)
    (Chicago/London, 1984), p. 53.
14 The "perfectibilist" posture is most often referred to as the medieval
    "rationalist" posture, for reason, as opposed to will, is held to be
    seeking natural perfection. See J. B. Korolec, "Free Will and Free
    Choice," in Cambridge History of Later Medieval Philosophy, pp. 629–41.
15 Marsilius' teaching was condemned in Avignon on October 27, 1327,
    shortly after the authorship of his work became known; he then fled to
    the court of Ludwig of Bavaria. No reconciliation between Marsilius
    and the papacy was to take place before Marsilius' death in 1342/3.
16 See William of Ockham, Dialogus, Pars Ia, V, c.17, 486. For a full
    analysis of the reasons underlying Ockham's rejection of the Petrine
    Doctrine at various stages throughout his career, see Arthur S.
    McGrade, The Political Thought of William of Ockham: Personal and
    Institutional Principles (Cambridge, 1974); Georges de Lagarde, La
    naissance de l'esprit laique au déclin du moyen age, vol. 5: Guillaume
    d'Ockham: critique des structures ecclésiales (Louvain, 1963), pp. 87–127.
17 See William of Ockham, Dialogus, Pars Ia, VI, c.100, 634.
18 See a biography of Ockham's intellectual life, Gordon Leff, William of
    Ockham: The Metamorphosis of Scholastic Discourse (Manchester/Totowa,
    NJ, 1975).
19 See Gordon Leff, Medieval Thought: St. Augustine to Ockham (London,
    1959), pp. 279–94.
20 William of Ockham, Dialogus, Pars Ia, VI, c.100, 634.
21 William of Ockham, De potestate et juribus romani imperii Book II, Part
    III, III, c.18, 953.
22 See William of Ockham, Dialogus, Pars Ia, VI, c. 97, 614, 618, and
    c.99, 624.
23 See Jasper Hopkins, Nicholas of Cusa on Learned Ignorance: A Translation
    and Appraisal of De docta ignorantia (Minneapolis, MN, 1981).
24 Armard A. Maurer, Medieval Philosophy (Toronto, 1982), pp. 310–24.
25 Cited in Paul E. Sigmund, Nicholas of Cusa and Medieval Political
    Thought (Cambridge, MA, 1963), p. 266.
26 "The Decree of the Council of Constance, 'Sacrosancta' (April,
    1415)," in Documents of the Christian Church, tr. and ed. Henry Betten-
    son (London, 1944, rpt. 1959), pp. 188–9.
27 For accounts of the Council of Constance, see John H. Mundy and
    Kennerly M. Woody, eds, The Council of Constance: The Unification of
    the Church (New York, 1969).

Chapter 8   Domains of Abstract Thought

 1 Augustine, The City of God XI, 26, tr. Marcus Dod (New York,
    1950), pp. 370–1.

2 The biographical case of Socrates is a historical illustration of this point. More universally considered, a compromise of any body of thought with theology might take one of several forms: the body of thought comes under supernatural influences; assumptions about God, etc. are deemed to be a truth which the ideas cannot contradict; the ideas take into account the existence of the theology; the ideas of theology become the object of inquiry in another body of thought; or the ideas make appeal to theology. See William Wallace, *The Elements of Philosophy: A Compendium for Philosophers and Theologians* (Staten Island, NY, 1977), pp. 5–6, 185–7.

3 See David Knowles, *The Evolution of Medieval Thought* (London, 2nd ed., 1988), pp. 187–98.

4 See, for example, A. C. Pegis, *St Thomas and the Problem of the Soul in the Thirteenth Century* (Toronto, 1934).

5 See Eileen Serene, "Demonstrative Science," in *The Cambridge History of Later Medieval Philosophy: From the Rediscovery of Aristotle to the Disintegration of Scholasticism 1100–1600*, eds Norman Kretzmann et al. (Cambridge, 1982), pp. 496–517.

6 See James A. Weisheipl, "Classification of the Sciences in Medieval Thought," *Medieval Studies* 27 (1965), pp. 54–90.

7 Peter Damian's (1007–72) identification of "model" learned individuals, Benedict of Nursia, Gregory the Great, Jerome, and Martin of Tours, points to the fact that the distinction was maintained into the Middle Ages as one of social class, rather than as a marker of servile status or not. See Karl F. Morrison, "Incentives for Studying the Liberal Arts," in *The Seven Liberal Arts in the Middle Ages*, ed. David L. Wagner (Bloomington, IN, 1986), pp. 32–5.

8 Aristotle, *Nicomachean Ethics*, Book X, ch. 9 (1181b 2–7).

9 Hugh of St Victor, *The Didascalicon of Hugh of St Victor: A Medieval Guide to the Arts*, tr. and ed. Jerome Taylor (New York, 1961), Book II, ch. 20, p. 75.

10 There is a considerable latitude in classifiers' use of terms such as "art" and "practical science." See Hugh of St Victor, *Didascalicon*, Book II, ch. 20, p. 75, "These sciences . . . ," and Weisheipl, "Classification," pp. 75–8.

11 "Every mechanical art is intended for man's *consolation* or for his comfort; its purpose, therefore, is to banish either *sorrow* or *want*; it either *benefits* or *delights*, according to the words of Horace. . . ." St Bonaventure, *On Retracing the Arts to Theology (De reductione artium ad theologiam)*, in *Tria Opuscula, Breviloquium, Itinerarium mentis ad Deum, De reductione artium ad theologium* (Quarrachi, 1911), 2.

12 For example, the early twelfth-century *De diversis artibus* of Theophilus Presbyter included instructions on bell founding, glass making, and oil paints. See Theophilus Presbyter, *De diversis artibus, The Various Arts*, tr. C. R. Dodwell (London, 1961), or Theophilus, *On Divers Arts: The Treatise of Theophilus*, trs John G. Hawthorne and Cyril S. Smith (Chicago, 1963).

13 See Elizabeth Whitney, *The Mechanical Arts: Medieval Ideas on Technology* (Ann Arbor, MI, 1985).

14 Hugh of St Victor, *Didascalicon*, Book I, ch. 9, p. 56.

15 Hugh of St Victor, *Didascalicon*, Book I, ch. 9, p. 56.

16 See Jean Dunbabin, "The Reception and Interpretation of Aristotle's Politics," in *Cambridge History of Later Medieval Philosophy*, pp. 723–37; Anthony Black, "The Individual and Society," in J. H. Burns, ed., *The Cambridge History of Medieval Political Thought c.350–1450* (Cambridge, 1988), pp. 588–606; Nicholai Rubinstein, "Marsilius of Padua and Italian Political Thought of His Time," in *Europe in the Late Middle Ages*, eds J. R. Hale et al. (Evanston, IL, 1965), pp. 44–75.

17 *Nicomachean Ethics*, Book VIII, ch. 10 (1160a 31–6).

18 *Nicomachean Ethics*, Book VI, ch. 6 (1140b 30–3).

19 See Serene, "Demonstrative Science," pp. 496–517.

20 Ernest Moody, *The Logic of William of Ockham* (New York, 1935), p. 303.

21 Hugh of St Victor, *Practica geometriae (Applied Geometry)*, xx, in *The Medieval Latin Tradition of Practical Geometry*, ed. Frederick Homann (Milwaukee, WI, forthcoming 1992).

22 See Lon B. Shelby, "The Geometrical Knowledge of Medieval Master Masons," *Speculum* 47, 3 (1972), pp. 393–421.

23 The clergy sensed the feelings their distance evoked without understanding the motivation. "'Antiquity relates that laymen show a spirit of hostility towards the clergy,' wrote Pope Boniface VIII in 1296, 'and it is clearly proved by the experience of the present time.'" Paul Johnson, *A History of Christianity* (London, 1976), p. 191.

24 Steven Ozment, *The Ages of Reform 1250–1550: An Intellectual and Religious History of Late Medieval Reformation Europe* (New Haven/London, 1980), p. 219.

25 Alister E. McGrath, *Reformation Thought: An Introduction* (Oxford, 1988), p. 137.

26 "in divinis intellectualiter versari oportebit;" Henry Chadwick, *Boethius: The Consolations of Music, Logic, Theology, and Philosophy* (Oxford, 1981), p. 110.

Conclusion

1 David L. Jeffrey, "The Self and the Book: Reference and Recognition in Medieval Thought," in *By Things Seen: Reference and Recognition in Medieval Thought*, ed. David L. Jeffrey (Ottawa, 1979), p. 1.

2 Gordon Leff, "Christian Thought," in *The Mediaeval World*, eds David Daiches and Anthony Thorlby (London, 1973), p. 191.

3 David Daiches and Anthony Thorlby, eds, *The Mediaeval World*, p. 11. See also Clyde L. Manschreck, *A History of Christianity in the World: From Persecution to Uncertainty* (Englewood Cliffs, NJ, 1974), p. 47.

4 Leff, "Christian Thought," p. 191.

5 David Knowles, *The Evolution of Medieval Thought* (London, 2nd ed., 1988), p. 309.

6 In many instances, the treatment of these studies had not risen above the level of abstraction it had found among the Romans and Greeks through whose languages and texts the Renaissance scholars approached them directly.

Annotated Bibliography

Annotations

1   Early Christianity and Biblical Scholarship
2   Liberal Arts and Medieval Paedagogical Institutions
3   Classical Learning
4   Judaic and Arabic Learning
5   Languages and Literature
6   Medieval Philosophy
7   Medieval Science
8   Medieval Religion and Theology
9   Medieval Intellectual Expression (general and particular)

5 R. W. Ackerman, *Backgrounds to Medieval English Literature* (New York, 1968).

1 A. Alfodi, *The Conversion of Constantine and Pagan Rome* (London, 1948).

9 G. H. Allard and S. Lusignan, *Les arts mécaniques au moyen âge* (Montréal, 1982).

1 R. Altaner, *Patrology* (Freiburg/Edinburgh/London, 1960).

5 G. K. Anderson, *The Literature of the Anglo-Saxons* (Princeton, NJ, 1966).

6 A. H. Armstrong, ed. *The Cambridge History of Later Greek and Early Medieval Philosophy* (Cambridge, 1967).

2 E. J. Ashworth, *The Tradition of Medieval Logic and Speculative Grammar* (Toronto, 1978).

3 A. Badawi, *La transmission de la philosophie grecque au monde arabe* (Paris, 1968).

1 O. Bardenhewer, *Geschichte der altchristlichen Literatur* (5 vols: Freiburg, 1962).

5 H. Barrett, *Boethius, Some Aspects of his Times and Work* (Cambridge, 1940).

6 L. Baudry, *Guillaume d'Occam, sa vie, ses oeuvres, ses idées sociales et politiques* (Paris, 1949).

3 ——, *Le Problème de l'origine et de l'éternité du monde dans la philosophie greque de Platon à l'ère chrétienne* (Paris, 1931).

5   A. C. Baugh and T. Cable, *A History of the English Language* (Englewood Cliffs, NJ, 1978).
5   A. C. Baugh and K. Malone, *The Middle Ages*, in *A Literary History of England*, vol. 1 (London, 1967).
3   C. Baumker, *Der Platonismus im Mittelalter* (Munich, 1916).
5   R. Benson et al., eds, *Renaissance and Renewal in the Twelfth Century* (Cambridge, MA, 1982).
5   N. Blake, *The English Language in Medieval Literature* (London, 1977).
2   P. Boehner, *Medieval Logic: An Outline of Its Development from 1250 to c.1400* (Chicago, 1952).
6   T. J. de Boer, *The History of Philosophy in Islam*, tr. E. R. Jones (London, 1933).
5   Boethius, *The Consolation of Philosophy*, tr. and rev. by H. F. Stewart and E. K. Rand (Cambridge, MA, 1953).
6   F. Bottin, *La sienza degli Occamisti: La scienza tardo-medievale dalle origini del paradigma nominalista alla rivoluzione scientifica* (Rimini, 1982).
1   W. Bousset, *Kyrios Christos* (Gottingen, 1935).
3/4 I. Brady, *A History of Ancient Philosophy* (Milwaukee, WI, 1959).
6   E. Bréhier, *La philosophie au moyen âge* (Paris, 1949).
8   A. Breuer, *Der Gottesbeweis bei Thomas und Suarez: Ein wissenschaftlichen Gottesbeweis auf der Grundlage von Potenz und Aktverhaltnis oder Abhängigheitsverhältnis* (Freiburg, 1930).
1   P. Brown, *Augustine of Hippo: A Biography* (Berkeley and Los Angeles, 1969).
5   F. Brunot, *Historie de la langue française des origines à 1990*, vol. 1 (Paris, 1966).
5   C. Buridant, "*Translatio medievalis*: Théorie et pratique de la traduction médiévale," *Travaux de linguistique et de littérature* 21, 1, pp. 81–136.
9   J. H. Burns, ed., *The Cambridge History of Medieval Political Thought c.350–1450* (Cambridge, 1988).
5   J. A. Burrow, *Medieval Writers and Their Work: Middle English Literature and its Background 1100–1500* (Oxford, 1982).
2   G. L. Bursill-Hall, *Speculative Grammars of the Middle Ages* (The Hague, 1971).
8   D. A. Callus, *The Condemnation of St Thomas at Oxford* (Westminster, MD, 1946).
2   ——, *Introduction of Aristotelian Learning to Oxford* (London, 1944).
5   *Carmina Burana*, set to music by C. Orff, recorded on Deutsche Grammophon (1966).
5   J. Carney, *Medieval Irish Lyrics, Selected and Translated* (Dublin/Berkeley, 1967).
5   G. Chaucer, *Works*, ed. F. N. Robinson (Boston, MA, 1957).
5   H. J. Chaytor, *From Script to Print: An Introduction to Medieval Vernacular Literature* (Cambridge, 1945).
8   M. D. Chenu, *La théologie comme science au XIIIe siècle* (Paris, 1969).
8   ——, *Toward Understanding St Thomas*, trs. A. M. Landry and D. Hughes (Chicago, 1964).

[4] H. Cherniss, *Aristotle's Criticism of Plato* (1944).

[8] J. Chevalier, *La penseé chrétienne, des origines à la fin du XVIe siècle*, vol. 2 of *Histoire de la pensée* (Paris, 1956).

[7] M. Clagett, *Archimedes in the Middle Ages* (4 vols: vol. 1, Madison, WI, 1964; vols. 2–4, Philadelphia, 1976–80).

[7] ——, *The Science of Mechanics in the Middle Ages* (Madison, WI, 1959).

[5] M. T. Clanchy, *From Memory to Written Record: England 1066–1307* (London, 1979).

[2] A. B. Cobban, *The Medieval Universities: Their Development and Organisation* (London, 1975).

[6] F. Copleston, *A History of Medieval Philosophy* (London, 1972).

[3] F. M. Cornford, *Plato's Theory of Knowledge* (London, 1935, rpt. 1973).

[5] ——, *Plato's Cosmology* (New York, 1937, re-ed. 1957).

[9] G. G. Coulton, *Studies in Medieval Thought* (New York, 1965).

[3] P. Courcelle, *Les lettres grecques en occident de Macrobe à Cassiodore* (Paris, 1948).

[7] A. C. Crombie, *Augustine to Galileo* (2 vols in 1: Cambridge, MA, 1959).

[7] ——, *Robert Grosseteste and the Origins of Experimental Science 1100–1700* (Oxford, 1953).

[7] H. L. Crosby, *Thomas of Bradwardine, His "Tractatus de Proportionibus", Its Significance for the Development of Mathematical Physics* (Madison, WI, 1955).

[7] W. C. Curry, *Chaucer and the Medieval Sciences* (New York, 1960).

[5] E. R. Curtius, *European Literature and the Latin Middle Ages*, tr. W. R. Trask (New York, 1953; rpt Princeton, NJ, 1973).

[6] U. Dahnert, *Die Erkenntnislehre des Albertus Magnus gemessen an den Stufen der "abstractio"* (Leipzig, 1933).

[5] D. Daiches and A. Thorlby, eds, *The Mediaeval World (Literature and Western Civilisation*, Vol. 2: London, 1973).

[9] R. C. Dales, *The Intellectual Life of Western Europe in the Middle Ages* (Washington, DC, 1980).

[7] ——, *The Scientific Achievement of the Middle Ages* (Philadelphia, 1973).

[2] L. J. Daly, *The Medieval University, 1200–1400* (New York, 1961).

[3] J. Daniélou, *Platonisme et théologie mystique* (Paris, 1953).

[7] C. Dawson, *Medieval Essays* (New York, 1959).

[8] M. Deanesly, *A History of the Medieval Church* (London, 1954).

[8] A. Dempf, *Die Hauptform mittelalterlicher Weltanschauung; eine geisteswissenschaftliche Studie über die Summa* (Munich/Berlin, 1925).

[8] Dionysius the Areopagite, *On the Divine Names and the Mystical Theology*, tr. C. E. Rolt (New York, 1920).

[1] E. R. Dodds, *Pagan and Christian in an Age of Anxiety* (Cambridge, 1965).

[2] H. F. Dondaine, *Le corpus dionysien de l'Université de Paris au xiiie siècle* (Rome, 1953).

[6] P. Dronke, ed., *History of Twelfth-Century Western Philosophy* (Cambridge, 1988).

[2] E. S. Duckett, *Alcuin, Friend of Charlemagne* (New York, 1951).

[7] P. Duhem, *Le système du monde; histoire des doctrines cosmologiques de Platon à Copernic* (7 vols: Paris, 1913–56).

[7] S. C. Easton, *Roger Bacon and His Search for a Universal Science* (Oxford, 1952).

[9] E. Eisenstein, *The Printing Press as an Agent of Change* (2 vols: Cambridge, 1979).

[4] W. K. Ferguson, *The Renaissance in Historical Thought, Five Centuries of Interpretation* (Boston, 1948).

[1] J. Festugière, *Les moines d'Orient* (Paris, 1961).

[7] N. W. Fisher and S. Unguru, "Experimental Science and Mathematics in Roger Bacon's Thought," *Traditio* 27 (1971), pp. 353–78.

[6] K. Flasch, *Das philosophische Denken im Mittelalter: Von Augustin zu Machiavelli* (Stuttgart, 1986).

[3] J. Fontaine, *Isidore de Séville et la culture classique dans l'Espagne Wisigothique* (2 vols: Paris, 1959).

[8] A. Forest, F. van Steenberghen, M. de Gandillac, *Le Mouvement doctrinal du IXe au XIVe siècle*, vol. 13 in *Histoire de l'Eglise depuis les origines jusqu'à nos jours*, ed. A. Fliche and V. Martin (Paris, 1951).

[8] E. L. Fortin, *Christianisme et culture philosophique au cinquième siècle* (Paris, 1959).

[9] P. Frankl, *The Gothic: Literary Sources and Interpretations through Eight Centuries* (Princeton, NJ, 1960).

[1] W. H. C. Frend, *The Donatist Church, a Movement of Protest in Roman North Africa* (Oxford, 1952).

[1] ——, *The Rise of Christianity* (Philadelphia, 1984).

[6] M. de Gandillac, *La Philosophie de Nicolas de Cues* (Paris, 1941).

[9] M. de Gandillac, J. Fontaine, J. Chatillon et al., eds, *La pensée encyclopédique au moyen age* (Neuchatel, 1966).

[1] J. Gaudement, *L'Eglise dans l'Empire romain (IVe–Ve siècle)* (Paris, 1958).

[4] H. Gibb, "The Influence of Islamic Culture in Medieval Europe," in *Change in Medieval Society*, ed. Sylvia Thrupp (Toronto, 1964, rpt. 1988), pp. 155–67.

[2] M. Gibson, ed., *Boethius; His Life, Thought and Influence* (Oxford, 1981).

[6] E. Gilson, *Being and Some Philosophers* (Toronto, 1952).

[8] ——, *The Christian Philosophy of St Thomas Aquinas*, tr. L. Shook (New York, 1956).

[6] ——, *History of Christian Philosophy in the Middle Ages* (London/New York, 1955, rpt 1978).

[6] ——, *Jean Duns Scot: Introduction à ses positions fondamentales* (Paris, 1952).

[8] ——, *Reason and Revelation in the Middle Ages* (New York, 1936).

[3/4] ——, "Les Sources Greco-Arabes de l'Augustinisme Avicennisant," *Archives doctrinales et littéraires du Moyen Age* 4 (1929), i.

[2] P. Glorieux, *La littérature quodlibétique de 1260 à 1320* (2 vols: Paris, 1925/35).

[2] ——, "L'enseignement au Moyen Age, techniques et méthodes en usage

à la faculté de théologie," *Archives d'historie doctrinale et littéraire du Moyen Age* 35 (1968), pp. 65–186.

2 ——, *Répertoire des maîtres en théologie de Paris au XIIIe siècle* (2 vols: Paris, 1933–4).

1 M. Goguel, *Jésus* (Paris, 1950).

4 A. M. Goichon, *La philosophie d'Avicenne et son influence en Europe médiévale* (Paris, 1944 re-ed. 1951).

9 J. Gonsette, *Pierre Damien et la culture profane* (Louvain, 1956).

6 M. Grabmann, *Die Geschichte der scholastischen Methode* (2 vols: Freiburg i. Breisgau, 1909/11).

5 R. F. Green, *Poets and Princepleasers: Literature and the English Court in the late Middle Ages* (Toronto, 1980).

1 S. L. Greenslade, *Schism in the Early Church* (London, 1953).

3 T. Gregory, *Platonismo medievale: Studi e Ricerche* (Rome, 1958).

6 R. Guelly, *Philosophie et théologie chez Guillaume d'Ockham* (Louvain, 1947).

4 J. Guttman, *Philosophies of Judaism* (London, 1964).

1 H. Hagendahl, *Latin Fathers and the Classics* (1958).

3 O. Hamelin, *La théorie de l'intellect d'après Aristote et ses commentateurs* (Paris, 1953).

8 A. von Harnack, *History of Dogma* (New York, 1958).

1 ——, *Mission und Ausbreitung des Christentums in den drei ersten Jahrhunderten* (2 vols: Leipzig, 1924).

3 C. H. Haskins, *The Renaissance of the Twelfth Century* (Cambridge, MA, 1972).

2 ——, *The Rise of Universities* (New York, 1923).

7 ——, *Studies in the History of Medieval Science* (Cambridge, MA, 1924).

6 D. J. B. Hawkins, *A Sketch of Medieval Philosophy* (London, 1946).

2 D. P. Henry, *The Logic of St Anselm* (Oxford, 1967).

2 ——, *Medieval Logic and Metaphysics* (London, 1972).

1 K. Heussi, *Der Ursprung des Monchtums* (Tubingen, 1936).

8 L. Hödl, "Geistesgeschichtliche und literarkritische Erhebungen zum Korrektorienstreit (1277–1287)," *Recherches de théologie ancienne et médiévale* 33 (1966), pp. 81–114.

5 K. L. Holzknecht, *Literary Patronage in the Middle Ages* (Philadelphia, 1923).

6 J. Hopkins, *A Concise Introduction to the Philosophy of Nicholas of Cusa* (Minneapolis, MN, 1978).

6 M. Horten, *Die Philosophie des Islam in ihrem Beziehungen zu den philosophischen Weltanschauungen des westlichen Orients* (Munich, 1924).

9 J. Huizinga, *The Waning of the Middle Ages*, tr. F. Hopman (London, 1924).

4 J. Husik, *A History of Medieval Jewish Philosophy* (New York, 1916).

3 E. von Ivanka, *Plato Christianus: Übernahme uund Umgestaltung des Platonismus durch die Väter* (Einsiedeln, 1964).

1 W. Jaeger, *Early Christianity and Greek Paideia* (Cambridge, MA, 1961).

3 ——, *Theology of the Early Greek Philosophers* (Oxford, 1947).

[6]   E. Jeauneau, *La philosophie médiévale* (Paris, 1975).

[2]   ——, *Lectio philosophorum: recherches sur l'Ecole de Chartres* (Amsterdam, 1973).

[9]   D. L. Jeffrey, ed., *By Things Seen: Reference and Recognition in Medieval Thought* (Ottawa, 1979).

[1]   P. Johnson, *A History of Christianity* (London, 1976).

[2]   A. G. Jongkees, "*Translatio studii*: les avatars d'un thème médiéval," *Miscellanea Mediaevalia in memoriam Jan Frederick Niermeyer* (Groningen, 1967), pp. 41–51.

[3]   F. F. Kampe, *Die Erkenntnistheorie des Aristoteles* (Leipzig, 1870).

[1]   J. N. D. Kelly, *Early Christian Doctrines* (London, 1958).

[6]   L. Kennedy, "The Nature of the Human Intellect according to St Albert the Great," *Modern Schoolman* 37 (1960), pp. 121–37.

[8]   A. Kenny, *The Five Ways: St Thomas Aquinas' Proofs of God's Existence* (London, 1969).

[1]   H. T. Kerr, *The First Systematic Theologian, Origen of Alexandria* (Princeton Pamphlets, 11: Princeton, NJ, 1958).

[6]   D. Knowles, *The Evolution of Medieval Thought* (London, 2nd ed., 1988).

[1]   W. L. Knox, *St Paul and the Church of the Gentiles* (Cambridge, 1939).

[6]   J. Kloch, *Nicolaus von Cues und seine Umwelt* (Heidelberg, 1948).

[6]   N. Kretzmann, A. Kenny, and J. Pinborg, eds, *The Cambridge History of Later Medieval Philosophy: From the Rediscovery of Aristotle to the Disintegration of Scholasticism 1100–1600* (Cambridge, 1982).

[6]   P. O. Kristeller, *Renaissance Philosophy and the Medieval Tradition* (Latrobe, PA, 1966).

[9]   G. Ladner, *The Idea of Reform: Its Impact on Christian Thought and Action in the Age of the Fathers* (New York/London, 1959, re-ed. 1967).

[9]   G. de Lagarde, *La naissance de l'esprit laique au déclin du moyen age* (Paris, 5 vols: Louvain 1956–70).

[2]   M. L. W. Laistner, *Thought and Letters in Western Europe, AD 500–900* (Ithaca, NY/London, 1931 re-ed. 1957).

[8]   G. Leff, *Bradwardine and the Pelagians* (Cambridge, 1957).

[6]   ——, *Medieval Thought: St Augustine to Ockham* (London, 1959).

[6]   ——, *William of Ockham: The Metamorphosis of Scholastic Discourse* (Manchester/Totowa, NJ, 1975).

[5]   M. D. Legge, *Anglo-Norman Literature and its Background* (Oxford, 1963).

[5]   C. S. Lewis, *The Discarded Image: An Introduction to Medieval and Renaissance Literature* (Cambridge, 1964).

[6]   A. de Libera, *La philosophie médiévale* (Paris, 1989).

[7]   D. C. Lindberg, ed., *Science in the Middle Ages* (Chicago History of Science and Medicine: Chicago/London, 1978).

[3]   A. C. Lloyd, "Neoplatonic Logic and Aristotelian Logic," *Phronesis* 1.1, pp. 58–72 and 1.2, pp. 146–60.

[5]   F. Lot, "A quelle époque a-t-on cessé de parler latin," *Bulletin Du Cange* 6 (1931), pp. 97–159.

[9]   O. Lottin, *Psychologie et morale aux XIIe et XIIIe siècles* (5 vols: vols 1–4,

Louvain, 1942–54; vol. 5, Gembloux, 1959).

[1] H. de Lubac, *Exégèse médiévale: Les quatres sens de l'écriture* (2 vols: Paris, 1959–64).

[6] D. E. Luscombe, *The School of Peter Abelard: The Influence of Abelard's Thought in the Early Scholastic Period* (Cambridge, 1969).

[5] S. Lusignan, *Parler vulgairement: Les intellectuels et la langue française aux XIIIe et XIVe siècles* (Paris, 1987).

[4] D. B. MacDonald, *The Development of Muslim Theology, Jurisprudence and Constitutional Theory* (New York, 1903).

[9] E. P. Mahoney, ed., *Medieval Aspects of Renaissance Learning* (Durham, NC, 1974).

[7] A. Maier, *An der Grenze von Scholastik und Naturwissenschaft* (Essen, 1943).

[7] ——, *Die Vorläufer Galilies im 14. Jahrhundert* (Rome, 1949).

[7] ——, *Metaphysische Hintergrunde der spätscholastischen Naturphilosophie* (Rome, 1955).

[7] ——, *Zwei Grundprobleme der scholastischen Naturphilosophie* (Rome, 1951).

[7] ——, *Zwischen Philosophie und Mechanik* (Rome, 1958).

[9] K. Malone and A. C. Baugh, *The Middle Ages: A Literary History of England* (New York, 1948, rpt. 1967).

[6] P. Mandonnet, *Siger de Brabant et l'averroisme latin au XIIIe siècle*, vols 6 and 7 of *Les philosophes belges* (Louvain, 1908–11).

[5] M. Manitius, *Geschichte der latienischen Literatur des Mittelalters* (3 vols: Munich, 1911–31).

[6] J. Marenbon, *Early Medieval Philosophy (480–1150): An Introduction* (London, 1983).

[6] ——, *Later Medieval Philosophy (1150–1350): An Introduction* (London, 1987).

[9] J. Mariétan, *Problème de la classification des sciences d'Aristote à s. Thomas* (Paris, 1901).

[9] R. Mark, *Experiments in Gothic Structure* (Cambridge, MA/London, 1982).

[2] H. I. Marrou, *Saint Augustin et la fin de la culture antique* (Paris, 1938).

[9] A. Martindale, *The Rise of the Artist in the Middle Ages and Early Renaissance* (London, 1972).

[6] A. Masnovo, *Da Guglielmo d'Auvergne a san Tommaso d'Aquino* (3 vols: Milan, 1946).

[6] A. A. Maurer, "Boethius of Dacia and the Double Truth," *Medieval Studies* 17 (1955), pp. 233–9.

[6] ——, *Medieval Philosophy* (New York, 1962; The Etienne Gilson Series 4: Toronto, 2nd ed., 1982).

[6] A. S. McGrade, *The Political Thought of William of Ockham: Personal and Institutional Principles* (Cambridge, 1974).

[2/5] R. McKitterick, *The Frankish Kingdoms under the Carolingians 757–987* (London, 1983).

3 P. Merlan, *From Platonism to Neoplatonism* (The Hague, 1960).

3 L. Minio-Paluello, "Les traductions et les commentaires aristotéliciennes de Boèce," *Texte und Untersuchungen zur Geschichte der altchristlichen Literatur* 64 (1957), pp. 358–65.

3 ——, *Opuscula: the Latin Aristotle* (Amsterdam, 1972).

7 H. G. Mollard, "Medieval Ideas of Scientific Progress," *Journal of the History of Ideas* 39 (1978), pp. 561–77.

1 A. Momigliano, ed., *The Conflict between Paganism and Christianity in the Fourth Century* (Oxford, 1963).

6 E. Moody, *The Logic of William of Ockham* (New York, 1935).

9 B. Morrall, *Political Thought in Medieval Times* (New York, 1962).

9 C. Morris, *The Discovery of the Individual, 1050–1200* (New York/London, 1972).

2 J. Murdoch and E. Sylla, eds, *The Cultural Context of Medieval Learning* (Dordrecht, 1975).

6 A. V. Murray, *Abélard and St Bernard: A Study in Twelfth Century "Modernism"* (Manchester/New York, 1967).

4 E. A. Myers, *Arabic Thought and the Western World in the Golden Age of Islam* (New York, 1964).

4 S. H. Nasr, *An Introduction to Islamic Cosmological Doctrines* (Cambridge, 1964).

7 O. Neugebauer, *The Exact Sciences in Antiquity* (Providence, RI, 1957).

6 J. H. Newell, *The Dignity of Man in William of Conches and the School of Chartres in the Twelfth Century* (Durham, NC, 1978).

2 L. Obertello, *Severino Boezio* (2 vols: Genoa, 1974).

6 D. J. O'Connor, ed., *Critical History of Western Philosophy* (New York, 1964).

6 J. J. O'Meara, *Eriugena* (Cork, 1969).

2 N. Orme, *English Schools in the Middle Ages* (London, 1973).

6 F. Overbeck, *Vorgeschichte und Jügend der mittelalterlichen Scholastik* (Basel, 1917).

6 J. Owens, *The Doctrine of Being in the Aristotelian Metaphysics: A Study in the Greek Background of Medieval Thought* (Toronto, 1951).

5 *The Oxford Book of Latin Medieval Verse*, ed. F. J. E. Raby (Oxford, 1959).

5 *The Oxford Book of Medieval English Verse*, eds C. and K. Sisam (Oxford, 1970).

2 L. J. Paetow, *The Arts Course at Medieval Universities, with Special Reference to Grammar and Rhetoric* (Champaign, IL, 1910).

9 E. Panofsky, *Abbot Suger on the Abbey Church of St. Denis and Its Art Treasures* (Princeton, NJ, 1946).

9 ——, *Gothic Architecture and Scholasticism* (New York, 1957)

8 J. M. Parent, *La doctrine de la création dans l'école de Chartres* (Paris/Ottawa, 1938).

2 H. R. Patch, *The Tradition of Boethius: A Study of his Importance in Medieval Culture* (New York, 1935).

[9] J. Paul, *Histoire intellectuelle de l'occident médiéval* (Paris, 1973).

[6] J. Paulus, *Henri de Gand, essai sur les tendances de sa métaphysique* (Paris, 1938).

[5] D. Pearsall, *Old English and Middle English Poetry* (London/Boston 1967).

[6] A. C. Pegis, "St Bonaventure, St Francis and Philosophy," *Medieval Studies* 15 (1953), pp. 1–13.

[6] ——, *St Thomas and the Problem of the Soul in the Thirteenth Century* (Toronto, 1934).

[8] J. Pelikan, *The Christian Tradition: A History of the Development of Doctrine* (4 vols: Chicago/London, 1978).

[9] N. Pevsner, "The Term 'Architect' in the Middle Ages," *Speculum* 17 (1942), pp. 547–62.

[6] F. Picavet, *Rocelin, philosophe et théologien* (Paris, 1911).

[6] J. Pieper, *Scholasticism, Personalities and Problems of Medieval Philosophy* (New York, 1960).

[2] J. Pinborg, *Logik und Semantik im Mittelalter: ein Überblick* (Stuttgart, 1972).

[9] R. L. Poole, *Illustrations of the History of Medieval Thought and Learning* (New York, 1960).

[9] J. M. Powell, ed., *An Introduction to Medieval Studies* (Syracuse, NY, 1976).

[3] M. dal Pra, *Scoto Eriugena ed il neoplatonismo medievale* (Milan, 1941).

[4] G. Quadri, *La philosophie arabe dans l'Europe médiévale* (Paris, 1947).

[6] J. F. Quinn, *The Historical Constitution of St Bonaventure's Philosophy* (Toronto, 1973).

[5] F. J. E. Raby, *A History of Christian Latin Poetry* (Oxford, 1927).

[2] E. K. Rand, *Founders of the Middle Ages* (Cambridge, MA, 1920).

[2] H. Rashdall, *The Universitites of Europe in the Middle Ages*, eds F. M. Powicke and A. B. Emden (3 vols: Oxford, 1936 re-ed. 1959).

[6] J. Reiners, *Der Nominalismus in der Frühscholastik* (Munster, 1910).

[4] E. Renan, *Averroès et l'Averroisme* (Paris, 1861).

[9] P. Renucci, *L'aventure de l'humanisme européen au moyen age (IVe– XIVe siècle)* (Paris, 1953).

[2] P. Riché, *Les écoles et l'enseignement dans l'occident chrétien de la fin du Ve siècle* (Paris, 1979).

[5] M. Richter, *Sprache und Gesellschaft im Mittelalter* (Stuttgart, 1979).

[6] L. M. de Rijk, *La philosophie au moyen âge* (Leiden, 1985).

[8] L. J. Rogier, R. Aubert, and M. D. Knowles, eds, *Nouvelle histoire de l'église* (Paris, 1963–75).

[1] W. Rordorf, *Der Sonntag, Geschichte des Ruhe- und Gottesdiensttags im altesten Christentum* (Zurich, 1962).

[1] S. Runciman, *The Medieval Manichee: A Study of the Christian Dualist Heresy* (Cambridge, 1947).

[7] S. Sambursky, *The Physical World of Late Antiquity* (London, 1962).

[7] G. Sarton, *Introduction to the History of Science* (3 vols in 5: Baltimore, 1927–48).

⁸ T. Save-Soderberg, *La religion des Cathares: Etude sur le Gnosticisme de la basse-antiquité et du moyen âge* (Uppsala, 1949).

⁴ E. Schurer, *Geschichte des jüdischen Volkes im Zeitalter Jésu Christi* (3 vols: Leipzig, 1964).

¹ E. Schwartz, *Zur Geschichte des Athanasius* (Berlin, 1959).

⁶ A. D. Sertillanges, *The Foundations of Thomistic Philosophy*, tr. G. Anstruther (St Louis, MO, 1931).

⁴ M. M. Shariff, ed., *A History of Muslim Philosophy* (2 vols: Wiesbaden, 1963).

⁶ D. E. Sharp, *Franciscan Philosophy at Oxford in the Thirteenth Century* (Oxford, 1930).

³ J. Shiel, "Boethius' Commentaries on Aristotle," *Medieval and Renaissance Studies* 4 (1958), pp. 217–44.

⁶ C. L. Shircel, *The Univocity of the Concept of Being in the Philosophy of Duns Scotus* (Washington, DC, 1942).

¹ M. Simon, *Les premiers chrétiens* (Paris, 1967).

² N. Siraisi, *Arts and Sciences at Padua: The Studium of Padua before 1350* (Toronto, 1973).

¹ B. Smalley, *The Study of the Bible in the Middle Ages* (Oxford, 1952 rpt. 1983).

⁸ R. W. Southern, *The Making of the Middle Ages* (London, 1953).

⁸ ——, *Saint Anselm and his Biographer, a Study of Monastic Life and Thought, 1059–c.1130* Cambridge, 1963).

³ F. van Steenberghen, *Aristotle in the West: the Origins of Latin Aristotelianism*, tr. L. Johnston (Louvain, 1955, 2nd ed., 1970).

⁶ ——, *La philosophie au XIIIe siècle* (Louvain, 1966).

⁴ M. Steinschneider, *Die arabischen Übersetzungen aus dem Griechischen* (Graz, 1960).

⁴ ——, *Die Europaischen Übersetzungen aus dem Arabischen bis Mitte des 17. Jahrhunderts* (Graz, 1956).

⁴ ——, *Die hebraischen Übersetzungen des Mittelalters und die Juden als Dolmetscher* (Berlin, 1893).

⁵ M. Stevens and J. Mandel, eds, *Old English Literature: Twenty-two Analytical Essays* (Lincoln, NB, 1968).

⁷ B. Stock, *Myth and Science in the Twelfth Century: A Study of Bernard Sylvester* (Princeton, NJ, 1972).

⁵ B. M. H. Strang, *A History of English* (London, 1970).

⁵ M. Swanton, *English Literature before Chauver* (London/New York, 1987).

⁷ L. Thorndike, *A History of Magic and Experimental Science* (8 vols: New York, 1923–58).

⁹ W. Treadgold, ed., *Renaissances before the Renaissance: Cultural Revivals of Late Antiquity and the Middle Ages* (Stanford, 1984).

¹ H. E. W. Turner, *The Pattern of Christian Truth: A Study in the Relations between Orthodoxy and Heresy in the Early Church* (London, 1954).

⁶ M. M. Tweedale, *Abailard on Universals* (Amsterdam, NY, 1976).

⁶ F. Ueberweg and B. Geyer, *Die patristische und scholastische Philosophie,*

vol. 2 of *Grundriss der Geschichte der Philosophie* (Berlin, 1928).

[9] W. Ullmann, *The Individual and Society in the Middle Ages* (London, 1967).

[9] ———, *Medieval Political Thought* (Harmondsworth, England, 1965, rpt. 1979).

[4] G. Vajda, *Introduction à la pensée juive du moyen âge* (Paris, 1947).

[6] A. van de Vyer, "Les etapes du dévelopement philosophique du Haut Moyen Age," *Revue Belge de Philologie et d'Histoire* 8 (1929), pp. 441–3.

[6] C. G. Verbeke and D. Verhelst, eds, *Aquinas and Problems of his Time* (Louvain, 1976).

[2] J. Verger, *Les Universités au moyen âge* (Paris, 1973).

[6] P. Vignaux, *Philosophie au Moyen Age* (Albeuve, Switzerland, 1987).

[2] D. L. Wagner, ed., *The Seven Liberal Arts in the Middle Ages* (Bloomington, IN, 1986).

[7] W. A. Wallace, *Causality and Scientific Explanation* (2 vols: Ann Arbor, MI, 1972).

[2] L. Wallach, *Alcuin and Charlemagne* (Ithaca, NY, 1959).

[4] R. Walzer, *Greek into Arabic: Essays on Islamic Philosophy* (Oxford, 1962).

[4] W. Montgomery Watt, *Islamic Philosophy and Theology* (Islamic Surveys, I: Edinburgh, 1964).

[8] E. H. Wéber, *La controverse de 1270 à l'Université de Paris et son retentissement sur la pensée de S. Thomas d'Aquin* (Paris, 1970).

[6] J. A. Weisheipl, "Albert the Great and Medieval Culture," *The Thomist* 44 (1980), pp. 481–501.

[9] ———, "Classification of the Sciences in Medieval Thought," *Medieval Studies* 27 (1965), pp. 54–90.

[2] ———, "Curriculum of the Faculty of Arts at Oxford," *Medieval Studies* 26 (1964), pp. 143–85.

[2] ———, "Developments in the Arts Curriculum at Oxford in the Early Fourteenth Century," *Medieval Studies* 28 (1966), pp. 151–75.

[7] ———, "The Place of John Dumbleton in the Merton School," *Isis* 50 (1959), pp. 439–54.

[7] ———, ed., *Albertus Magnus and the Sciences: Commemorative Essays 1980* (Toronto, 1980).

[3] W. Wetherbee, *Platonism and Poetry in the Twelfth Century* (Princeton, NJ, 1972).

[9] E. Whitney, *The Mechanical Arts in the Context of Twelfth and Thirteenth Century Thought* (Ann Arbor, MI, 1985).

[9] ——— *Paradise Restored: The Mechanical Arts from Antiquity Through the Thirteenth Century* (Philadelphia, 1990).

[3] H. Wierwzowski, *The Medieval University: Masters, Students, Learning* (Princeton, NJ, 1966).

[1] G. G. Willis, *Saint Augustine and the Donatist Controversy* (London, 1950).

[7] C. Wilson, *William Heytesbury: Medieval Logic and the Rise of Mathematical Physics* (Madison, WI, 1956).

[5] P. Wolff, *Les origines linguistiques de l'Europe occidentale* (Toulouse-le-Mirail, 1982).

[6] M. de Wulf, *History of Medieval Philosophy* tr. E. C. Messenger (London, 1938).

[8] E. Zellinger, *Cusanus-Konkordanz unter Zugrundelegung der philosophischen und der bedeutendsten theologischen Werke* (Munich, 1960).

[6] A. Zimmermann, *Ontologie oder Metaphysik? Die Discussionen über den Gegenstand der Metaphysik in 13. und 14. Jahrhundert* (Leiden, 1965).

[9] —— ed., *Antiqui und Moderni. Traditionsbewusstsein und Fortschrittsbewusstsein im späten Mittelalter* (Berlin/New York, 1974).

Index